GOVERNOR WILLIAM C. SPROUL OF PENNSYLVANIA
SIGNS THE WOMAN SUFFRAGE RATIFICATION
RESOLUTION, JUNE 24, 1919.

Left to right: Harry McDevitt, Mrs. Lawrence Lewis, Governor Sproul, Dr. Frederick Rasmussen, Ella Reigel.

LIFTING THE CURTAIN

The State and National Woman Suffrage Campaigns
In Pennsylvania As I Saw Them

By

CAROLINE KATZENSTEIN

DORRANCE & COMPANY
PHILADELPHIA

JK
1911
P4
K3

36740

DEDICATED

To my sister Josephine, (Mrs. Wilton W. Blancké) with gratitude for her encouragement, constructive criticism, and invaluable assistance in the preparation of this book.

ACKNOWLEDGMENTS

I wish to express my gratitude to Mr. Harrison W. Fry (one of the "cub" reporters assigned to cover Woman Suffrage many years ago, and now Editor in charge of Religion and Education on the Philadelphia *Evening Bulletin*) for reading the body of the manuscript and making helpful suggestions.

To Mr. Cleo C. West, an Associate Manager of the Prudential Insurance Company of America, for his careful review of the Life Insurance story in the Appendix.

To Mr. Add B. Anderson, Secretary and Business Manager of the School District of Philadelphia, and Mr. Harry Kephart, Assistant Secretary of the School District of Philadelphia, for data relating to public school teachers throughout Pennsylvania.

To Mr. William F. Brophy, Assistant Actuary of the Philadelphia Life Insurance Company, for help in the reproduction of some of the old photographs.

To Reference Departments of the Free Library of Philadelphia.

To Mr. Nell B. Stevens, General Librarian of the Pennsylvania State Library.

To Mr. John J. Rehr of the Legislative Reference Bureau, Harrisburg, Pa., and to Mr. S. Edward Hannestad, Director of that Bureau.

To the Library of the Philadelphia *Inquirer;*

To the Library of the Philadelphia *Evening Bulletin.*

C.K.

PREFACE

After women were enfranchised throughout the United States in 1920, I was urged to write a story of the woman suffrage campaigns in Pennsylvania, both State and national. As fate had placed me in a strategic position at a critical time in the development of the movement in the Keystone State, it seemed that perhaps I was the logical one to undertake this work. But for some reason the task did not appeal to me. Perhaps the events were too recent to make a review of them seem likely to prove of interest to the public. However, as the years have passed, and as many of the distinguished leaders in that gallant fight have died, it seems more and more fitting that some official record of the work that they and others in the rank and file of the movement accomplished should be preserved.

In presenting this record of Pennsylvania's work, as I saw it during the ten years immediately preceding the passage of the Federal Woman Suffrage Amendment, I have, I hope, been able to add material of sufficient interest and of sufficient historical value to make the writing of another book on the subject worth while. During those years, I was closely associated with State and national leaders, and was in charge of various centers from which the campaigns were directed.

For more than two years I was Executive Secretary for the Pennsylvania Woman Suffrage Association from the opening of State Headquarters in Philadelphia in 1910 until they were moved to Harrisburg in 1912. Then I served as Executive Secretary for the Eastern District of

Pennsylvania, which took over immediately the headquarters just relinquished by the State Association, and I continued that work until about the middle of 1914. From that time until nearly a year after the proposed amendment to the Pennsylvania Constitution was defeated in November, 1915, I was Executive Secretary of the Equal Franchise Society of Philadelphia and took charge of that organization's headquarters from its opening until it closed. From 1916 to 1920, I was Executive Secretary of the Pennsylvania Branch of the National Woman's Party. Also I was a member of the Membership Committee of the National American Woman Suffrage Association for two years, beginning that work in the fall of 1911.

In this record, I have given little space to statistics because such data are often uninteresting, and also because the available figures on the suffrage campaigns in Pennsylvania would so inadequately indicate the actual work accomplished that they would rather misrepresent the campaigns than give a true picture of them. There were in 1910 comparatively few active suffrage workers, and they were so busy trying to overcome extreme conservatism, indifference, prejudice, and organized opposition that they did not, I think, feel it worth while to spend time in building up a statistical record of their work. In my second annual report as Corresponding Secretary of the Pennsylvania Woman Suffrage Association, I emphasized this point when I said it had seemed better to make two converts to the Cause than to make one convert and keep a record of the case. I have, on the other hand, given considerable space to letters because they were a very vital part of the work and they emphasize the spirit behind it.

However, as I recently delved into my voluminous files, I found important official and personal letters relating to my work in the campaigns that are of such a complimentary nature the thought of making them public is embarrassing. On the other hand, there are other communications that are unfavorably critical; and perhaps one group may balance the other. Anyway, they are both part of the record, and as they relate to me in my several official capacities rather than to me as an individual I hope I may not be considered bold in using some of the first-mentioned group.

In writing this book, I have had, in addition to data on the woman suffrage movement from its earliest days until the time when this account begins, many official records that originated in or came to the principal Pennsylvania centres of which I had charge during the campaigns. They include minutes of meetings, official reports, correspondence with suffrage leaders and other prominent persons, press clippings, literature published by the National American Woman Suffrage Association, literature published by the National Woman's Party (first called the Congressional Union for Woman Suffrage), press bulletins and biographical sketches from these two organizations, and copies of press bulletins that I, in my capacity as Chairman of Publicity for several suffrage organizations, prepared.

C.K.

INTRODUCTION

Lifting The Curtain is a vivid, first hand account of the last dramatic period of the campaign for the political emancipation of American women. It gives a detailed picture of this historic movement, especially in the region around Philadelphia—always a center for activities for the freedom of women, from the time of Lucretia Mott until the final suffrage victory in 1920.

Caroline Katzenstein took a leading part in the campaign she describes. All that she sets forth in *Lifting The Curtain* was a part of her own life. Hence the peculiarly stirring quality of the book as well as its value as an authoritative document.

There is a great need for a book such as *Lifting The Curtain*. It will be of value as a source book to students, teachers, historians. All who want to know something about the movement that led to the enfranchisement of American women will find here the inside story. It is a much clearer and more accurate portrayal of the suffrage campaign than that presented in the history text books used today in schools and colleges.

Lifting The Curtain is of value also in bringing tribute to a wonderful band of women to whom all American women owe a great debt. It is right that the memories of these gallant leaders should be honored and that the women of today should recognize and appreciate their heritage. This is the real reason that this book was written.

ALICE PAUL

CONTENTS

ix

ILLUSTRATIONS FACING
PAGE

PART I

1

THE PIONEERS—OUR INHERITANCE
AND INSPIRATION

In the national election of November, 1954, approximately 48,000,000 women in the United States were eligible to vote in what may be one of the most crucial elections ever held in the history of our country. We are facing a global conflict that threatens civilization itself. How many of these women realize the debt of gratitude they owe to courageous women who won for them the priceless right of the franchise? If they knew the history of the struggle of the suffrage pioneers, and of the generations of other Suffragists that succeeded them and continued the fight, might they not value more highly their own political freedom?

With the hope of stimulating a true appreciation of this freedom, I shall turn back the pages of history for a few centuries and recount some of the outstanding achievements of women that contributed to woman's enfranchisement.

All through the ages, some thoughtful women have, I believe, had an impulse to share with their menfolk the responsibilities of life outside the home as well as within it. Conspicuous among such women, and among the first in our country was Mistress Margaret Brent, of Maryland. She was heir to Lord Calvert, the brother of Lord Baltimore, and executor of the estates of both in the Colony.

As representation in the Maryland Legislative body was based on property, she demanded, in 1647, "place and voyce." After several hours of heated debate, her petition was denied. Thus was established a precedent that other Legislatures found easy to follow when women later petitioned for "place and voyce."

More than a century later, in the historic year of 1776, women gave evidence that the "spirit of independence" was as strong in them as in men. In March of that year, Abigail Adams wrote to her husband, John Adams, in the Continental Congress: "I long to hear that you have declared an independency, and, by the way, in the new code of laws which I suppose it will be necessary for you to make, I desire you would remember the ladies and be more generous and favorable to them than were your ancestors. Do not put such unlimited power into the hands of husbands. Remember all men would be tyrants if they could. If particular care and attention are not paid to the ladies we are determined to foment a rebellion, and will not hold ourselves bound to obey any laws in which we have no voice or representation."

Despite Abigail Adams' admonition to her husband, when the Constitution was adopted the rights of women were in no way considered.

In 1826, just fifty years after Mrs. Adams' stirring appeal, a beautiful and educated young Scotchwoman, Frances Wright, came to the United States. Through years of lecturing, she brought the subject of Woman Suffrage before the public for the first time. The public's response, however, was one of almost universal derision.

Another foreigner, eloquent Ernestine L. Rose, daughter of a Polish rabbi, was able by her lectures on the "Science of Government" to draw crowded houses in all sections of the country. An advocate of the full enfranchisement of women, she was one of the first to urge women to obtain the repeal of laws that adversely affected their interests. In the winter of 1836-7, she circulated a petition in Albany, N. Y., for a law that would enable a married woman to hold property. Able to get only five signatures, including those of men as well as women, she took the petition to the Legislature and addressed that body in behalf of such a law. For years, Ernestine L. Rose worked steadily along these lines.

In addition to these women from abroad, a number of women from the United States began to demand political rights for women. Among them were Margaret Fuller, Lucy Stone, and Lucretia Mott.

Early in the nineteenth century women were drawn into the Anti-Slavery movement as well as into the movement for equal rights for women. Two South Carolina women, Sarah and Angelina Grimke, took the decisive step of emancipating their slaves in 1828, and by stirring speeches in the North aroused favorable public support for the anti-slavery cause. Soon thereafter, William Lloyd Garrison joined the movement and the American Anti-Slavery Society was formed. From the beginning of this Society, women were active in the campaign to free the slaves, and the names of the leaders among them soon became widely known. Prominent among them was Lucretia Mott. But when the women, recognizing their own rights, began to take part in the business meetings and public debates of the Anti-Slavery organization, the opposition became so violent that in 1839 the Society was split on this point.

Nearly all of the men that carried the abolition of slavery to success, the group that comprised Garrison, Phillips, Piermont, Pillsbury, Thompson, Foster, Stanton, and Gerrit Smith, espoused the rights of women and thereafter gave genuine support to the woman's rights campaign.

In the summer of 1840, Lucretia Mott was sent as a delegate from an American Abolition Society to a World's Anti-Slavery Convention in London. With Mrs. Mott were Elizabeth Cady Stanton, Mary Grew, five other women and several men, among whom were Wendell Phillips, William Lloyd Garrison, Nathan P. Rogers, Henry B. Stanton, and James G. Birney.

The men managing this London meeting were in a panic when they discovered that America had chosen some women delegates and that they were actually present in that capacity. Such a thing had never before been heard of! Had these women any right to take part in the proceedings? *Certainly not.* Why should they? There was no precedent. Seriously the question was considered. After two long days of bitter discussion, a verdict was reached excluding the women. The duly accredited women delegates from America had no standing at the London Convention, but they were permitted to sit in the gallery where they could be seen but not heard.

This high-handed action aroused much indignation among the Americans and among some of the British present. Two of the American delegates, William Lloyd Garrison and Nathaniel P. Rogers, refused, by way of protest, to attend the Convention except as spectators.

The treatment accorded the women delegates from America stirred them to a keener realization of woman's humiliating position as a disfranchised class. Also it laid the foundation for a beautiful friendship between Elizabeth Cady Stanton and Lucretia Mott, which stimulated and strengthened their work for Equal Rights for Women in the years to come.

In July, 1848, Lucretia Mott and her sister, Martha C. Wright, attended the yearly Meeting of Friends in Western New York, at Waterloo. Here Mrs. Stanton joined them

DR. ANNA HOWARD SHAW

President, National American Woman Suffrage Association

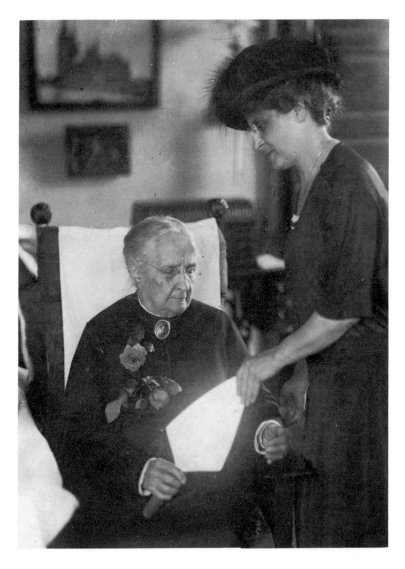

MRS. CHARLOTTE L. PEIRCE AND
CAROLINE KATZENSTEIN

Mrs. Peirce, who contributed a trowel to be used in laying the cornerstone at the dedication of headquarters of the National Woman's Party in Washington, D.C., May 21, 1922, delegated Miss Katzenstein to represent her.

at the home of Mrs. Mary Ann McClintock, where plans were made to organize a movement devoted especially to woman's rights. On a Sunday morning the four women prepared their now famous Resolutions and Declaration of Sentiments. A two-day convention to discuss "the social, civil, and religious condition and rights of woman" was arranged for July 19th and 20th in the Wesleyan Chapel, at Seneca Falls, New York.

A Call to this convention was sent to the county papers, but the four women did not dare to sign it!

James Mott, Lucretia Mott's husband, presided at the meeting. Addresses were made by the four callers of the Convention, by Frederick Douglass, and by several other men prominent in the locality. After discussion, the Resolutions were adopted and the Declaration of Sentiments was signed by one hundred men and women. Some of these signers withdrew their names when "the storm of ridicule began to break."

A look at the legal position of women at that period, 1848, will emphasize the need for a campaign such as the pioneers had planned. For some reason, or lack of it, married women were more discriminated against than single women. The handicaps upon women at the time of the Seneca Falls Convention are summarized in the historic 1848 "Declaration." Here are a few of the discriminations against women to which attention was then called:

> He [man] has made her, if married, in the eye of the law, civilly dead.
> He has taken from her all right in property, even to the wages she earns.
> He has made her, morally, an irresponsible being, as she can commit many crimes with impunity, provided they be done in the presence of her husband. In the covenant of marriage, she

is compelled to promise obedience to her husband, he becoming, to all intents and purposes, her master—the law giving him power to deprive her of her liberty, and to administer chastisement.

He has so framed the laws of divorce, as to what shall be the proper causes, and in case of separation, to whom the guardianship of the children shall be given, as to be wholly regardless of the happiness of women—the law, in all cases, going upon a false supposition of the supremacy of man, and giving all power into his hands.

After depriving her of all rights as a married woman, if single, and the owner of property, he has taxed her to support a government which recognizes her only when her property can be made profitable to it.

It should be emphasized that the meeting at Seneca Falls was not a Woman Suffrage Convention, but a Women's Rights Convention, and that the privilege of the franchise was only one of the rights that these pioneers were demanding. It was, in fact, the only one of the "Resolutions" not unanimously adopted. Mrs. Stanton and Frederick Douglass, however, held out so stoutly for the suffrage resolution that it was included with the others.

As reasonable as were the demands for equality made by women at that first meeting of its kind in recorded history, it took rare courage to make them. The Convention was undertaken with genuine anxiety. And there were serious misgivings in the hearts of its planners as to their ability to handle a public meeting. Also they were worried about the public's reception of the demands they would make.

Elizabeth Cady Stanton is described by her daughter, Harriot Stanton Blatch, as having been so filled with terror at the thought of directing a convention and of addressing a large audience that she longed to run away. The principle and ideal involved, however, helped her to overcome her fears. But when Lucretia Mott sent word she might not be able to attend the meeting on account of the illness of her husband, Mrs. Stanton felt she was facing almost more than she could bear. After all, though, Mrs. Mott arrived with her husband and soon heard from Mrs. Stanton's own lips the wording of that *alarmingly bold* demand for the franchise for women. Mrs. Mott's almost impatient reply was, "Oh Lizzie! If thou demandest that, thou wilt make us ridiculous! We must go slowly."

The press was bitter in its denunciations of the 1848 Resolutions. One newspaper that represented the general tone of the press wrote:

> This bolt is the most shocking and unnatural incident ever recorded in the history of humanity; if these demands were effected, it would set the world by the ears, make confusion worse confounded, demoralize and degrade from their high sphere and noble destiny women of all respectable and useful classes, and prove a monstrous injury to all mankind.

However, just four years later, in 1852, when Lucretia Mott presided at a Woman's Rights Convention in Syracuse, New York, the *Syracuse Standard* paid her the following compliment:

> It was a singular spectacle to see this Quaker matron presiding over a convention with an ease, grace, and dignity that might be envied by the most experienced legislator in the country.

At this meeting, Susan B. Anthony may be said to have begun her public appearance as an advocate of woman's rights, a leadership that lasted half a century.

Mrs. Charlotte L. Peirce was the last survivor of the Seneca Falls Convention and its only participant that lived to cast a vote. One of a family of fourteen children, Mrs. Peirce, then Charlotte Woodward, found herself at an early age face to face with the realities of life. At fifteen, she left home and taught school "five sessions."

In 1848, she was living in Waterloo, N. Y., just four miles from Seneca Falls, and was greatly stirred by the published Call to the Convention. She and a few friends excitedly planned to attend it, and early Wednesday morning, July 19, in a democrat wagon drawn by farm horses, were on their way. When they arrived at Wesleyan Chapel where the meetings were to be held, they found about fifty men crowded before the locked doors although men were not invited to the first day's sessions!

When Charlotte Woodward returned to her boarding house and began to tell her fellow boarders about her thrilling experience, she happened to mention the fact that Frederick Douglass, a speaker at the Convention, had come back with the Waterloo party in their wagon. A man at the table, shocked by her double boldness in attending a woman's convention and in being associated with Frederick Douglass, said, "Young ladies who do such things cannot expect attention from gentlemen." Her quick reply was, "Gentlemen had better wait until their attention is desired."

Fortunately, the man of her choice, Dr. C. N. Peirce, whom she met in Philadelphia, (her home for about seventy years) was not only deeply interested in her efforts to improve the status of woman, but, like her, was also an ardent abolitionist. Throughout their long and happy married life their constructive work in various fields added lustre to the name of Philadelphia.

Shortly after the Pennsylvania Legislature had ratified the Federal Woman Suffrage Amendment, I asked Mrs.

Peirce, then in her 90th year, if she expected to vote when ratification of the Amendment was completed. She replied, "I'll vote if I have to be carried to the polls."

From 1852, conventions for the rights of women and for the rights of Negroes were held in many parts of the United States. The movement for the emancipation of women made steady progress until the breaking out of the Civil War, which filled the public thought to the exclusion of practically all other questions. But Susan B. Anthony, though an ardent abolitionist, continued always with the crusaders for the emancipation of women. In her mind, war or no war, the campaign for woman's emancipation should go on. Although Elizabeth Cady Stanton did not at the time see eye to eye with Susan B. Anthony on this point, she later stated that she realized her mistake.

At the close of the war, the question of the rights of the Negro slaves seemed to be uppermost in the public mind. It was called the Negro's hour. The 13th Amendment to the National Constitution emancipated the Negro from slavery; the 14th Amendment gave him civil rights; the 15th Amendment granted him the franchise. The franchise for women was forgotten; civil rights for women were forgotten.

The Equal Rights Association, formed before the Civil War to promote the interests of both Negroes and white women, was changed in 1869 into an organization for the rights of women. This was at the close of a meeting of the Equal Rights Association, in New York City, attended by women from nineteen States. The women met May 15, 1869, and formed a new organization, called the National Woman Suffrage Association. Its object was to work for the emancipation of women, especially for an Amendment to the National Constitution, which would enfranchise women. Elizabeth Cady Stanton was made President and Susan B. Anthony was put on the Executive Committee.

Because of a division of opinion on tactics, Lucy Stone, Julia Ward Howe, and others issued a call for a Convention to meet in Cleveland, Ohio, in November, 1869. At this Cleveland convention, the American Woman Suffrage Association was formed, with Henry Ward Beecher as President, and Lucy Stone as Chairman of the Executive Committee. This group centered its work on obtaining suffrage for women through amendments to State constitutions. Both organizations held annual national conventions.

In 1890, the two organizations united, keeping in the name of the combined group the two names *National* and *American* and calling itself the National American Woman Suffrage Association. The new organization worked by both methods to obtain woman suffrage—through an amendment to the National Constitution and through amendments to the Constitutions of the States. Mrs. Stanton was elected its president; Miss Anthony, vice-president-at-large; and Lucy Stone, chairman of the Executive Committee.

In 1892, Mrs. Stanton, because of advancing age, resigned the presidency, and Susan B. Anthony was elected as her successor. The Rev. Anna Howard Shaw was elected vice-president. When at the age of 80 Miss Anthony resigned the presidency, in 1900, Mrs. Carrie Chapman Catt was elected to that office. Four years later, in 1904, Mrs. Catt, feeling unable to serve longer, was succeeded by Dr. Shaw.

Dr. Shaw, before beginning her work for the political enfranchisement of women, had learned from personal experience the difficulties women had to overcome in entering the professional world. Here, as in her suffrage work, she demonstrated her splendid fighting spirit. She received

a degree in medicine and one in theology. Although the
Methodist Episcopal Conference refused her ordination on
account of her sex, she was, nevertheless, ordained by the
Methodist Protestant Church. She had filled several pas-
torates in Massachusetts when, in 1888, she met Susan B.
Anthony. Thereafter she devoted her life to working for
woman suffrage.

When the Pennsylvania Headquarters were opened in
1910, it was to Dr. Shaw that we looked for guidance.

2

FIRST WOMAN SUFFRAGE HEADQUARTERS IN PENNSYLVANIA OPENED IN PHILADELPHIA 1910

If you believe in democracy and if you think women are human beings, you must believe in woman suffrage. To me the enfranchisement of women had always been as simple at that.

But in 1910, when I began my official suffrage work, I found that democracy was to many persons, then as now, only a name. I also found that while women were theoretically believed to be human beings they were not considered eligible to certain rights, privileges, and opportunities that give dignity and beauty to life—blessings the granting of which should not be questioned in any truly democratic community.

March 2, 1910, a long circular letter, signed by Mrs. Rachel Foster Avery, President of the Pennsylvania Woman Suffrage Association, Miss Jane Campbell, President of the Woman Suffrage Society of the County of Philadelphia, and a four-member Committee on Headquarters, was sent to Suffragists throughout Pennsylvania. It began, "We believe the time has come in Pennsylvania when the status of the suffrage work demands the establishment of state and county headquarters in Philadelphia."

(Prior to this time, suffrage work had been conducted from the homes of officers and members.) The letter said:

> It is estimated that suitable headquarters, centrally located, will cost between $400 and $500 rent per year. For about $40.00 per month we can secure a clerk who will be a moderately good stenographer and familiar with the typewriter, who can take charge of mail and sale of tickets for such lectures and entertainments as may be undertaken by the State and County Associations and other local suffrage bodies. We will need to have a telephone, a typewriter, and to provide for certain amount of stationery and postage. These items can be brought within a couple of hundred dollars annually. Our estimate is that a minimum sum of $1200 annually will be necessary to enable us to run the headquarters.

But seven months passed before our Headquarters could become a reality, and even then pledges for the modest sum of $1,200 to cover the year's budget had not been completed. As late, in fact, as December 10th, Emily Q. Atkinson, Chairman of Headquarters, felt it necessary to remind our members that pledges for only $864 had been received and to urge them to pledge the $336 balance needed.

December 13th, Alberta M. Goudiss, Press Chairman of the Philadelphia County Society, appealed by letter for help in getting subscribers to our National Official Organ, *The Woman's Journal*. After explaining that the expense of the new State and County Headquarters was "pressing very hard on local workers," she added:

> The *Journal* is offering a commission of $50.00 for one hundred new subscribers, if se-

cured before January 1st. Since the price of the
Journal has been reduced to $1.00 per year,
one can secure an excellent eight-page suffrage
newspaper for the moderate sum of two cents
per week. Thus far, we have secured 71 subscriptions. Can you not help us raise the remaining 29?

Suffragists had become so accustomed to the slow
process of educating the public that they seemed hardly
able to realize they were launching a genuine political
campaign and needed adequate funds to carry on. They
also needed a re-dedication of themselves to overcome the
indifference of many women, the opposition of large numbers of men and a small group of women anti-Suffragists,
and the antagonism and organized resistance of all too many
politicians. Sixty-two years had passed since the suffrage
pioneers had called their Convention of 1848 at Seneca
Falls, where they had stated the whole case for women
comprehensively. And yet Suffragists continued to show
amazing patience and to *plead* for a right unjustly denied
them instead of *demanding* it.

The plans outlined in the above letter of March 2, 1910,
became a reality the following October 7th, when the first
woman suffrage headquarters to be established in the Keystone State were opened at 208 Hale Building, S. W.
Corner of Chestnut and Juniper Streets, Philadelphia. I
was installed as its Executive Secretary. As the Pennsylvania Woman Suffrage Association, an auxiliary of the
National American Woman Suffrage Association, was then
forty-one years old, it was high time to inject into the
movement new life and to stimulate activity as only a
central home for it and its auxiliary societies could make
possible.

December 9th, the Equal Franchise Society of Philadelphia was invited to "share our comfortable quarters,"
and was offered, "on the payment of $100 into the Head-
quarters' Fund," desk space and other worth-while privileges. This offer was promptly accepted and our Headquarters thus became the official home of a State, a county,
and a city organization. The association of the three groups
was a happy one. Also, we managed somehow to pay all
our bills and to close the first year with a slight balance
on our books!

For a short time after we were settled in our new
Headquarters, things were rather quiet. Our large room,
with an abundance of windows, was a bright and cheerful
place for work, but being on the second floor in a building
with only two small elevators and a narrow, winding stair-
case it had its disadvantages. Friends could not drop in
easily, and the public, whose curiosity might have been
aroused if we had been located on the street floor, just
passed us by.

Miss Annie Heacock, of Wyncote, newly-appointed
Secretary of Headquarters Committee, had acted as secretary of the meeting held in Philadelphia, December 22,
1869, when the Pennsylvania Woman Suffrage Association
was organized. From her forty-one-year-old Minute Book,
I had a peep into the past and got at first-hand the following information on what took place on that historic
occasion.

Stimulated by the organization of the American Woman
Suffrage Association* in Cleveland, Ohio, the previous
November 24th and 25th, a group of leading Philadelphia
men and women met in the hall of the Mercantile Library,

---

* Later joined with the National Woman Suffrage Association to
become the National American Woman Suffrage Association.

10th Street above Chestnut, to organize an auxiliary of the new national association.

John K. Wildman read the call to the meeting, and Judge William S. Peirce, active in many reform movements in the past, served as its chairman. John K. Wildman, Miss Ramborger, Clementine John, Ellen M. Child, and Passmore Williamson were chosen as a committee of five to draft the new Association's constitution. Mary Grew, who began her work for freedom as Corresponding Secretary of the Philadelphia Female Anti-Slavery Society in 1834, who was one of the founders of the New Century Club of Philadelphia, and who later served as President of the Pennsylvania Woman Suffrage Association for twenty-three years, addressed the meeting.

I feel impelled to call the reader's especial attention to two outstanding facts in Miss Heacock's minutes. The first is that a man presided at the meeting that organized the Pennsylvania Woman Suffrage Association, and that two men were on the committee of five that drafted the organization's constitution. The second is that members of the Society of Friends were conspicuous at this meeting.

Now, in order to link the meeting in the hall of the Mercantile Library in Philadelphia, December 22, 1869, to the opening of the Suffrage Headquarters in Pennsylvania in 1910, I shall give a few historical facts. Mary Grew was made the first president of the new State association. When, in 1892, Miss Grew resigned at the age of 80, she was succeeded in the presidency by Mrs. Lucretia L. Blankenburg, who held that office many years. Mrs. Blankenburg was the wife of Rudolph Blankenburg, Philadelphia's reform Mayor, whom the newspapers called the Old Dutch Cleanser.

Prior to 1892, Philadelphians identified with the suffrage movement belonged to the State Association. But in the fall of that year it was decided to make the Pennsylvania Association a delegate body. As that barred individual memberships, the Philadelphia members formed a county organization. Miss Grew was asked to lead the new organization, but as she felt unable to assume the necessary duties of an active officer, she accepted only the honorary presidency. However, it was largely due to her counsel and influence that the new society had its successful beginning. After Miss Grew's death in 1896, the office of honorary president was abolished. The first president of the County Society was Miss Jane Campbell, who was annually re-elected and was, I believe, the Society's only president. It was Miss Campbell, who joined with Mrs. Rachel Foster Avery in sending out that letter in 1910, already mentioned, urging the opening of our first State and County Headquarters in Philadelphia.

As Suffragists in Pennsylvania were working for an amendment to the National Constitution at the same time they were working for an amendment to the State Constitution, the new Pennsylvania Headquarters served as a center for both campaigns.

Before bringing to a close the story of the opening of Pennsylvania's first woman suffrage headquarters, we should, I think, review briefly the advances the movement had made in the period between the early years of the pioneers and the time around which this book begins.

From 1848 the campaign for woman suffrage was carried on with increasing interest until in 1910 there were five fully enfranchised States. *Wyoming was the first place in recorded history where women went to the polls on equal terms with men.* Here is a list of those five States and the years in which they enfranchised women:

Wyoming.....	1869	Idaho........	1896
Colorado	1893	Washington...	1910
Utah	1896		

Simultaneously with this progress in the States, there was conducted a campaign for an amendment to the United States Constitution for the purpose of granting suffrage to women similar to that granted Negroes after the Civil War by the 15th Amendment. A Woman Suffrage Amendment was introduced in the Senate by Aaron Augustus Sargent, Senator from California, January 10, 1878.* This action was taken at the request of Susan B. Anthony, Elizabeth Cady Stanton, and other suffrage leaders.

While some of the western States were enfranchising their women, the movement was also making progress in some foreign countries as the following listing will show:— New Zealand, in 1893, granted full suffrage to all women; in 1902, full suffrage to women was granted throughout Federated Australia; in 1906, Finland granted full suffrage to all women. (At that time, Finland was a subordinate State under Russia.)

In addition to the five States already mentioned that had granted full suffrage to women, there were other parts of the United States where some form of partial suffrage had been given women, as follows:

SCHOOL SUFFRAGE was granted certain classes of women, subject to various restrictions, in:

Kentucky......1838		Montana 1887	
Kansas........1861		New Jersey....1887	
Michigan 1875		North Dakota..1887	

---

* See appendix for record of vote on this Amendment, the 19th when it was ratified, August 18, 1920, called the Susan B. Anthony Amendment.

Minnesota..... 1875	South Dakota.. 1887
New Hampshire 1878	Arizona 1887
Oregon 1878	Oklahoma 1890
Massachusetts.. 1879	Connecticut 1893
Vermont 1880	Ohio 1894
New York..... 1880	Delaware 1898
Mississippi 1880	Wisconsin 1900
Nebraska 1883	

SUFFRAGE on TAXATION and BONDING propositions was granted certain classes of women, subject to various restrictions in:

Montana 1887	New York..... 1901
Iowa 1894	Kansas 1903
Louisiana 1898	Michigan 1908

MUNICIPAL SUFFRAGE was granted to women in Kansas in 1887.

With this injection of the world picture of woman's enfranchisement up to and a little beyond the opening of State Headquarters in Philadelphia, we can see that Pennsylvania women needed abundant faith and hope to believe in the possibility of woman's ever securing full political equality with man.

3

OUR FIRST YEAR AT HEADQUARTERS . . .
THE PRESS BECOMES OUR ALLY
1910-1911

The women at the head of the State Association in 1910 were Mrs. Rachel Foster Avery of Swarthmore, President; Mrs. Mary B. Luckie of Chester, Vice-President; Miss Katharine Collison of Philadelphia, Corresponding Secretary; Miss Jane Campbell of Germantown, State Member of the Executive Committee of the National American Woman Suffrage Association; Mrs. Mary Churchman Morgan of Philadelphia, Recording Secretary; Miss Matilda Orr Hays of Wilkinsburg, Treasurer. The Auditors were Mrs. Robert D. Coard of Pittsburgh, and Rebie Van Artsdalen of Ivyland.

Mrs. Avery brought to her State work a long experience of active participation in the national field. For twenty-one years, from 1880 to 1901, she had served as Corresponding Secretary of the N. A. W. S. A.*

There was a very friendly atmosphere at Headquarters and a cordial relationship among the officers. But of them all, the one to whom I felt most indebted for guidance and advice was Mrs. Morgan. Her fearlessness, courage, and calm wisdom were a constant source of inspiration. Her Quaker training and thinking seemed to make action a

---

* National American Woman Suffrage Association.

OFFICERS OF PENNSYLVANIA WOMAN
SUFFRAGE ASSOCIATION

Left to right, top row: Annie Heacock, Jane Campbell, Lida Stokes Adams. *Middle row:* Rachel Foster Avery, Ellen H. E. Price. *Bottom row:* Mary Churchman Morgan, Emily Q. Atkinson, Caroline Katzenstein.

MRS. LUCRETIA L. BLANKENBURG

A President of the Pennsylvania Woman Suffrage Association, and Philadelphia's First Lady, 1911-1916.

natural and easy outcome of the spirit that stirred within her. The mother of three children, she wished to influence the legislation that affected not only her own home and children, but homes and children everywhere.

Soon there were two changes in our official family. Mrs. Avery resigned as State President, and Miss Collison, as Corresponding Secretary. Mrs. Ellen H. E. Price succeeded Mrs. Avery as President, and I became the Corresponding Secretary. Mrs. Price had unusual qualifications for her suffrage work. She belonged to the generation of women that had to prove the right to higher education, not only for themselves but for their sex. As a college graduate, as a teacher, as the wife of a college professor and the mother of two teachers, and as one who had filled many important offices in work of the Society of Friends she had been an exponent of woman's power to serve effectively wherever her lot was cast—in the home, in the school, and in the community.

This year, an *Outline of the Legal Position of Women in Pennsylvania,* prepared by Alice Paul, which included changes in the law by the 1911 Legislature, was added to our literature department. The pamphlet had this introductory note by Owen J. Roberts, LL.D., who was then Professor of Law at the University of Pennsylvania:

> I have gone carefully over Miss Paul's work, and, in my opinion, it is entirely accurate, and very well arranged. The work has been carefully done, and there seems to be nothing to add to it. Its excellent features are its method of arrangement, and the shortness and clarity of the statement of the various propositions.

Many ways had been devised to help fill our war chest. We had on sale at Headquarters fancy articles, Suffrage

washcloths that stared the user in the face each morning
with "Taxation without representation is tyranny," and
Suffrage candy. An ardent young Suffragist, Olga Gross,
although occupied during the day with a position ordinarily
filled by a man, had made, principally at night, about two
hundred pounds of peanut brittle and given the profit on
this labor to pay for our telephone. Also, there was a
circulating library of books relating to women.

With an original allowance of $10, our Chairman of
Literature, Emily Q. Atkinson, had bought 26,284 pieces
of literature and also suffrage post cards, buttons, pins, note
paper, posters, blotters, rubber stamps,* baggage stickers,
etc. By making a small profit on our sales and by turning
the money over many times the Chairman of Literature
had paid bills amounting to $194.51.

Our income for the first year was made up of the
following items:

Pledges and contributions	$1,062.99
Rental of desk space by the Equal Franchise Society	90.00†
Premiums and commissions on subscription to the *Woman's Journal*	75.00
Sale of fancy articles	24.00
Interest on money in bank	7.67
Total	$1,259.66

As the cost of maintaining Headquarters, including rent,
salary, office supplies, furnishing, telephone, etc., had been

---

* Seemingly small ways of advertising the campaign were very
effective. Arthur Hassler, a member of a prominent musical family
and for many years leader of an orchestra, recently reminded me that,
during the suffrage campaign, even his bank checks were stamped with
VOTES FOR WOMEN.

† The annual rental of $100. was adjusted because the E.F.S. did
not join us when the Headquarters were first opened.

only $1047.08, we were able to close the first year's finan-
cial account with a balance of $212.58! Of course, much
more was spent than appeared on our books because members bore many of the expenses connected with their work,
such as paying trainfare to Harrisburg and other places,
but we had no way of reckoning these sums.

One day, soon after the opening of Headquarters,
some reporters came in to see us, and Miss Lida Stokes
Adams talked with them. She invited me to "listen in"
and see how an interview was conducted. That was my
training in newspaper work! Shortly afterward, I was
appointed chairman of publicity for the State Association
—a bit of evidence of our lack of trained workers. For a
time my new rôle was not a difficult one because we had not
planned anything sufficiently exciting to be of real interest
to the press. Also, in the eyes of the editors the "cub"
reporters were all that we rated. But this estimate of our
news value worked out better than it promised. The very
young and inexperienced reporters sent to Headquarters
appreciated the cordial welcome they received and our
willingness to explain the suffrage movement to them in
addition to giving them carefully prepared copy. They were
so anxious to succeed in their new profession that they
eagerly accepted a story when we had anything worth-
while to offer them. And they were, I think, much less
prejudiced against woman suffrage than many of the older
reporters.

Because of my own lack of experience in press work,
I planned from the first to avoid, if possible, being mis-
quoted and when I was asked for an interview I would
write a statement that the reporter could break up into an
interview when he went back to his office. As I kept a
carbon copy of these statements they have proved helpful
in the writing of this book.

Since there was practically no available fund for paid propaganda, I soon realized that the newspapers offered our main, almost our only, hope of success and I set out to cultivate the press and to establish a friendly relation with all the papers, even with those at first definitely opposed to us. Gradually, as our work began to take shape, and the papers learned better to know the caliber of our leaders, the editors would occasionally ask of them an expression of opinion on public questions not directly related to our campaign.

Also, when a distinguished visitor who was in favor of woman suffrage came to Philadelphia I would seek him or her out for an interview at our Headquarters and would invite the reporters to come in at the appointed hour to meet the visitor. This was not only a means of propaganda for us, but it was a convenience to the newspapers and it added to the importance of Headquarters. I recall especially the success of an interview with Forbes Robertson, the famous English actor, whose niece, Beatrice Forbes Robertson Hale, was one of our speakers. Mr. Robertson was in Philadelphia to fill a theatrical engagement that had been eagerly awaited by the public, and a statement from him was sure to attract wide attention. As it was more convenient for Mr. Robertson to be seen at his hotel, I rounded up the reporters and went with them to make sure there would be no hitch in obtaining the interview. Gradually our relation with the press grew friendlier and friendlier and our news was considered of some value. Occasionally we were honored by a visit from an editor. It may not be amiss here to look a bit into the future to show how this friendly relationship developed.

In 1913, at the Pennsylvania Woman Suffrage Association's convention in Pittsburgh, I was asked to take part in a discussion on press work and shall quote a part of what I said at that time:

Since Suffrage Headquarters were opened in Philadelphia a little more than three years ago, there has been a wonderful change in the attitude of the local press toward us. From a feeling of bare tolerance, there has developed not only an interest in our work but a feeling of sympathy toward the Cause. There is now, I think, only one newspaper in Philadelphia that is really anti-suffrage, while several are not only friendly, but strongly pro-suffrage. Nor is this change felt only at the city desk. Even the telephone operator has learned to respect us. Three years ago, when I called up a newspaper to give in a *valued* item, the wire brought back a supercilious operator's disconcerting announcement of our call, "Suffragettes calling." Today, the operator knows the press chairman's name and announces it to the paper. She may even say, "Good morning, do you wish to speak to the City Editor?" This sounds unimportant, but to have developed from a despised collective mass into a specific human being with a real appellation is a significant advance. The change is partly due, I think, to the fact that the newspapers have learned to know us. They have seen that we are a sane, determined group of workers bent on carrying out a great reform. And we have discovered that behind the powerful institution known as the press there are real human beings, who can be reached if properly approached.

In return for courtesies we have shown them, the Philadelphia papers are most considerate and generous to us. It is not infrequent that one paper will make, free of charge, enough copies of a photograph to furnish all the other city papers. Four of the five morning papers and all three of the afternoon papers accord me the privilege of a regular reporter in the use of the reverse phone call. In fact the press work in Philadelphia is carried on with no special appropriation of money at all and the slight expense attached to it comes out of a small account for incidental expenses.

During the discussion I emphasized the fact that I thought it was just as important to express appreciation of a good newspaper report as to complain of an unsatisfactory one.

In about one year's time after the opening of Headquarters, the Executive Secretary was able to report the organization of ten counties into twenty-seven suffrage societies. Adding to these the twelve Ward Equal Suffrage Leagues in Philadelphia, all of which were auxiliary to the Woman Suffrage Society of the County of Philadelphia, Pennsylvania had a total of thirty-nine suffrage organizations.

State Headquarters had not only stimulated interest in the campaign, but had greatly simplified our work. Our hearing before the Senate and the House at Harrisburg, March 14, 1911, would have been practically impossible without this central place for work. Thousands of letters and notices were sent all over the State and volunteer workers helped to accomplish this work at a minimum cost.

Next in importance to the hearing, was the open-air campaign in Philadelphia during which twenty-one meetings were held in different parts of the city between July 25th and September 30th. But this story deserves a separate chapter, and will be told in the one that follows.

The Pennsylvania Woman Suffrage Association's interesting 43rd annual Convention was held in Philadelphia, November 23, 24, and 25, 1911. Through the courtesy of Mayor Rudolph Blankenburg, four of the morning and

afternoon sessions of the Convention were held in the
Mayor's Reception Room, City Hall. Prominent among
the Convention speakers were Dr. Anna Howard Shaw;
Dr. Harvey W. Wiley, United States Chemist; Dr. George
Edward Reed, ex-president of Dickinson College; and
Mrs. Emmeline Pankhurst, the famous suffrage leader of
England.

I closed my report on our first year's work with these
hopeful words:

> We have an active Hospitality Committee,
> which arranges from time to time delightful re-
> ceptions to enable new members to meet the older
> workers. It has been a real joy to see how all
> classes of women meet on the common ground of
> suffrage. We are actually learning "team-work."
> If the future did not seem full of promise, if the
> emancipation of women were impossible instead
> of sure, I should still think the Cause worth
> working for if only to teach women the splendid
> development that comes from co-operation in a
> great work.

4

PENNSYLVANIA'S FIRST OPEN-AIR SUFFRAGE CAMPAIGN 1911

In the summer of 1911 the suffrage movement in Pennsylvania received an unexpected and most significant contribution when two brilliant young college women, Alice Paul of New Jersey and Lucy Burns of New York, offered their services gratis to inaugurate and conduct an open-air suffrage campaign in the Keystone State. This generous offer, made to Mrs. Ellen H. E. Price, the new State President, was gratefully accepted and Alice Paul was authorized to take charge of the work. Miss Paul's official position was Chairman of a Committee on Open-air Meetings for the State Association. In her notice to the editor of the *Woman's Journal*, she wrote, July 26, 1911, "The first open-air suffrage meeting ever held in Philadelphia took place last night." After giving some details of the meeting, she added, "This is the beginning of a vigorous open-air campaign which the State Association will conduct in this city during the summer months. Two meetings will be held every night this week in various parts of the city and later when the movement is well started, meetings will be held twice a week or oftener." She closed her news item with this comment, "Several hundred men and women gathered around the speakers, listening attentively and with apparent cordiality from beginning to end."

Before I make a more detailed report on these first open-air meetings, the reader will, I believe, be interested in knowing something of the background of Miss Paul and Miss Burns. Alice Paul, born of a long Quaker ancestry, and descended from the Penn and other distinguished families connected with the founding of Philadelphia, was born in Moorestown, New Jersey, a few miles from Philadelphia. She attended Quaker school in Moorestown, was graduated from Swarthmore College in 1905, the New York School of Social Work in 1906, and received an M.A. degree from the University of Pennsylvania in 1907. In 1907, 1908, and 1909, she was a student in Berlin, Germany, and at Woodbrooke School for Religious and Social Work in England, and at the University of Birmingham and the University of London, in England. While helping in the suffrage campaign in Philadelphia in 1911, she was a Fellow at the University of Pennsylvania working for her Ph.D. degree, which she received the following year.

Lucy Burns was born in Brooklyn, New York. She was graduated from Vassar College in 1902; studied English at Yale University 1902-3; taught English at Erasmus Hall High School in Brooklyn 1904-06; and studied in Berlin and Bonn, Germany, 1906-09. From 1909 to 1912, she worked for the Women's Social and Political Union in the campaign that organization was waging to enfranchise the women of England. It was while she was on a visit to her family in 1911, that she took time out to aid the woman suffrage movement in Pennsylvania.

Although Miss Paul and Miss Burns had gone to Europe to continue their studies at various universities, they both found themselves in 1909 caught in the aggressive campaign being waged by suffragists in England, and they volunteered to help in the ranks of Mrs. Emmeline Pankhurst's group, the Women's Social and Political Union.

In the early summer of 1909 on the occasion of a deputation to the Prime Minister, led by Mrs. Pankhurst, Miss Paul and Miss Burns were both arrested and they met for the first time at the Bow Street Police Station in London. As the case was appealed, no one was imprisoned. But later in that summer when the two young women were speakers at an open-air meeting outside the famous Limehouse meeting in London held by Lloyd George, they were arrested with other speakers and were imprisoned in Holloway Jail. After their release from Holloway, they were again arrested for speaking at an open-air meeting in Glasgow, Scotland. As the charges were not pressed by the Glasgow authorities, all the women were released without being sentenced. A little later, that same summer, they were arrested for taking part in an open-air meeting in Dundee, Scotland, and this time both were imprisoned. However, because of a hunger strike, they were released after a few days. In November, 1909, Miss Paul was arrested for taking part in a suffrage demonstration at the Guild Hall in London on the occasion of the Lord Mayor's Banquet. This time, she was imprisoned in Holloway Jail, London, for a month.

Now let us return to the beginning of our open-air meetings in Philadelphia, the first of which was held Tuesday, July 25, 1911, and see some of the things that took place before and after they began.

In order that we might start out together that first night, seven of us met at the Suffrage Headquarters, 208 Hale Building. In addition to Miss Paul and Miss Burns, our little band included Mrs. Mary Churchman Morgan; Mrs. Margaret C. Klingelsmith, a lawyer, and, at the time, librarian of the University of Pennsylvania Law Library; Miss Center, Mrs. Klingelsmith's sister; and Olga H. Gross.

In 1911, Philadelphia was still using some of the old

type summer cars similar to the park trolley cars that were discontinued in 1946. They had running boards on each side of the car and riders stepped from these boards into the cars. The seats ran across the car instead of length-wise. As there were only a few passengers in the car when we started out, we were able to have two rows of seats all to ourselves near the front and to talk freely without fear of being overheard.

Contrary to our usual custom of seeking all the publicity possible for our activities, no advance notices had been sent to the press. The reason was that we thought it best not to ask for a police permit to hold the meeting for fear it might be refused us. (Such a meeting had never before been held in Philadelphia's history.) After we had demon-strated that there was no danger to the public in permitting women to hold open-air suffrage meetings at specially selected intersections where there was sufficient space not to interfere with traffic, it would seem ridiculous for the authorities to refuse us this privilege. This reasoning proved sound and we were able thereafter to get a permit in advance of our meetings and thus to be strictly law-abiding! Well, anyway, here we were this first night start-ing out to do something a bit irregular from a legal point of view and no one knew better than Miss Paul the possible consequences. She therefore explained the situation to us as we rode along and she posed this question: "If the police interfere with our meeting, shall we offer resist-ance?" With her keen psychological insight, she did not mean this question to invite a general discussion on to-do or not-to-do and she clinched the subject by quickly adding, "If the police threaten to arrest us and we offer no resist-ance, it will mean the end of open-air suffrage meetings in Philadelphia." To her rhetorical question, "Shall we offer resistance?" there was not a dissenting voice. And there was no apparent hesitancy about facing the unpleasant possibilities.

From the street car, we went direct to the Washington Hotel at 7th and Dauphin Streets where a one-horse cart had already been hired for the evening and a very kindly driver had been assigned us—all for the modest sum of $1.50. We had earlier procured a frame about one yard square that had been used by a sandwich-man. This frame had been covered with yellow sateen at a cost of 30¢, and Olga H. Gross had been able to get *Votes for Women* painted on it in bold, black letters free of charge.

But as we neared Front and Dauphin Streets, the corner selected for our meeting, I am frank to confess that I seemed to develop a sort of *Jack and the Beanstalk* complex, because the policeman on the beat near our corner appeared to grow taller and taller and bigger and bigger the closer we got to him. To me he seemed to be not just an arm of the law but the whole body of it! And when I looked around and saw our little band of *conspirators,* the possible battle we were facing seemed as if it might be a very unequal combat. Neither Miss Paul nor Mrs. Klingelsmith weighed, I think, more than a hundred pounds. And while others in our party were more robust looking, Lucy Burns seemed to offer the most effective resister if resistance should become necessary. She was of statuesque build, with a mass of lovely red hair arranged in a braid on top of her head, and her irresistible smile should have disarmed any policeman, no matter what his size. But the law is the law, and an officer, no matter how gallant, might feel he had to do his duty. However, Mrs. Morgan's civic work had taught her many things and her level head came to the rescue with a suggestion that eased the tension. Shortly before the meeting began, she called me aside and said that because I was needed at headquarters I must not stand the chance of being arrested. She said that if we got into trouble with the police I should hurry to a public telephone and call her husband, Mr. George Morgan, and tell him to come down and put up bail for all of us that needed it. Mr. Morgan, Sunday Editor of the Philadelphia *Record,* was not only a devoted husband, but a good friend of the Cause, and we knew we could count on his prompt response to his wife's message.

And now the exciting moment had arrived. Miss Paul and Miss Burns were driving up in the little cart, and Olga Gross was with them guarding the *Votes for Women* placard. The cart was to serve as a rostrum for the speakers, and the placard, soon to be unveiled, was to whet the curiosity of the crowd and quickly to acquaint them with the purpose of the meeting. We came, they saw, we conquered! The crowd gathered around us and soon numbered, I think, about three hundred persons. Miss Paul opened the meeting and introduced Mrs. Morgan who spoke on the "Woman in the Home." Mrs. Klingelsmith spoke next, and Miss Burns closed the meeting with her usual delightful and convincing talk. The crowd paid remarkable attention, seemed genuinely interested, and asked a number of questions. Beatrice Brown of New York who had joined us at the place of meeting, assisted Olga Gross and me in milling through the crowd and giving out suffrage leaflets and copies of the *Woman's Journal.*

After all our anxiety, the kindly policeman did not interfere with our meeting in any way. Perhaps his inexperience in facing such an unusual situation as the one we presented made him unable to think his way out with clarity and speed. Or maybe he was just fine enough to take a big view of what was happening and saw no reason to interfere with our demonstration. Anyway, our meeting was a great success and we were started on a new and most effective way of making our appeal to the public.

As it was fairly late when our meeting closed, Mrs. Morgan acted as my chaperon back to headquarters and stayed until I had telephoned the exciting news to the press. When I picked up the telephone and said, "Philadelphia has had its first open-air suffrage meeting," it seemed to me that there was more interest at the city desks than I had ever before been able to arouse. At that time, Philadelphia had five morning papers, the *Inquirer, North American, Press, Public Ledger,* and *Record.* And there were three afternoon papers, the *Bulletin, Telegraph,* and *Times.* I can locate no clippings of this July 25th meeting and neither the *Inquirer* nor the *Bulletin* (Philadelphia's only remaining newspapers in 1954 of the eight published in 1911) could help me when I asked recently if they had any clippings on it in their files. They did not maintain in 1911 the excellent clipping system they have today. I can quote from only one of the eight Philadelphia papers of 1911. In Miss Paul's news item to the *Woman's Journal* to which I have already referred, she used the following quotation from the *Public Ledger* of July 26, 1911:

> The appearance of the wagon with its women speakers very soon attracted a large crowd, which throughout the course of the evening meeting displayed intense interest in the proceedings, and at the unusual spectacle of a street corner meeting in this city.
>
> The arguments of the Suffragist leaders were listened to with rapt attention, and frequent questions were asked, but there was no disturbance.
>
> The spectacle of a woman with a wagon for a platform pleading for the use of the ballot was so novel that the audience was quick to re-

spond to the points made by the speakers, who received a cordial reception, mingled with cheers when telling points were made.

The following evening, July 26, Alice Paul, Lucy Burns, Mrs. Morgan, Olga H. Gross, and I met again at the Washington Hotel, drove in our "One-hoss shay" to Front and Diamond Streets, and had even a better meeting than the evening before. Mrs. Morgan was the chairman, and Alice Paul and Lucy Burns the speakers. Olga Gross and I again distributed leaflets and this time took up a collection. A resolution appealing to the Elections Commission for favorable action on Woman Suffrage was passed by a large majority. According to my original notes on this meeting, Mr. Mitchell of the *Press* gave us excellent publicity on the telephoned report of it to his paper after the meeting.

Our third meeting, held July 27, at the corner of Germantown and Lehigh Avenues, was the best one so far. This time, we had notified the press in advance of the meeting and reporters and photographers were on hand to cover it. Again the Washington Hotel provided transportation to the meeting for the same five Suffragists of the evening before. Mrs. Morgan introduced not only Alice Paul and Lucy Burns, but Olga H. Gross, who spoke for the working girl. When the resolution addressed to the Elections Commission was offered, it met with practically unanimous approval. Also the collection was larger than the evening before. Plainly, we were making progress in our appeal for public support of granting women the use of the ballot.

For our fourth open-air meeting, we selected the north side of City Hall Plaza. To the five regular workers, we had two additions, Mrs. Robert Keen and my sister, Ida Katzenstein. We had asked the Socialists, who were accustomed to hold open-air meetings, to rent us a stand for our speakers, but they generously lent it instead. Our chairman, Mrs. Morgan, made a short talk and so did Olga Gross. Lucy Burns then spoke for about one hour and was followed by Alice Paul, who spoke for about an hour and a half. During all this time, the crowd listened attentively. Then the meeting was thrown open for questions from the audience, and Alice Paul was wonderful both in handling the crowd and in answering questions. One man, apparently drunk, interrupted many times during the question period, but he was unable to interfere with Alice Paul's control of the meeting, and his questions were courteously answered. The *Press* reporter, who told us he had been sent to write the meeting up comically, promised not to do this, and, at the close of the meeting, at Alice Paul's request, he carried our sign back to Headquarters for us. When slips were offered for names of sympathizers and supporters of our campaign, a lawyer added to his signature a statement that he should be glad to aid the Cause.

Saturday, July 29, our fifth meeting was at the corner of Germantown and Girard Avenues. I was chairman, and the speakers were Mrs. Morgan, Dr. Earnest Stevens, Paulette Boheme, Lucy Burns, Virginia P. Robinson, and Alice Paul. We were much moved by a poorly dressed woman who, when the collection was taken, emptied her pocketbook of its sixteen cents to aid in the campaign. Because of the Saturday night crowd and the presence of a number of children on the street, the meeting was the noisiest one we had had, but our speakers were able to stand the strain on their vocal cords and the evening was successful.

For our sixth open-air meeting, Monday, July 31, we invaded West Philadelphia at 40th Street and Lancaster Avenue. Mrs. Morgan, chairman, introduced as her first speaker Jennie Rantz, a self-supporting young girl, who was not only an ardent Suffragist but an able and very intelligent speaker upon whom we could depend for help in the years ahead of us. Three other speakers, Paulette Boheme, Lucy Burns and Virginia P. Robinson, helped to make the evening memorable.

Once when the press later in the campaign began to lag in giving us publicity, and needed stimulation, Alice Paul planned a special "stunt" to arouse newspaper interest, and asked Mrs. Mary Churchman Morgan and me to carry out her plan. We were told to leave our homes in the very early morning, before the wheels of industry had begun to turn, and to give the public a thought for the day.

Supplied with a box of cakes of chalk, not sticks, Mrs. Morgan and I, around four A.M., met and started out on our publicity mission. We hurried down to the center of Philadelphia and, on as many wide sidewalks as time allowed us, we wrote in large letters our slogan, VOTES FOR WOMEN. As it did not take long to write just three words, we were able to cover considerable space in a comparatively short time. And the newspapers also covered considerable space in reporting this mysterious defacement of the city's sidewalks. Thus we had chalked up another publicity victory without any raid on our slim treasury.

Night after night, Miss Paul and Miss Burns spoke at open-air meetings in various parts of Philadelphia and continued to draw large crowds and to arouse much interest. And the press was not slow in seeing the effectiveness of this new way of appealing to the public for woman's enfranchisement and in grasping its news value. Unfortunately, it took some time to develop good speakers for the outdoor work among the local Suffragists and Miss Paul felt keenly the need to accomplish this. One Saturday afternoon, after closing hours at our Headquarters, she and I lingered to do some work and to discuss the open-air campaign. She asked me to speak at the evening meeting although she must have known, I think, that I had no talent at all in that direction. When she saw my reaction to her request, she explained, "The papers will get tired of reporting as speakers only Alice Paul and Lucy Burns, Lucy Burns and Alice Paul. We need to have new names to keep up their interest." It seemed like an impossible assignment for me as the very thought of addressing a street crowd made my heart pump so loud that I thought a person near me could have heard it. And yet, as I hated to say no to our leader, I tried to muster courage to do my part. I put my arms on the table and rested my head on them while I struggled to see if I could overcome the dread that filled me. Finally, I looked up and said, "Miss Paul, I am going through the tortures of the damned." She didn't come over and try to comfort me and she did not try to make the task seem a light one. She answered simply in her calm, imperturbable way, "We've all done that." Finally, she explained, "It doesn't make any difference what you say at the meeting. Even if you only introduce Miss Burns and me, it will give the papers another name to use." I promised to play my part as "local color" and to be "another name," and, in preparation for this important role, I developed a genuine headache thus lessening my likelihood of being effective in the slightest degree in making a convert to woman suffrage.

Night after night, the papers sent reporters and photographers to cover our meetings. Miss Paul's pale face and frail body made a striking contrast to Miss Burns' ruddy complexion and sturdy frame.

At one of our evening meetings, a group of street urchins, who were small enough to be at home asleep in their beds, mounted a little box near our corner and displayed a crudely-made placard on which was written VOTES FOR BOYS. At the top of their voices they screamed their slogan for a few minutes, thus adding to the strain on the throats of the women, who were already struggling against the regular street noises. But the competition was not serious and the children soon tired of their fun and left us in control of the crowd.

As the campaign progressed, we not only "influenced people," but we "made friends" in abundance. One of the most needed contributions to our work was the construction of some specially-made movable platforms for the speakers. These ingenious contrivances were, I believe, actually conceived by Mrs. Katherine G. Halligan and they were just one of her many gifts to the Cause. They were several feet high, very sturdily built but not too heavy to be rolled easily on their low wheels. The speakers could, with little difficulty, climb up the well-graded steps to the platform, and be just properly elevated above the crowd. Mr. Ryerson W. Jennings, one of our ardent champions, let us store one of these HALLIGAN STUMPSTERS in his Little Hotel Wilmot which was located on South Penn Square within a stone's throw of City Hall Plaza, our happy hunting ground for central city campaigning. All we had to do was to get a boy to roll a HALLIGAN STUMPSTER to a selected spot and we were ready to call the meeting to order. And what an improvement the street meetings were over meetings we had held in halls! No rent, no paid speakers (a luxury we indulged in occasionally), no notices to be sent to members, practically no expense at all. Also, the audiences we reached on the street were largely persons who would not have taken the time to go to an indoor suffrage meeting, but who would listen to our appeal when presented without any inconvenience to them. And, as most of them were men, we were able to educate voters in whose hands our fate rested. As fine as many of the indoor meetings were, they were largely attended by members of suffrage organizations. The most the leaders could expect to accomplish from them was to stimulate the members to renewed interest in the campaign, to raise small sums of money, obtain publicity, and, of course, to get a few converts to the Cause. Often the results achieved were meager and discouraging, considering the effort and expense involved.

The open-air meetings made suffrage history, and the 1911 summer campaign came to a brilliant close September 30th in the most fitting of places—Philadelphia's Independence Square, a spot hallowed in our nation's history. From five stands, the following eighteen speakers, in turn, addressed an estimated crowd of 2000 persons from 3 P. M. until 5:30:

> Dr. Anna Howard Shaw, our National President.
> Miss Harriet May Mills, President of the New York State Woman Suffrage Association.
> Dr. George Edward Reed, ex-President of Dickinson College.
> Miss Inez Milholland, a Vassar graduate, chosen on account of her beauty to lead the New York suffrage parade.
> Miss Eleanor Brannan, granddaughter of Charles A. Dana, founder and editor of the New York *Sun*.
> Miss Emily Pierson of Connecticut, an M.A. from Columbia University.
> Dr. Earl Barnes, formerly professor at Leland Stanford University.
> Miss Alberta Hill from Australia.
> Mrs. Rheta Childe Dorr, author of *What Eight Million Women Want*.
> Mrs. William L. Colt, Vice-President of the West

Chester County Suffrage Association in New York.

Rev. Arthur Hilton, of the Baptist Church.

Miss Jane Campbell, President of the W.S. Society of the County of Philadelphia.

Miss Florence Sanville, Secretary of the Pennsylvania Consumers' League.

Mrs. Louis N. Robinson, graduate of Swarthmare and Columbia.

Mrs. Leonard Averett, a young and attractive local speaker.

Miss Beatrice Brown, of New York, who helped at our first open-air meeting.

Mrs. Mary Churchman Morgan, Recording Secretary of the Pennsylvania W. S. Asso.

Miss Alice Paul, at that time a Fellow at the University of Pennsylvania.

I hope at least some of the many thousands of women that in recent years have taken part in the sale of Liberty Bonds, in getting blood donors for the Red Cross, and in other worth-while public work, have realized with gratitude that in 1911 two brave young women blazed the trail for them and helped to make their open-air work easier and more effective.

5

PENNSYLVANIA PARTICIPATES IN WORK OF MEMBERSHIP COMMITTEE OF NATIONAL AMERICAN WOMAN SUFFRAGE ASSOCIATION 1911-1913

In October, 1911, the N. A. W. S. A. held its annual convention in Louisville, Kentucky. As Mrs. Ellen H. E. Price was unable to attend the convention, I was sent as her proxy. In my capacity as head of the Pennsylvania delegation, I found the convention a thrilling experience because I was placed temporarily on the National Executive Committee, and was thus given an opportunity to take part in conferences with such leaders as Dr. Anna Howard Shaw, Mrs. Carrie Chapman Catt, Miss Jane Addams, and Dr. M. Carey Thomas.

I had been asked to make a short talk on District Organization, but was taken entirely by surprise when it was announced at one of the evening meetings that the Pennsylvania Headquarters had been awarded a silver cup for sending in the largest number of subscriptions to the *Woman's Journal* during the year. This cup was to be kept at our Headquarters until the next national convention, when it would be awarded to the person securing the most subscriptions during that year. Also I was given, as a souvenir, a five-dollar gold piece that had once belonged to Susan B. Anthony.

Although I returned to Philadelphia with happy

memories and added enthusiasm, I had been given a difficult assignment which entailed much work. I had been asked to serve on the Membership Committee of the N.A.W.S.A.

The five members of this Committee were scattered over a wide territory, and voting had to be done by mail. Miss Laura Clay of Kentucky was Chairman. Other members were Miss Harriet May Mills, President of the New York State Woman Suffrage Association, Mrs. Huntley Russell, first Vice-President of the Michigan Woman Suffrage Association, Mrs. Susan W. Fitzgerald of Massachusetts, Recording Secretary of the N.A.W.S.A., and I.

Miss Laura Clay, whose grandfather, General Green Clay, was one of the early immigrants from Virginia in the days when Kentucky was still a part of that State, was born in Madison County, in the family home built by her grandfather. A practical farmer, she managed about 275 acres of this homestead that came down to her by inheritance. In 1888, she helped to organize the Kentucky Equal Rights Association, and was chosen its first president, a position to which she was re-elected for many years. With woman suffrage as its ultimate aim, the association devoted most of its time to securing improved laws for women and children, and succeeded in having many discriminatory laws against women repealed. Also, the organization secured the opening of several colleges to women, the requirement of women physicians in the women's wards of State Insane Asylums, and a law making fathers and mothers joint guardians of their minor children.

Shortly after the Louisville Convention, Miss Clay sent us rules for carrying on our work and, in her communication, quoted from a letter of November 10, 1911, she had received from the corresponding secretary of the N.A.W. S.A. In referring to an application for membership from

an Indiana association, Mrs. Mary Ware Dennett, as
quoted by Miss Clay, had written:

> I am very sorry that the question of admitting
> limited suffrage associations did not come up be-
> fore the convention at the executive committee.
> This Indiana association, of which Dr. Graham
> is president, stands for restricting suffrage; so
> also does Miss Mary Winsor's association in
> Philadelphia, and it seems to me a knotty prob-
> lem to decide whether or not the National Asso-
> ciation can admit them.

Because this chapter covers a little more than two years,
and is concerned with two subjects that vitally affected both
State and national suffrage campaigns, I shall give considerable space to it.

One of these subjects deals with the wisdom, or unwisdom, of attempting to limit the franchise, before women,
through the use of the ballot, could join with men in
deciding what, if any, limit should be imposed. The other
subject concerns an effort to interpret properly the meaning of the Constitution of the N.A.W.S.A. in regard to
the admission of organizations applying for membership
in it.

As to limiting the franchise, I had always understood
that the National Association was seeking merely to remove
the sex qualification from the franchise laws and was not
attempting to make any other change in them. I, therefore,
wrote to Miss Clay, December 9, 1911, expressing doubt
as to the eligibility of the Indiana Equal Restricted Suffrage
Association to become an auxiliary of the N.A.W.S.A.

January 24, 1912, Miss Clay wrote to her committee
members, "Give your opinion and vote whether or not
Associations working for suffrage with qualifications other

than those now required for men shall be eligible for membership."

My strong conviction that we should support the National Association in its stand that it was unwise for women to consider limiting the franchise before they had won the right to vote, made my reply to Miss Clay's question somewhat vehement. Here it is:

> I vote NO. To my mind, we are trying to do away with sex disqualification. We want women put on the same political plane with men. If that position is a good one, the women and men can rejoice on their way; if it happens to be an unfortunate one, they should work out some reform together. Why should men alone have the right to limit the franchise for *both* men and women? If in our future Democracy persons with harelip are to be disfranchised, then let women so afflicted have the right to register their disapproval and be disfranchised by a fair majority.

October 30, 1912, Miss Clay wrote to the Membership Committee:

> I have received an application for membership from Miss Mary Winsor, in behalf of the Pennsylvania Limited Suffrage League, of which she is president. . . . I notified Miss Winsor that the fact that her League was *limited* would cause inquiry from our Committee. She assures me that Woman Suffrage is the chief object of the League, though it stands also for excluding the criminal of both sexes, and an educational qualification for both. She has sent a certified list of more than three hundred members; and at my suggestion, has already sent on dues to the National, as I knew I could not write my letters to

our Committee in time for her to do so after the answers were received.

As the scattered members of Miss Clay's Committee had less than a month left in which to take action on Miss Winsor's application before the N.A.W.S.A. would hold its annual Convention in Philadelphia, I wrote immediately (Nov. 1, 1912) to all of them and sent a copy of this letter to Miss Clay. I felt the Committee as a whole should know that neither our National President nor our State President approved the admission of the Pennsylvania Limited Suffrage League to membership, and I sent the members copies of letters in our files at Headquarters from both these officials.

Here is our State President's letter of May 6, 1912:

My dear Miss Winsor:

In reply to your favor of the 2nd inst., I enclose a copy of the Constitution of the Pennsylvania Woman Suffrage Association.

The fact that your Society is a non-dues paying Club will not affect its eligibility to either auxiliaryship or affiliation with the State Association.

But we, as an organization, stand for universal suffrage (however much latitude may be allowed to individual conviction) and all our auxiliary societies must conform to this principle. . . .

Trusting that I have made this clear to you— and with the hope that we may be able to meet on common ground and work together for democracy, I am

Yours sincerely,
E. H. E. Price.

And here is a copy of our National President's letter of May 31, 1912:

My dear Miss Katzenstein:

Thank you for your letter and the copy of Mrs. Price's.

I believe Miss Winsor has sent a request to become affiliated with the N.A.W.S.A., but I have not heard yet just what has been done with the request, whether or not it will be accepted by the committee. Miss Winsor, I think, is a very sincere and earnest person, but I cannot help feeling that her limited suffrage ideas are very harmful and that their very plausibility makes them so. And, while I have no fear she will ever be able to affect the National Association, or persuade our body to in any way speak for limited suffrage, nevertheless I fear that there will be a great deal of time wasted and unpleasant feeling developed in regard to it. I do wish she would give it up and join in for full suffrage, because it is absolutely useless to advocate her theories for they could not get passed by any legislature this side of Judgment Day, and it is particularly difficult at legislative hearings. . . .

Faithfully yours,
Anna H. Shaw.

Again, on June 10, 1912, Mrs. Price wrote on the subject:

My dear Miss Winsor:

The following resolution was passed unanimously by the Executive Board at its regular monthly meeting held June 6, 1912:

"Whereas, believing that the platform of the Pennsylvania Limited Suffrage League is inimical to that of the Pennsylvania Woman Suffrage Association, and that, by confusing the minds of the people it tends to weaken the forces for Woman Suffrage,

Be it resolved, That this Executive Committee request the Pennsylvania Limited Suffrage League, through its President, Miss Mary Winsor, to withdraw its bill for a Limited Suffrage now in the hands of the Elections Commission and refrain from presenting any similar bill to the coming Legislature."

Hoping that your association will see the wisdom of such a course and will join forces with us in the effort to secure Votes for Women before pushing your propaganda for a limited suffrage for both men and women, I am

Very sincerely yours,

Ellen H. E. Price, President.

Before closing my letter to the Membership Committee, I added a part of a conversation I had had with Judge Edward Biddle, who drew up the Limited Bill, which was presented at the same legislative hearing before which our Bill came in 1911. Judge Biddle admitted that the Limited Bill was not practical, and said, "And now you will like to ask me why I have worked for the Bill." To my reply that that was just what I should like to ask, he said, "I shall have to waive an answer."

The Pennsylvania Limited Suffrage League was refused membership in both the National and the State association. The controversy over limited suffrage in Pennsylvania then died a natural death and members of the organization joined with other Suffragists in trying to win VOTES FOR WOMEN on the same terms as granted to men.

Now let us take up the second subject—the correct interpretation of the National's Constitution as it related to applications for membership.

Miss Clay, in a letter dated January 24, 1912, had written the members of her committee they might expect to receive some applications for membership direct from the corresponding secretary of the N.A.W.S.A., and in explanation she wrote:

> It was agreed between Mrs. [Mary Ware] Dennett and your chairman that when applications for membership were received at National Headquarters, she would make and send copies to each member of our Committee.

July 2, 1913, Mrs. Dennett sent us the following letter:

> I am enclosing a copy of the application for membership in the National Association from the Congressional Union for Woman Suffrage of Washington, D. C. and am sending the certified list of 300 members to Miss Clay, the chairman.

This is the application Mrs. Dennett enclosed:

June 26, 1913.

Mrs. Mary Ware Dennett,
505 Fifth Avenue,
New York, N. Y.

My dear Mrs. Dennett:—

I am enclosing a list of 300 members of the Congressional Union, which you said was necessary in order to become affiliated with the National. Our full name is "The Congressional Union for Woman Suffrage." Our headquarters are 1420 F Street, N.W., Washington, D.C. Our Committee is as follows:—

Miss Alice Paul, N.J., Chairman,
Mrs. Crystal Eastman Benedict, Wisc.
Miss Lucy Burns, N.Y.
Mrs. Lawrence Lewis, Jr., Pa.
Mrs. Mary Beard, N.Y.

My recollection is that you said we were to

pay $30 upon entering. Please let me know if this is correct and I will have it sent at once.

Are there any other details concerning which we should send information before joining?

Very sincerely yours,
(Sgd.) Alice Paul,
Chairman Congressional Union.

In her letter of July 9, 1913, Miss Clay wrote in part:

I have written to Miss Paul that the application is not sufficiently regular to be laid before our Committee, and have asked her to supply the deficiencies so that I could submit it to the Membership Committee. . . . When I receive an application sufficiently regular to justify presenting it to you I will write for your vote on the admission of the Congressional Union for Woman Suffrage of Washington, D. C.

July 21st, I replied to Miss Clay's letter and said that if Miss Paul satisfied her that the Congressional Union for Woman Suffrage had properly applied for membership, I should take pleasure in voting "yes" to admit them because I thought they were doing splendid work.

August 11th, 1913, Miss Clay, in her circular letter to us, wrote, "You will find enclosed copy of a letter from the Congressional Union which is in answer to a letter from me." As she then discussed the Congressional Union's letter at length, it will, I believe, make the discussion clearer if I give the Congressional Union's letter first. This is it:

July 19, 1913.

My dear Miss Clay:
In accordance with your request, I have looked up the minutes of the Louisville convention with regard to the membership committee.

In compliance with rule 1 of the membership committee, as printed in these minutes, I am enclosing a certified list of the members of the Congressional Union.

Rule 2 refers to state organizations and does not therefore affect our association.

Rule 3 defines a suffrage organization as one whose main object is to secure suffrage for women. This is the purpose of the Congressional Union.

Rule 4 merely refers to questions which the membership committee feels unable to decide and mentions no requirements for any association applying for membership.

You inquire whether we wish to become auxiliary as a local, state, or national society. We wish to become an Auxiliary under Article 3, Section 1, of the Constitution which states that "any other Suffrage Organization of not less than 300 members may become auxiliary to the National American Woman Suffrage Association and thus secure representation in the annual Convention, by paying annually into the treasury, ten cents per member." We are not a National society in the usual sense of the word as we aim to assist in merely one particular phase of the National's work. Neither are we a local or a state society, as we have members in different parts of the country.

You also inquire concerning the election of officers. Our officers are chosen by our Committee from among its members, as are the officers of the Woman's Political Union of New York, for instance.

You further inquire whether the Congressional Union will be bound by the decisions of the N.A.W.S.A. If the Congressional Union is an auxiliary of the National Association it will of course be bound by the decisions of the convention in the same way as are all other auxiliaries.

We will be glad to send any further information which you may desire.

Very Sincerely yours,

Alice Paul,

Chairman Congressional Committee.

To continue quotations from Miss Clay's letter of August 11, 1913, to the Membership Committee:

On referring to Art. 3, Section 1, I believe you will concur with me that it relates to local associations, or associations less than state associations. Since the Congressional Union gathers its members from many or all of the states I rule that it is essentially a national society and as such can be admitted only on a two-thirds vote of the Executive Committee, as provided for in Art. 3, section 2 of the Constitution. I have written to this effect to Miss Paul and to Mrs. Dennett, or rather to the Board of General Officers, through Mrs. Dennett. If it had not been for the labor of writing, I should have been glad to consult all the members of the Committee before making this ruling; but as in case of our being unable to settle any point the reference would have to be to the Ex. Com. the result would have been the same, even if the members of my committee do not agree with my ruling, while I am confident that they will agree with it after a careful study of the provisions of the constitution.

The letter [Alice Paul's] was accompanied by a certified list of 436 members, of whom 179 are not residents of the District of Columbia. I think they are from about fifteen states.

I am glad this question is not to be decided by our small committee but by representatives of all the states, since it concerns the interests of so many of them. Of course, it is neither possible nor desirable that the Congressional Union should be prevented from organizing and working its own plan of Congressional action. But I think it is very desirable that the National should continue to occupy a position where it can give or withhold its endorsement of any Congressional work. It could not do so if it had as an auxiliary an association which can act independently of the decisions of the National Convention. I may say that when the question comes up to me as one of the Ex. Com. I shall vote against the admission of the Congressional Union. It seems to me only just that all the states which have auxiliaries in the National should have some voice in the conduct of work before the U. S. Congress; and some of those states do not endorse the form of the amendment now before the Congress.

In Miss Clay's letter of October 8, 1913, to her Committee, she repeated her former "ruling" that the Congressional Union for Woman Suffrage was essentially a "National body," and that the Constitution of the N.A. W.S.A. reserved to its Executive Committee decision on the eligibility of "National bodies" to membership in the N.A.W.S.A.

She said that she had written a similar letter to the Board of General Officers of the N.A.W.S.A. and had requested a ruling on the proper way to handle the Congressional Union's application for membership. Here is the reply Miss Clay received from Mrs. Dennett, a copy of which she sent us. Mrs. Dennett's letter was dated September 5, 1913:

Your letter of Aug. 11th to the Board, in reference to the admission of The Congressional Union to the National Association has been acted upon by the board, and the members are unani-

mously agreed that, since Sec. 1, of Article III
of the Constitution does not define the character
of "any other suffrage organization of not less
than 300 members" by prescribing its membership
as national or state or any other sort, the Congressional Union is plainly consistent with the
terms of the Constitution in making its application for membership. Even if the Congressional
Union were defined as a National organization
(and its own officers do not thus define it) it
would be under no obligation to join the National, according to either section 2 or section 6
of Article III, if it preferred to join under section
1 of Article III.

The Board, therefore, considers it quite unnecessary to submit the question to the Executive
Committee. If, however, you should find, on consulting all the other members of your committee
that they did not agree with the Board, and a
majority should still wish to have the question
laid before the Executive Committee, the vote
will be duly submitted from Headquarters by the
President.

Feeling, apparently, firmly convinced that she was right
in regard to the course the Congressional Union should follow in making its application for membership in the
N.A.W.S.A., Miss Clay submitted three questions on that
subject to her Committee in her October 8th letter. Here
are the questions and my reply to them:

(1) Do you think the characteristics of the
Congressional Union are those of a local, or
State, or National Society?

I agree with Miss Paul when she says that the
Congressional Union is not a National Society
in the usual sense of the word, as its aim is to

assist in merely one particular phase of the National's work. The fact that the Official Board of the N.A.W.S.A. do not see in it a rival and are unanimous in agreeing that it "is plainly consistent with the terms of the Constitution in making its application for membership," under Section I, Article 3, seems to me to strengthen Miss Paul's claim.

With its membership drawn from over 15 States, and its acknowledged aim to secure a Federal Amendment, the Union is plainly neither a State nor a local society.

(2) Do you think the Membership Committee has authority to admit a National Society to auxiliaryship?

According to the present Constitution, I should say that the Membership Committee has authority to admit a National Association as an auxiliary to the N.A.W.S.A. if it applied for membership under Article 3, Section 1. The words "or any other suffrage organization of not less than 300 members" are certainly clear, whether it is wise or not to have two ways in which National Associations may become auxiliary.

(3) If the opinion of the Committee is not unanimous on its power to admit the Congressional Union, do you think this difference of opinion comes under the rule that differences in a Committee shall be referred to the Executive Committee, or do you think a simple majority should decide the Committee's power in this instance?

As I understand it, the majority vote of a committee is binding and would settle questions of policy as well as all other questions.

October 24, 1913, Miss Clay discovered that a mistake had been made in the appointment of members on the Membership Committee, and wondered if some technicality, which had escaped her, might be found to correct the error.

Dr. Shaw found the needed technicality as the following letter from her, dated October 30, 1913, will show:

Dear Miss Katzenstein:—

Miss Clay's rather remarkable discovery when it is almost too late to remedy it, is unfortunate . . . and the only way I can see out of it is to get our National Board to appoint as members of the Membership Committee, people who are members of the National Executive Committee. That would remove you from the committee, but I am very glad you have been on it so long this year.

You see, when we re-appointed the old members of the EX committee, who had been members of the Executive Committee at the time they were appointed, we did not recognize the fact that they were not then members of the Executive for this year, in fact we had not been informed of that event, so did not know, and in placing your name on the committee we made a mistake, because it should have been either the State President or Miss Jane Campbell.* We have decided to put Miss Campbell on in your place and to put somebody else on who is near enough so that we can get in connection with them quickly, and submit to them the findings of the previous Membership Committee, and ask the new members to confirm the action of the old members.

Since . . . we have accepted their [Congressional Union's] dues and they understood they

---

* Miss Jane Campbell was State Member of the Executive Committee of the National American Woman Suffrage Association.

were admitted, it would be an outrage for them to come and find they were not admitted. So, will you co-operate with us and see Miss Campbell and explain the position to her, and ask her to telegraph us her acceptance of the findings of the majority of the Committee? This will admit, besides the other societies, the Union in Washington and it will be a perfectly legitimate method.

Of course we were wrong not to investigate in regard to the legitimacy of the members of the committee, but it seems to me that Miss Clay, as Chairman of the Committee, was quite as wrong as we were, since she had not half so much work to do and yet did not discover, until almost too late, that she was not properly appointed.

You have doubtless received Miss Clay's letter and understand all about what I am writing of in a very great hurry, but I know your interest in the cause well enough and your interest in admitting these societies and know you will not hesitate to do everything you can to put Miss Campbell right and get her vote in favor of the admission of these societies. If she will simply say in a telegram that she votes to confirm the acceptance of all the societies which you had previously voted upon, that will settle Pennsylvania all right in the matter.

Faithfully yours,
(Signed) Anna H. Shaw.

Here is my reply to Dr. Shaw's letter:

October 31, 1913.

Dr. Anna Howard Shaw,
505 Fifth Avenue,
New York City.
My dear Dr. Shaw:

Although I have just returned from the State Convention in Pittsburgh, and am almost too

tired to think, I hasten to answer your letter of
Oct. 30th.

The mail brought not only your letter but one
from Miss Clay and I am enclosing a copy of
my reply to Miss Clay.

I tried to reach Miss Campbell by long distance call to Pittsburgh but was told that she
had left the Pittsburgh office and would not return. I, therefore, sent her a special delivery
letter and tried to make it clear that the matter
was one needing urgent attention. In my letter,
I asked her to meet me tomorrow at one o'clock.
If she can do this you may be able to receive a
telegram from her Saturday afternoon.

Although I have several times called attention
to the fact that I was, in my opinion, ineligible to
serve on the Membership Committee, this opinion
was never confirmed and I, therefore, trusted
that everything was all right.

Regretting this serious annoyance and hoping
that it may be straightened out, I am,

Cordially yours,

Caroline Katzenstein.

Miss Jane Campbell was just the right person to help
in straightening out a complication of this sort. I recall
another incident when her quick thinking and acting at a
suffrage meeting arranged to be held at her home, 413 W.
School House Lane, Germantown, saved the day. For some
reason, partly, perhaps, because the day was rainy, only
four women attended the meeting. As Miss Campbell was
very well known, reporters were sent out to cover it. Now,
it would not have done to let this seeming lack of interest
in woman suffrage get to the papers and Miss Campbell
rose to the occasion. She left the meeting to see the reporters, explained that it was a closed meeting and promised, if they would wait, to give them news on what took

place as soon as she could. When she later returned, she told the representatives of the press that an election had been held and gave them the results of this vote. Every woman present had been unanimously elected to office, but Miss Campbell left out the word *every*. And so the day was saved!

Thus ended my two years of work on the Membership Committee of the National American Woman Suffrage Association, an assignment which had been interesting, but of which I was glad to be relieved. During that time, our Committee had acted on applications from the north, east, south, and west. The list included the Minnesota Equal Suffrage League, Portland Equal Suffrage League of Oregon, Political Equality League of Wisconsin, Louisiana Woman Suffrage Party, Florida Equal Franchise League, Just Government League of Maryland, State Equal Franchise League of Maryland, Washington Suffrage League, Everybody's Equal Suffrage League of Oregon, Woman's Franchise League of Indiana, Ohio Equal Franchise Association, The Massachusetts Political Equality Union, Political Union of New Jersey, Montana State Equal Suffrage Association, Equal Suffrage Association of Hawaii, Women's Political Union (New York), Woman Suffrage Party (a New York organization with, I think, over 45,000 members), Montana Equal Suffrage State Central Committee. In the last three listed organizations were such distinguished leaders as Mrs. Harriot Stanton Blatch, daughter of Elizabeth Cady Stanton, Mrs. Carrie Chapman Catt, and Miss Jeannette Rankin, of Montana, who was later to become the first woman member of the United States Congress.

6

*PENNSYLVANIA HEADQUARTERS GROW IN
SIZE AND IMPORTANCE . . . HEARING
BEFORE ELECTIONS COMMISSION
1912*

Our second year at the State Headquarters was very encouraging. Thanks to the press, our activities in Pennsylvania were widely advertised. For instance, a letter addressed to "The Sec. of the Woman Suffrage Association of America" came to us from Palestine, Texas. It was an inquiry about available literature on Woman Suffrage, a subject the writer said would be one of the "uppermost questions in the State of Texas" and would be debated in all the high schools of the State.

And from Stem, North Carolina, a gentleman sent us a letter he had received from his Representative at Washington, D. C., in reply to a request for literature on Woman Suffrage. The Congressman regretted that there were "no such publications issued by the Government at all" and added, "You might be able to secure something on the subject by writing to the Secretary of the Womans Suffrage League of Philadelphia, Pa. This is about the only source from which you could procure information on the subject to my knowledge."

Although the literature published by the National Association enabled us to answer all ordinary questions on woman suffrage with comparative ease, we occasionally had requests for more data than we had, and I was compelled to refer the inquirer to some other source, or sources, of information. A case in point was a letter from a lady who wrote, "Kindly mail me all available information at hand, which and how many states now have Suffrage and what practical results thus far, how many women hold elective and appointive office, and are they filling those offices creditably."

In order further to advertise the Cause and to increase our literature fund, we added some novelties of our own to those supplied by the National; such as blotters, pencils, wash-cloths, sashes, hatpins, attractively-boxed tea, etc. During this second year, the literature department handled 86,166 pieces of literature, 7,837 buttons and pins, and paid bills amounting to $553.97. It had managed through the sale of its novelties, by making small profits on individual sales of literature, and by occasional small gifts from persons realizing the importance of this part of the work, not to call upon the State for any financial help. One day we received fifty-eight orders and requests for literature.

Headquarters had become a sort of clearing house for the State and outside places as well. One of each morning's duties was to re-address mail that came from far and near. A letter could come to Philadelphia with no other address than *Mary Smith, a Suffragette,* and be fairly sure of reaching its destination. During the year, one hundred and eighty-one subscriptions to the *Woman's Journal* were sent to Boston.

We established an official organ for the State, the *Pennsylvania Suffrage News,* with the hope that each society might keep in close touch with its sister groups and that all of them might thus be stimulated to make good reports. By the end of November we had a subscription

list of one thousand, and in the latest issue had advertisements amounting to $70.00.

Without being solicited by us, *The Delineator,* in May,
published a notice of one of our most valuable pamphlets,
Outline of the Legal Position of Women in Pennsylvania,
and in consequence orders came to us from many distant
States; Brentano's New York store wrote to inquire about
it; and the Children's Bureau at Washington ordered it.

Because of our increased activities, it became necessary
to double the size of our Headquarters by renting an adjoining room.

In response to an appeal for help from a neighboring
State where an active campaign was in progress, we lent
Ohio our field secretary, Mrs. Ida Porter Boyer, and paid
her salary and expenses for the last two months of that
State's campaign.

Also, when New York State had its big suffrage parade,
May 4, 1912, Pennsylvania sent a delegation to take part
in it. Two special railroad coaches were required to carry
the group from the Keystone State.

A hearing before the Elections Commission was held
March 22, 1912, in the Common Council Chamber, City
Hall, Philadelphia. Although the results of that hearing
were not made public for some time, we were convinced
that our proposed Amendment to the State Constitution
would be favorably recommended to the Legislature. This
belief was based largely on the fact that every political
party but one in the State had a Woman Suffrage plank in
its platform, and even that party had, at its convention,
passed a resolution in favor of woman suffrage. But the
Elections Commission, at its hearing, was taking no chances
on letting Suffragists win without proving their mettle.
Here are quotations from the regulations imposed by the
Commission and signed by its secretary, Mr. Wm. H. Hays:

All speakers to be required to direct their attention principally to the questions:

1. Do the majority of women desire the right of suffrage, and what statistics are available as a basis of judgment on this question?
2. Will the right of suffrage, if granted, be exercised generally by women, and what statistics are available on this point?
3. Will the exercise of suffrage by women result in a benefit to the community, and what statistics are available on this question.

Each of the three associations named is requested to file with the Commission printed briefs, giving a synopsis of the respective arguments, and giving out accurate statistics of results in communities where the experiment has been tried. These briefs should be filed at the hearing; but at all events not later than fifteen days after the hearing.

The speaker's full name and address must be announced distinctly when introduced.

A list, giving the full name, address, and topic, of each speaker, also the approximate time to be consumed by the speaker, must be furnished to the Secretary of the Commission before the hearing begins.

Let us analyze these questions:

Question #1. Even if this question referred only to the women in Pennsylvania, a complete answer to it would have required a poll of all the women in the State and enough favorable replies from them to constitute a majority of the whole.

Question #2. This question, relating to the *possibility* of Pennsylvania's enfranchisement of her women, seemed to presuppose in us a power of divination that we did not possess, and made a request for the presentation of statistics on conditions that did not exist.

Question #3. We could, of course, have given statistics on what women had accomplished in those States where they had been enfranchised sufficiently long to help in passing desirable legislation, but these figures could be no guarantee that the same good results would be duplicated in Pennsylvania if its women were granted the right to vote.

We felt we had as much right to express our ignorance at the polls as the men had, and that we should not be required to show, in advance of our enfranchisement, the beneficial effect our vote might have on the "community."

What magic the women that first won their enfranchisement must have had when there were no statistics on which to base their plea for justice!

At the Hearing, the Pennsylvania Woman Suffrage Association, the Pennsylvania Limited Suffrage League, and the Pennsylvania Association Opposed to Woman Suffrage were each allowed one hour to present arguments. The two first-named organizations spoke in favor of their respective bills before the Legislature; the anti-suffrage organization spoke against both full suffrage and limited suffrage for women. In rebuttal, each organization was given one-half hour.

The speakers representing the Pennsylvania Woman Suffrage Association, led by Dr. Anna Howard Shaw, must have impressed the Commission favorably because our bill for full suffrage was given a favorable vote by the 1913 Legislature. We had now officially launched our campaign, and we had two years in which to prepare to go before the 1915 Legislature for the needed second favorable vote by that body before the question of Woman Suffrage could be submitted to the voters of the State.

We had now reached the stage when more emphasis

should be laid on political work and less on educating the public. To do that work, we needed more funds and we set about raising them. One method of accomplishing this was pleasurable as well as profitable—theatre benefits. The chairman of the Committee of Finance, Mrs. Anna Lowenburg, raised $1,030,00 on two plays, EVERYWOMAN, and BUNTY PULLS THE STRINGS. Also, ELECTION DAY, a play written by Mrs. Wilfred Lewis, President of the Equal Franchise Society, was successfully given at the New Century Club.

During the year $5,500.00 in round numbers was raised, and the retiring treasurer was able to hand over to the new treasurer, again in round numbers, $1,500.00. As usual, a number of contributions did not pass through the treasurer's books. A need arose and some generous member filled it.

The Pennsylvania Woman Suffrage Association at its annual convention in Harrisburg, November 18, 1910, had voted approval of the method of organization by political districts rather than by clubs and societies and had recommended to the newly elected executive board that a committee be appointed to take immediate action toward organizing a Woman Suffrage Party in Pennsylvania. The following day plans were made to carry out the recommendation, and Mrs. Anna M. Orme, Vice-President of the State Association, was made Chairman of the Woman Suffrage Party. Mrs. Orme worked with zeal to make the Party a success. Closely associated with her in this work was Lida Stokes Adams, Chairman of Legislation. As the new organization did not disturb any existing suffrage groups, it met with immediate approbation. In 1912, the Woman Suffrage Party received 210 replies from candidates for the Pennsylvania Legislature to this question:

> If you are elected will you support a bill in the Legislature providing for the referendum for a constitutional amendment granting full suffrage to women, upon the same terms upon which it is now given to men?

Many of the candidates not only answered the question in the affirmative, but expressed enthusiastic belief in the reform. Some simply replied that they had already signed Woman Suffrage Party slips.* A few were evasive, but even they seemed to think it best to go on record as not opposed. For instance, a gentleman from Franklin County wrote:

> I have always felt that taxation without representation was unfair. I may, therefore, be expected to give the matter of Woman Suffrage the same careful consideration I would give to any question which was agitating the public mind.

The replies as a whole were, however, so encouraging they were printed in pamphlet form for campaign material —a 28-page document.

The Woman Suffrage Party should not be confused with the National Woman's Party whose Headquarters were located in Washington, D. C. Neither organization was a political party in the ordinary sense of those words. They were non-partisan in character and had but one aim— the enfranchisement of women. One group was trying to amend the State Constitution, the other the national Constitution.

---

* Membership in the Woman Suffrage Party carried no dues and was open to men as well as women.

7

NATIONAL AND STATE CONVENTIONS HELD IN PHILADELPHIA . . . STATE HEADQUARTERS MOVED TO HARRISBURG
1912

As the annual conventions of both the National and State Associatons were held in Philadelphia in November, 1912, the National's preceding the State's, Pennsylvania's 44th convention was devoted only to business. However, Ellen H. E. Price, our President, and other members of the Board that signed the Call, Anna M. Orme, Mary Churchman Morgan, Caroline Katzenstein, Matilda Orr Hays, Mary M. Coard, Ellen M. Thomas, and Jane Campbell, were looking toward the future with enthusiasm. Reference was made in the Call to the adoption of constitutional amendments, November 5, 1912, granting full suffrage to women in the three States of Kansas, Oregon, and Arizona; to the endorsement of woman suffrage by local political parties; to the friendly attitude of the press; to the eagerness with which suffrage literature and speakers were sought; to the activity of women in political campaigns; and to the breaking down of prejudice. All of these things, the Call pointed out, indicated early victory. It closed with this appeal for support:

The women of Pennsylvania may secure the franchise in 1915 if they all work together to

effect organization in every legislative district in
the State. Let this be our aim for the coming
year, and let every Suffragist and every delegate
feel her share of responsibility in carrying out this
plan. Come and let us take counsel together in
the City of Brotherly Love, in the interest of the
Cause to which we are dedicated.

Three business sessions were held in Westminster Hall
in the Witherspoon Building on the afternoon and evening of
November 26th and the morning of November 27th, 1912.
The Convention's decision to have the State Headquarters
located in Harrisburg seemed a wise one not only on account
of the central location of the State's Capital, but because
the active legislative campaign we were waging for a
Suffrage Amendment to the Pennsylvania State Constitution made our ability to keep in close touch with the
Legislature of prime importance.

In order to assist in the election of new officers, a
number of us holding key positions in the State refused
to allow our names to be placed in nomination.

The new State officers were chosen largely from the
western and central parts of the State. Mrs. Frank M.
Roessing became the new president, and Mrs. Price, the
retiring president, was elected as an auditor on the new
Board.

Among prominent Suffragists living in Harrisburg were
Mrs. Mabel Cronise Jones, President of the Central Penn-
sylvania Woman Suffrage Association, Dr. Ruth A. Deeter,
Mrs. J. Sharon MacDonald, and that strong supporter
of the enfranchisement of women, Bishop James Henry
Darlington.

The removal of State Headquarters from Philadelphia
to Harrisburg lessened neither the activities of Suffragists

in the eastern part of the State nor public interest in their work. The former State offices in the Hale Building were taken over by the Eastern District of Pennsylvania as was explained in a letter sent out shortly after the Convention by Miss Lida Stokes Adams, who had been elected Eastern Vice-President. In addition to Miss Adams' name, the only ones listed on the new stationery were Dr. Anna P. Sharpless, Treasurer, Miss Helen Moore Fogg, Recording Secretary, and Miss Caroline Katzenstein, Executive Secretary. Miss Adams wrote:

Our State Convention in Philadelphia, November 26-27, 1912, decided for the good of our Cause, to transfer State Headquarters from Philadelphia to Harrisburg.

A conference of local leaders held in Philadelphia, December 3, 1912, was unanimously of opinion that Headquarters should be maintained also in Philadelphia for the work in this section of the State; and, looking to that end, a Council was formed for the purpose of maintaining Headquarters and stimulating organization throughout the Eastern District of Pennsylvania, which comprises:

Berks	Lancaster	Philadelphia
Bradford	Lebanon	Pike
Bucks	Lehigh	Schuylkill
Carbon	Luzerne	Susquehanna
Chester	Monroe	Wayne
Delaware	Montgomery	Wyoming
Lackawanna	Northampton	

It is estimated that the annual cost of maintenance—based upon the greatest economy consonant with efficiency—including rent, salaries, telephone, and incidentals will be over $2,000.00.

The Philadelphia *Public Ledger* on Sunday, November 17, 1912, carried a page on Woman Suffrage. Under the caption, EXTENT AND WORKING OF WOMAN SUFFRAGE ABROAD, in letters so large they went across the entire top of the page, was a long article by Mrs. Carrie Chapman Catt. This article, which was accompanied with a photograph of Mrs. Catt and which was introduced with a statement by the paper that "her appearance at the National Convention will be hailed with delight by all," took up more than half the page.

Under the caption, *Open Discussion of the Question Shall Women Have the Right to Vote,* the lower part of the page carried a FOR and AGAINST on the subject, and I was asked to supply the FOR side. The *Ledger's* lead on my contribution was, *Coming National Convention Regarded in the Light of "Expert Testimony" as to What Women Are Doing and Can Do.* This, I think, was a kind way to accept what I will admit was about as bold a way of getting free advertising as I had ever attempted. Here it is:

> The victory of November 5 * demonstrates clearly that the time for theorizing on woman suffrage has nearly passed and that the great duty before women today is to fit themselves for the citizenship that will soon be theirs.
>
> That men are awakening to their responsibility in this educational movement is shown in many ways. Especially is this noticeable in the organizations that have recently sprung into being. There are now an international, a national, and many State men's leagues for woman suffrage, and our own University has lately taken this forward step and numbers among its charter

---

* November 5, 1912, the States of Kansas, Oregon, and Arizona adopted Constitutional Amendments granting full suffrage to women.

members some of the most advanced thinkers in Pennsylvania's chief seat of learning.

To Suffragists, the emancipation of woman is a matter of such simple justice and the consequent elevation and development that must come from a participation in public affairs seems so plainly desirable that it is difficult for them to understand how intelligent persons can oppose it. And yet they know that there are some intelligent and sincere persons that actually believe, with the ballot in the hands of woman, chivalry will die, wives will neglect their husbands and children, and all sorts of direful things will happen. In short, the emancipation of woman will place a capital "R" before evolution and make of this beautiful world a howling wilderness.

With every sign pointing to the fact that this great change in woman's condition is soon to take place everywhere, the Pennsylvania Woman Suffrage Association is prepared to offer some "expert testmony" on the subject. From November 21 to 26 it will act as hostess to the National American Woman Suffrage Association during its annual convention in Philadelphia, and a rare opportunity of hearing distinguished men and women from this country and abroad will be given. Meetings will be held mornings, afternoons, and evenings in Witherspoon Hall, and, although the evening meetings will be the greatest attractions, every session will be full of interest, and the public, both men and women, are invited to attend.

I should like especially to call attention to the Thanksgiving mass meeting to be held in the Metropolitan Opera House, November 24, at 3 P. M., and to say that this is the only meeting during the convention for which tickets will be necessary. Tickets may be had for the asking at our headquarters, 208 Hale Building, Juniper and Chestnut Streets, any time between 9 and 5, and at the Opera House from 10 to 3 the day of the meeting.

The following facts about the convention will, I believe, interest your readers:—The suffrage situation is more interesting this year than ever before in the entire 64 years of its history. The number of delegations entitled to sit in this year's convention is about 45% greater than last year. There are now ten States that have won equal suffrage, and the time when the opposition in the other States will go down like a house built of cards is rapidly coming.

The meetings at the national convention will vary in character all the way from a great out-door rally in Independence Square on the opening day, at noon, to a Thanksgiving service on Sunday afternoon in the Metropolitan Opera House. The regular business sessions and the evening meet-ings will be held in Witherspoon Hall, and Mayor Blankenburg will give an official welcome to the convention at the opening session, November 21, at 2:30 P. M.

The opening night is campaign night, when speakers will be heard from all the successful campaign States. On this night, also, the presi-dent, Dr. Anna Howard Shaw, will give her an-nual address.

The second evening is Men's Evening. The program is entirely in the charge of the National Men's League for Woman Suffrage. Not a woman will speak that whole evening. Mr. James Lees Laidlaw, president, will preside, and among the speakers will be Reginald Wright Kauffman, Jesse Lynch Williams, Witter Bynner, A. S. G. Taylor, Frederic C. Howe, George Lynch Peabody, Judge Dimner Beeber, and the Rev. James Bratton Mythan.

The program for the third evening is pre-sented entirely by the National College Equal Suffrage League, the president of which is Miss

M. Carey Thomas, President of Bryn Mawr College. There will be a lively tilting of words between the two opposing teams, made up entirely of college people. The anti-suffragists, however, will have to be actresses to the extent that they will assume their parts. The pro-suffrage debaters need play no rôle.

Monday evening there will be two distinguished speakers, each with a world-wide reputation. One is the Baroness Von Suttner, the great advocate of international peace and winner of the Nobel prize, and the other is Mrs. Carrie Chapman Catt, President of the International Woman Suffrage Alliance. Mrs. Catt has just returned from her year-and-a-half trip around the world.

The Sunday afternoon mass meeting in the Opera House will probably be the largest indoor suffrage meeting held in the history of Philadelphia. The speakers will be Anna Howard Shaw, Jane Addams, Julia Lathrop, the newly appointed head of the Children's Bureau, and W. E. B. DuBois, Editor of *The Crisis*. There will be 66 ushers for the enormous auditorium. They will be garbed in a uniform devised for the occasion. The background of the stage will be a huge world map showing the progress of suffrage up to date. All the suffrage territory is painted dark red. The hemispheres float in a gorgeous blue, which will serve as a background for the speakers and distinguished guests, and for the choruses that will lead the music.

The Independence Square meeting at noon (weather permitting) on November 21 is exciting a great deal of interest for the place in which the meeting is held gives an opportunity for a kind of program that is peculiarly appropriate. The original Women's Declaration of Rights at *Seneca Falls*, 1848, will be read, and

Mrs. Charlotte L. Peirce, the only living signer, will be formally presented with a bouquet of flowers. The Suffragists wish they could have the privilege of ringing the old Liberty Bell, but the danger of widening its historic crack makes that bit of enthusiasm impossible. Nevertheless, the spirit of '76 will not be lacking.

The speakers for this meeting are coming from all over the country, from the Far West, the Middle West, New England, New York, and these, added to the Philadelphians, who so successfully made their debut in out-of-door speaking in the Independence Square meeting a year ago, will make a showing so brilliant that the listener may feel distracted trying to decide to which of the five platforms, from which speaking will go on simultaneously, he will give his attention.

In another effort to arouse public interest in the national convention, I asked Mrs. Rudolph Blankenburg, wife of Philadelphia's Mayor, to let me arrange an interview with the press for her on woman's fight for freedom. Mrs. Blankenburg was not only Philadelphia's "First Lady," but she had won distinction in her own right long before her husband's election. Also she could look back with pride on ancestors whose achievements in behalf of woman's progress were significant. Her mother, Dr. Hannah Myers Longshore, a member of the first graduating class of The Woman's Medical College of Pennsylvania, was a pioneer among women physicians and through her skill and devotion won high rank in her profession. And it was largely through another ancestor, Dr. Joseph S. Longshore, Mrs. Blankenburg's uncle, that the founding of Pennsylvania's great medical college for women was made possible.

Here are excerpts from Mrs. Blankenburg's interview:

During the past quarter of a century I have personally observed the gradual change in everything that pertains to the treatment of women. The early days of the struggle have been described to me over and over again by my mother, who lived when woman's position was truly primitive and when the entering wedge had scarcely been placed in the opening that has sprung today into a chasm between past prejudice and present custom.

The term suffragist was unknown fifty years ago. Then the women who enlisted in the fight for freedom were not merely asking for the ballot. They were asking for their rights as human beings. They were asking for the right to call the clothes on their backs their own, for the right to their own children, for the right to their own wages and inheritance, for the right to live normal lives. They were struggling against the inheritance of the past which made women the chattels of men, to be willed or given away at pleasure. It is only since 1848 that women in this country have had the right to own and control their own property and wages. Up to that time married women were not even legally entitled to their clothing.

The passage of laws giving women these inestimable privileges was followed by laws granting them the privilege of opening their own bank accounts, and in 1897 the legislature made it legal for women to incorporate for purposes of learning, charity, benevolence, or religion. This was a great step and was naturally followed by undreamed-of advancement, but the women had to fight every inch of the way in their emancipation as the history of the pioneers in the professional and business life of the country will show.

Mrs. Blankenburg referred to the insults and antagonism her mother had to submit to because she determined to take her stand with men and acquire medical training. And Mrs. Blankenburg herself suffered similar harsh treatment because of her mother's professional work. When she was a little girl, a teacher forbade a neighbor's child to play with her because her mother was a "woman doctor."

Mrs. Blankenburg traced the evolution of women's clubs back to the Female Cent Society, the first missionary organization in which women were allowed to assemble and give their pennies, hoarded by a long period of self-denial, to the cause of advancing the education of the heathen. Continuing, she said:

> At these meetings, when they were first held, over one hundred years ago, the women were not allowed to read their reports because it was considered unladylike for them to raise their voices in public. They had to get the minister to attend their meetings and relate their progress for them. The next development in club life for women was their interest in the currency question and the anti-slavery movement. Gradually came the organization of Woman's Rights societies after the war and women found a lot of things to talk about when they got together and agreed that many changes must be made in their own status before they could be rightly considered as human beings. Of course they faced the same old bugaboos that the suffragists are laughing at today and that the anti-suffragists are pointing to in holy horror. They were told they were unwomanly, they were usurping man's rights and privileges, they were losing their femininity, and other stock phrases that were used to keep them "in their places." But the time had passed when they could be bribed to keep quiet with a trinket

or a silk dress—you know every man in the olden days gave his wife a silk dress when she signed a legal document—and woman's power and knowledge kept growing.

In order to enable the Pennsylvania Headquarters to handle the local press work for the National Convention, the temporary assistance of a stenographer was provided by the Chairman of Local Arrangements, Mrs. Lawrence Lewis. This work was begun seven weeks prior to the Convention and an effort was made to arouse special interest in this chief national suffrage event. We supplied the city editors with an abundance of photographs sent us from National Headquarters in New York, and with as much press copy as there was any hope of their using— in all about one thousand pages.

The Philadelphia newspapers responded most generously, doing us many favors in addition to giving us much space. Through their help, a new record for national suffrage conventions was established. Overflow crowds so large that the National Association would heretofore have been glad to claim them as first audiences marked the six-day convention as a whole.

8

HEADQUARTERS OF EASTERN DISTRICT
OF PENNSYLVANIA CONTINUES AS
ACTIVE CENTER
1913

The brilliant convention of the N.A.W.S.A. in 1912 had so aroused Philadelphia that a casual onlooker might have thought we had practically reached our goal. But those of us able to look behind the scenes knew that we still had much prejudice and opposition to overcome, and that our educational campaign had to be intensified.

Always faced with too small a campaign fund, and with a shortage of trained speakers and workers, we had to struggle under this double handicap. But we were by degrees learning the art of campaigning and our volunteer speakers were making up for their lack of training by their sincerity and their deep interest in the Cause. Who, for instance, could have been more convincing than one of our volunteers who brought back to Headquarters the following story on her method of *converting* one of her listeners?

Miss Hastings, one of a number of business women that had volunteered to speak at suffrage meetings, reported the following conversation with a man in her audience when she spoke in a small Pennsylvania town. He was sufficiently interested to wish to discuss the subject in detail at the close of the meeting and to emphasize why he was opposed. He felt that as he supported his wife and was thus the head of the family he was entitled to speak for the two of them on public questions, which were settled at the ballot box.

Miss Hastings listened with patience and hoped he would not mind if she asked him some personal questions. Her first inquiry was about his present and past earning power. Did he, as a married man, earn more than when he was single? His answer was "no." He was still earning fifteen dollars a week. Was he able to save anything when he was single? Again his reply was "no." Then Miss Hastings asked whether it had never puzzled him to understand how two persons could live on wages that had in the past proved barely sufficient for one person, and she began to teach this humble worker a simple lesson in economics. Her lesson ran like this. "When you were single, you went to the store and bought a work-shirt for seventy-five cents. Now, your wife buys three and a half yards of cotton cloth at ten cents a yard and makes a shirt for you. Doesn't she thus earn forty cents on each of these shirts she makes? When you were single, you ate in a restaurant, and part of the cost of your meals was the salary paid to the cook employed there. Now you buy, let us say, a barrel of flour for five dollars and your wife converts it into bread, biscuits, cakes, pies, etc., worth perhaps twenty-five dollars. Doesn't she earn the difference between the cost of the flour, plus a few other ingredients, and the good things she prepares with them? You formerly sent your soiled clothes to the laundry. Now your wife washes and irons them at home. Again, hasn't she earned the laundry charges? Incidentally, she mends your clothes and thus makes them last longer than they did when you were single. When you are ill, she nurses you and in this way may save you medical bills. Although your wife does not actually receive a salary, don't you really think that she earns her living and is a partner in building and maintaining your home?" The young man had to admit the logic of Miss Hastings' analysis of his wife's position as a wage earner. He confessed that he formerly thought he "actually owned the very clothes on his wife's back."

When one thinks of the time a busy woman had to give to make this one convert, it is easy to realize that the simple educational process put a severe tax on campaign workers and made the political emancipation of women seem almost hopeless at times. Of course Miss Hastings may have credited this man's wife with more ability than she actually possessed, but what she said was within reason and the ideally helpful woman she pictured surely had counterparts in many homes the country over. (It should be borne in mind that the cost figures she used applied to the years around 1913.)

Not only were we making progress in the field of public speaking, but our literature department, under the able management of Miss Rebecca D. Ernst, became a model for other suffrage headquarters. Miss Ernst came early and spent practically the entire day, taking her volunteer "job" with the seriousness of a paid employee and with the added enthusiasm of a worker for a great reform.

In 1913, increased newspaper interest was shown by requests from editors and from writers of feature stories for information and assistance. The following are instances of this closer tie between the press and Philadelphia's Headquarters for the Eastern District of Pennsylvania.

The Sunday editor of the *Public Ledger* telephoned to ask if we could furnish some suffrage articles for his paper. Soon he was sent an article by Mrs. Beatrice Forbes-Robertson Hale. This was published May 18th. June 1st, the *Public Ledger* used our second article, written by three New York women, Mrs. Harriet Burton Laidlaw, Miss

Inez Milholland, and Mrs. Suffren. I was surprised that this service was to bring Headquarters $15.00 from the newspaper. Woman Suffrage was becoming a marketable product!

The managing editor of the Philadelphia *Press* requested our help in obtaining a correspondent for his paper to cover the Budapest Congress of the International Suffrage Alliance. With assistance from National Headquarters, we suggested Mrs. Crystal Eastman Benedict, a brilliant young Suffragist. This service brought a letter of thanks from the *Press*.

For the excellent anti-suffrage cartoon that appeared in the *Saturday Evening Post* of May 3rd, we wrote letters of thanks to the editor, Mr. George Horace Lorimer, and to the cartoonist, Mr. Herbert Johnson. Mr. Lorimer sent a letter of thanks in acknowledgment of our letter to him. Through the generosity of a friend, we had a thousand copies of the cartoon printed and placed on sale at Headquarters.

Miss Mary Isabel Brush, a special writer for the New York *Press* and the Chicago *Herald,* came to Headquarters several times for suffrage data and for photographs of Philadelphia Suffragists.

Miss Elizabeth C. Hunter, formerly a reporter for the Philadelphia *Public Ledger,* was mailed information she requested for a special suffrage story that she was preparing for *Grit,* a publication with a circulation of a quarter of a million.

Acting on the suggestion of a newspaper man, we sent forty-eight letters to members of the G.A.R. asking them to say a word in favor of woman suffrage in their addresses on Memorial Day in public schools. In each letter, we enclosed a piece of suffrage literature and called special attention to a quotation from Abraham Lincoln who, as early as 1836, made this statement, "I go for all sharing the privileges of Government who assist in bearing its burdens —by no means excluding women."

Thanks to the press, our Headquarters were known outside the United States. The French Chamber of Deputies sent us a letter asking information on the woman suffrage movement in our country.

This report on our progress in the field of publicity should include a pleasant little story showing the genuinely friendly attitude of many of Philadelphia's leading newspaper men toward our campaign.

One day an editor hesitantly called my attention to what he considered a regrettable error by a suffrage leader of one of Philadelphia's Legislative Districts. The Suffrage Headquarters in that District had a sign-board on which the word *Legislative* had been abbreviated so that the sign read *Such-and-Such a Leg. District,* and this had caused derision among some of the men in the neighborhood. With genuine gratitude, I thanked the editor and promised to see that the mistake was corrected.

The public of 1954 no longer considers the mention of a woman's leg improper in polite society. The fame of one actress rests partly on the beauty of her legs, and both the daily press and magazines have in the past devoted much space to emphasizing and photographing them. But in the early part of the 20th century, if it ever became absolutely necessary to refer to a woman's leg it was called a *limb*.

Could it have been that persons opposed to the enfranchisement of women encouraged this taboo in order to instill into woman's mind the fear that if she ever dared to venture out too far from her "sacred sphere" into the larger world, she would be "out on a limb"!

Not only were we getting increased support from the

press and winning friends among its leaders, but we were also receiving unusual gifts and courtesies from business firms and individuals. H. H. Battles sent flowers to our meeting at the Empire Theatre when Mrs. Beatrice Forbes-Robertson Hale was our principal speaker. The firm of Coyle and Kelley, who had added the *Woman's Journal* to the other publications they sold, now took up the task of clipping three of Philadelphia's smaller newspapers for our pressbook—the *Star,* the *Item,* and the *News Post.* L. C. Smith & Brothers generously gave us the use of one of their typewriters for about a year. Mr. John Crum kindly offered us the use of a machine in his office when we had much addressing to do. For our week's exhibition of the *Voiceless Speech* at 716 N. Broad Street, the Keystone Window and House Cleaning Company cleaned the store for us free of charge; and Mr. A. Humphrys contributed two placards for the exhibition.

Miss Marion Mott, of Radnor, granddaughter of Lucretia Mott, gave a portrait of Mrs. Mott to Headquarters. It was hung with pride over our literature table.

A contribution from two Suffragists enabled us to subscribe to the *Woman's Journal* for three public libraries in Philadelphia.

Pathetically small ways were tried—not to fill our coffers, but to keep the bottoms from showing! And this struggle was not peculiar to Pennsylvania, but was felt in some degree at our National Headquarters in New York, and by the *Woman's Journal* in Boston. Here are some of the means we used to collect money:

Mite boxes were left at Headquarters by the Woman Suffrage Party to catch the unwary penny. Our wash cloths, with the inscription TAXATION WITHOUT REPRESENTATION IS TYRANNY, were making a hit. A New York worker wrote to inquire about their price by the gross—something I had to find out because they had, so far, been a contribution to Headquarters from Mrs. Gabriel H. Lang. From National Headquarters, we bought Woman Suffrage Playing Cards that came in two styles and were retailed at 25c a pack. At the request of the National Corresponding Secretary, Mrs. Dennett, I tried to interest Evans Drug Store and Hoskins Stationary Store in handling these cards, and succeeded in selling each of them a small order. Also we were able to buy attractive Woman Suffrage Calendars for 1914, which were edited by Dr. Shaw and which could be sold only through suffrage organizations. At the retail price of 50c, we could make a profit of 15c. Week after week, Martha Moore, a young graduate of Swarthmore College, stood at the corner of Broad and Chestnut Streets and bravely hawked the *Woman's Journal,* thereby helping us to send a few dollars now and then to our National Official Organ, as well as spreading the gospel of "justice to women."

To make our funds go as far as possible, we made a business contact with a stationer, who sold us office supplies at wholesale prices. And the Wanamaker Store granted us the same privilege that some other organizations had; we could buy things needed at Headquarters at a ten per cent discount.

Because Pennsylvania was now an active campaign State looking anxiously toward the hoped-for referendum in 1915, we did not let the vacation season of 1913 slow down our work. Special funds for open-air campaigning had been raised, and here and there a gift came in that had not actually been solicited. June 9th, Mr. Wilmer Atkinson telephoned to ask whether I could see him in his *Farm Journal* office. Before leaving on a trip to the West, he wished to make a contribution to suffrage, and gave me a check for $50.00 to be used where I thought it was most needed.

The Woman Suffrage Party made plans to display the "Voiceless Speech" during the summer months in store windows in various parts of the city. This effective method of propaganda drew large crowds, and these crowds were later given an opportunity to listen to open-air speeches in front of the stores when questions could be asked and answered.

Under the auspices of the Woman Suffrage Society of the County of Philadelphia, the Woman Suffrage Party, the Equal Franchise Society of Philadelphia, and smaller suffrage groups, 35 meetings were held during the month of June in Philadelphia, Radnor, Cynwyd, Merion, Wyncote, Wayne, Rosemont, Chester, Berwyn, Media, Kennett Square, Scranton, Honesdale, Glenolden, Norristown, and Concordville. A number of prominent speakers, some from outside the State, were obtained for special meetings. Mrs. Beatrice Forbes-Robertson Hale spoke in the Wayne Opera House and at a suffrage tea at the home of Mrs. George Horace Lorimer in Wyncote. Mrs. Raymond Brown of New York spoke at the Merion Cricket Club; Dr. Robert Brooks of Swarthmore was our speaker at Rosemont. Senator Helen Ring Robinson, of Colorado, and Mrs. Helen Hoy Greeley, of New York, spoke at many meetings in Philadelphia and nearby places.

But work at Headquarters was not confined to campaigning in the Eastern District of Pennsylvania. We co-operated with nearby States when important suffrage demonstrations were held, and, of course, we continued to work for the National Suffrage Amendment.

For instance, when New York had its big suffrage parade May 3, 1913, we needed a special coach to accommodate the Pennsylvania delegation that marched in that parade.

Again, June 28th, 1913, when a Roller Chair Suffrage Parade was held in Atlantic City, New Jersey, we helped in many ways to make it a success. About one-third of the paraders were from the Quaker City. On the train, at the station, and on the boardwalk, we sold suffrage novelties. Mrs. Anna Lowenburg, one of Philadelphia's active workers, obtained from the Mayor of Atlantic City a permit to hold the first open-air suffrage meeting ever held at that resort. And we prepared a special story for the Philadelphia papers to advertise another Roller Chair Suffrage Parade for July 9th in Ocean City, New Jersey.

SUFFRAGE WEEK in Philadelphia, October 6th to 13th, 1913, helped to make October one of the busiest months we had had. A woman suffrage study class, conducted by Mrs. Helen Hoy Greeley, held four weekly sessions; and preparations were made for the opening of the Suffrage Shop on the ground floor at 1721 Chestnut Street by the Woman Suffrage Party.

In an effort to stimulate nationwide interest in woman suffrage, Mrs. Charles W. Ruschenberger conceived the idea of having an exact copy of the Liberty Bell made, and offered to pay for it. This replica was called The Justice Bell. It was sent to Erie, Pennsylvania, for the Perry Celebration and proved to be one of the chief attractions in the suffrage division of the celebration. Upon request, it could be obtained for suffrage demonstrations anywhere in the country.

9

ANTI-SUFFRAGISTS ATTACK US
1913

On the eve of action in the Pennsylvania Senate on the proposed Woman Suffrage Amendment to the Pennsylvania Constitution, a curious incident occurred. Leaders of the anti-suffrage movement reported that on Sunday night, March 30, 1913, damage had been done to their Philadelphia headquarters and they used bitter words in ascribing to Suffragists the commission of this deed. We knew nothing about the incident until it was reported in the morning papers. Immediately, I gave out the following statement:

> Just why alleged depredations upon the anti-suffrage headquarters, said to have been committed Sunday night, March 30th, should not have been given publicity until Tuesday morning, April 1st, the time scheduled for the third and final reading by the Senate of the Woman Suffrage Bill, is giving Suffragists food for thought.
>
> The dignified and straightforward methods consistently pursued by our Association and the entire absence of anything approximating "militancy" has, we think, placed our movement in a position where it need not stoop to refute the charges brought against it by the leaders of the anti-Suffragists.
>
> Members of our Association, who have this morning visited the anti-Suffragists headquarters, assure us that the "damage" reported in some of

the morning papers is too slight to receive serious consideration and remind us that this is the first of April.

However, in the interest of lawful conduct by the community at large, we hereby offer the sum of two hundred dollars for information that will lead to the exposure, arrest, and conviction of the person or persons guilty of the alleged offense.

This statement was sent in my capacity as Executive Secretary of the Woman Suffrage Headquarters, 207-208 Hale Building, Philadelphia, and was dated April 1, 1913.

April 8th, Mr. Wilmer Atkinson, wrote to Miss Lida Stokes Adams, reviewing the case in detail and quoting statements by two prominent anti-Suffragists which had appeared in a Philadelphia newspaper. A statement by Mrs. Horace Brock, a leader of the anti-suffrage group, was quoted by Mr. Atkinson as follows:

Suffragists or suffragettes, whichever they choose to call themselves, it's their work undeniably. One would have thought they'd have had more sense than to play such tricks, practically on the eve of the State Senate's listening to their argument why women should vote! Such action as this proves conclusively why women should not vote.

Mr. Atkinson added that in "this same paper" Mrs. A. J. George, another anti-suffrage leader, is represented as having said:

Doubtless they will smash what windows they can. Doubtless they will blow up a few houses, and set fire to postoffices, and threaten the lives of a few public officials.

Despite all warnings, they are adopting the

militant methods of their English sisters. The present act is comparatively mild, but what will come remains to be seen.

This is an hysterical moment for these women. Poor things! They cannot help themselves. They are out beyond their depth; out in the wide rushing world, forgetting home, love, everything, in their wild, mad, heedless rush for the ballot. There's no doubt it was the suffragettes, she said. Who else under the sun could it be? It was work befitting Sunday, wasn't it?

Mr. Atkinson's indignation over the "outrageous charges" against Suffragists made him feel that we should "demand proof from Mrs. Brock and Mrs. George for their scandalous accusations" and he added:

Now, as a member of the Men's League for Woman Suffrage, and a life-long advocate of the cause, I feel deeply the humiliation of quietly resting under such serious and unwarranted charges and believing it a question for the Suffrage organization to meet by complete denial and utter repudiation of acts of violence of any kind and particularly the one in question.

Mr. Atkinson closed his letter to Miss Adams with this postscript:

P. S. I saw the statement you made in the morning papers and it is well, perhaps sufficient, but I hope you will consider the matter of a further statement as suggested above. I am sure it is the furthest from my wish to give you annoyance or trouble for like the rest of us you "have troubles of your own" no doubt.

I do not have Miss Adams' reply to Mr. Atkinson,

but I know that he called me on the 'phone and offered to give a reward of $100 for information that would lead to the exposure, arrest, and conviction of the guilty person or persons.

Somehow it did not seem to me possible that any considerable portion of the public could take too seriously the ridiculous, intemperate things the antis had said about us, although I might easily have pointed out to them that Suffragists believed they had a civic duty as well as a responsibility to their homes, and were sufficiently intelligent to plan their day so as to be able to perform the one duty without neglecting the other. And I might have given a few illustrations of this happy combination of private and public duty well done, although it would have been hard to select the illustrations when they were the rule rather than the exception.

I might, for instance, have called attention to Mrs. Charles Z. Klauder, who not only managed her lovely home and raised her two children with care, but who aided her husband, a distinguished architect, by acting as his chauffeur on business trips that required considerable time at the wheel, a job that he very much disliked. In addition, she took an active part in both the State and national suffrage campaigns. And Mrs. Eleanor B. Arrison who, left with two small children to raise on an inadequate income, used her needle to supplement her family income. Yet, she found time to be Chairman of the 5th Legislative District of the Woman Suffrage Party, and to answer many appeals for help from both the Pennsylvania and Washington headquarters. And Mrs. Leon Thomas Stern who, in addition to looking after the welfare of her husband and two sons, was a newspaper columnist, author of many books, an active civic worker, and an ardent Suffragist. And Mrs. S. Pancoast Levis, who combined with her many duties the job of being assistant to her husband in publishing the *Lansdowne News*. Also, she was for quite a long time Deputy United States Marshal in and for the Eastern District of Pennsylvania, in care of women jurors. She was said to be the first woman in the United States to hold such a position in a federal court. In the suffrage campaign, she represented the Woman Suffrage Party as Leader of the Borough of Lansdowne.

An unpleasant experience thus ended without seeming to have done us any real harm. We were never called upon for the $200.00 reward we had offered, and the Pennsylvania Legislature voted in 1913 in favor of the submission of the Woman Suffrage Amendment to the voters of the State.

10

NATIONAL ASSOCIATION HOLDS 45TH
ANNUAL CONVENTION IN WASHINGTON,
CONGRESSIONAL UNION IS HOSTESS
1913

Mr. Richard J. Beamish, Managing Editor of the Philadelphia *Press,* asked me to wire his paper one thousand words daily during the 45th Annual Convention of the N.A.W.S.A. held in Washington, D. C., November 29, 1913, through December 5th. This Convention was of especial significance for many reasons, principally perhaps because of two business propositions that were to be considered.

It was felt the time had come to adopt a new constituton designed to place the Association on a firmer financial basis. The old way had been for the annual convention to decide that the N.A.W.S.A. should maintain headquarters, publish literature, conduct a press bureau, help in the State campaigns, and, in general, keep up the work of a great organization. Then, the various State Associations and individuals pledged whatever they thought they could afford in support of the work. But the amount thus raised had never been enough to meet the year's expenses.

The new plan, drawn up by a revision committee, provided for the adoption of a budget, and for the assumption of financial responsibility by the affiliated, auxiliary, and associate members of the organization to cover that budget.

The other business proposition related to the founding of a corporation, capitalized at $50,000, to be known as the National Woman Suffrage Publishing Company, which would have charge of the printing of suffrage literature.

Also, the Convention was to have a report on the year's work of its Congressional Committee, which had established headquarters in the nation's capital, and which, under the chairmanship of Alice Paul, had done a remarkable job. The members of this Congressional Committee had, with the approval of the N.A.W.S.A., formed a new organization, known as the Congressional Union for Woman Suffrage, to assist in the work for a federal suffrage amendment, and it was this new organization that was to serve as hostess to the Convention.

It was hoped that during the Convention the assembled suffrage leaders of the United States would be able to secure from President Woodrow Wilson a favorable expression of opinion on woman suffrage that might be regarded as the Democratic Party's policy on the subject.

The Convention was to call upon the President to ask Congress, in his forthcoming message, to adopt the Woman Suffrage Constitutional Amendment as an Administration measure, and to urge Congress to take immmediate and favorable action upon it.

It was to call upon the United States Senate to vote in favor of the Suffrage Amendment then before it.

And it was to urge the Rules Committee of the House of Representatives to report favorably on the Resolution creating a standing Committee on Woman Suffrage in the House.

The business meetings on the opening day were followed by a luncheon at the National Hotel, during which short talks were sandwiched between the courses. Miss Marion Reilly, Dean of Bryn Mawr College, presided. Dr. Shaw, introduced as "Our Greatest Suffrage Orator," urged college women to feel their responsibility toward suffrage by organizing suffrage groups in all colleges for women, and by establishing a spirit of friendliness and understanding between the college woman and her sister, the wage earner. Miss Jane Addams spoke of the influence for good that had been manifested in Illinois since women had been granted the use of the ballot in Presidential elections just six months earlier. Lucy Burns spoke on the political strength of the Western women voters and said that one-fifth of the Senate, one-seventh of the House, and one-sixth of the electors came from States where women were voting on national questions.

Then Dr. Marion Smith of Philadelphia gave some interesting figures collected by Dr. Clyde King of the University of Pennsylvania for Mayor Rudolph Blankenburg. She said that $225,000,000 was spent for food every year in Philadelphia and that 90% of that money was handled by women. For all sorts of household expenses $750,000,000 was spent yearly in Philadelphia and most of this sum was handled by women. Dr. Smith pointed out that selling power was organized, while purchasing power was not.

In my first press story of the Convention, I emphasized the fact that both Dr. Shaw, our national president, and Miss M. Carey Thomas, founder and head of the National College Equal Suffrage League, hailed from Pennsylvania, and that Mrs. Lawrence Lewis of Philadelphia, one of the five members of the National Congressional Committee, had been asked to repeat the success she had achieved in 1912, when the National Convention was held in Philadelphia, and was again Chairman of the Committee on Local Arrangements.

Sunday, November 30th, marked the real opening of the Convention—a meeting for the public as well as the delegates. Although there was a charge of $2.00 for the better seats and $1.00 for a part of the gallery, the Columbia Theatre was packed and the waiting crowd at the door was invited to sit on the platform.

Above the platform, in letters so large that all could read, was the principal message of the Convention: "We Demand an Amendment to the Constitution of the United States Enfranchising Women."

Among the Sunday speakers were three women that earned their living by manual labor. Mary Anderson, organizer for the National Women's Trades Union League, spoke on the working woman and the ballot.

Margaret Hinchey, a New York laundry worker, pointed out that in New York women laundry workers worked for long hours for $3 to $4 a week. And New York children five years of age and less were paid 5 cents for making 540 forget-me-nots that required 1620 pieces in the making.

Rose Winslow, a weaver, struck a hard blow at philanthropic persons who, she said, spent their time in creating homes for working girls so as to make it possible for underpaid women to live in a semi-charitable institution. She said this effort could be better expended in securing for the wage earner an independent living wage. Through the use of the ballot, the wage earner could help herself and grow in the process, she concluded.

Helen Ring Robinson, State Senator from Colorado, followed with a scholarly speech proving that woman in striving for a voice in public affairs was only trying to preserve the home she had carefully built.

Miss Jane Addams, the last speaker, as usual won the heart of the audience, her very presence being a benediction. Our greatest woman voter declared that we were on the eve of a change in the science of government which would bring the voter into immediate relation with the needs of the community in which he lived. She added, "In the past, men have rallied to the call of their parties, now the voter is becoming a human being, not a cog in the political machine."

At the afternoon session December 1st, Dr. Shaw expressed the growing impatience of the older workers, and said that women the world over had been aroused and were demanding that every obstacle in the way of their complete development be removed. She averred that according to the Constitution of the United States women already possessed the right to vote, but were denied that privilege only through a misinterpretation of that document. The twist in the Constitution has come, she said, through a "twist in the minds of the twisters."

Mrs. Mary Ware Dennett, National Corresponding Secretary, reported the many suffrage victories of the year and added that proposed Amendments to State Constitutions had been introduced in 25 State Legislatures, and that there were only two States in which there were no suffrage organizations—South Carolina and New Mexico.

Miss Elinor Byrnes, National Press Chairman, made a report that astounded her hearers. It seemed impossible that one woman could have accomplished so much. The 10,000 columns of press clippings on exhibition showed only a part of the work of the press Bureau during the past eleven months. According to Miss Byrnes, Pennsylvania had the proud distinction of being the banner State in press work.

At the December 2nd session, the importance of the suffrage movement was emphasized by a letter received from the Chief Executive of Minnesota. Governor Eberhart invited the N.A.W.S.A. to hold its 1914 Convention in St. Paul. His invitation read: "It gives me great pleasure to second the invitation of the St. Paul Association of Commerce to your association to hold your next meeting in St. Paul and I can assure you on behalf of the entire State as well as the Twin Cities, that you will be given a most cordial welcome should you decide on this location."

Another invitation that added prestige to the Convention was to an "at home" at the residence of Mrs. Robert M. LaFollette, wife of the Senator from Wisconsin. The invitation read, "To meet Mrs. Catt, Dr. Shaw, the official board and the delegates to the National American Woman Suffrage Convention. Women of the Cabinet and Congressional circles in equal suffrage at home Friday, December 5, from four until seven o'clock."

But in spite of these courtesies, the day brought keen disappointment because President Wilson made no mention of woman suffrage in his message to Congress. At the evening meeting, Dr. Shaw called the Convention's attention to the fact that while the President had recognized the necessity for the extension of the ballot to the Filipinos, and had urged Territorial voters' rights for Alaska, he had failed to mention woman suffrage in his message. Dr. Shaw continued:

> President Wilson referred in his message to the fact that the time had come for an extension of greater social justice; and we women eagerly listened to this. We had hope that social justice would include some measure of political justice to the women of the country. I feel fully that measure of disappointment which, under the circumstances, is natural; for the time has come for the President to say a word in our behalf.
>
> We feel that President Wilson has fallen short of the greatest opportunity which has come to him or ever will come to him. No other President

has ever had such an opportunity. President Wilson had the opportunity of speaking a word which might ultimately lead to the enfranchisement of a large part of the human family. Even Lincoln, who, by a word, freed a race, had not this opportunity to release from the bonds one half of the human family!

I feel that I must make this statement as broad as it is for the reason that we at Budapest last year realized that womenkind throughout the world look to the United States to blaze the way for the extension of universal suffrage in every quarter of the globe. President Wilson has missed the one thing that might have made it possible for him never to be forgotten. I am saying this on behalf of myself and of my fellow officers.

When the discussion of the budget came up, the most debated point in the change in the constitution of the National Association, Pennsylvania made one of the many thousand-dollar pledges for the new year's work. The full amount was soon subscribed.

December 3rd was devoted largely to the Hearing before the Rules Committee of the House of Representatives on the appointment of a Woman Suffrage Committee in the House similar to the one already formed in the Senate. Heretofore woman suffrage hearings in the House had been held before the overworked Judiciary Committee, which year after year had failed to take definite action on the suffrage question.

Of the eleven members on the Rules Committee, only seven were present, but the committee room in the House Office Building was packed to the doors. Chairman Robert L. Henry in introducing Dr. Shaw said she would be in "charge of the proceedings." But before the proceedings actually began, Pennsylvanians had reason to be proud of one of their Congressmen, Mr. M. C. Kelly, who introduced the following resolution:

> Whereas: The question of equal suffrage is one of vital public interest, and the people of the nation have an inherent right to full knowledge of the action upon it by their representatives in Congress and the committees of Congress, therefore be it,
>
> Resolved, That all hearings upon this subject before the Rules Committee of the House of Representatives be open to the public and the final vote shall be a matter of public record.

After instructing the audience that no demonstration would be in order, Dr. Shaw, in a clear, ringing voice, told the Committee that she had not come to convert its members to the right of the people to have a voice in their own government, but to ask that a properly qualified committee be appointed to consider woman suffrage—a committee that was not overworked and that might at all times be ready to give ear to the suffrage question.

As the subject under discussion was one of world-wide importance, and was being considered by the leading nations of the world, Dr. Shaw urged that the House of Representatives go on record either for or against it. "Let us have some action, even if it be an adverse one," she said.

Mrs. Ida Husted Harper emphasized the difficulty of getting suffrage through amendments to the State Constitutions and ended her appeal by a reference to the historic suffrage parade on the 3rd of March, 1913. "Gentlemen of the Committee," she said, "you have not forgotten the suffrage parade in Washington last Spring, when troops from Fort Meyer had to be summoned to protect the women from the mob that closed in upon them. If you could have been in that procession and looked into the faces of that jeering, insulting, half-drunken line of men you would have realized what the mothers, wives, and daughters of this country are subjected to when they are compelled to plead with the individual voters to grant them the suffrage. Create for us our own Committee, one that will not be too busy or too indifferent to give our case the attention to which it is entitled, a Committee whose appointment will hold out to us the hope that ultimately our question will be considered by the National Congress which is elected to represent all the people, women as well as men."

In a most convincing way Miss Jane Addams gave many instances in which Congress had extended the franchise, the most conspicuous of which was the 15th Amendment. To some of the other instances she mentioned, important, if less far-reaching, Representative Hardwick of Georgia offered objections, which Miss Addams met satisfactorily or was willing to take from her list—a list long enough to impress any fair-minded body of men.

At this point, Mr. Pou of North Carolina suggested that the Committee on Election of President, Vice-President, and Representatives be given charge of the woman suffrage question. Another member of the Committee commented that that committee was a "dead" one. A short while later, Representative Garrett of Tennessee had to leave the hearing, but before going he had an opportunity to speak of the Elections Committee where, he said, bills are sometimes "quietly, gently, delicately, and reverently buried."

The next Suffragist to address the Rules Committee was Mrs. Desha Breckenridge, granddaughter of Henry Clay. In true Southern style, she referred to the Civil War, which deprived the South of the flower of its manhood.

With that loss to the electorate, and the illiterate colored vote that followed the war, Mrs. Breckenridge said that Kentucky was put so low in the scale of literacy that it stood in danger of "tipping off." Her State, she added, needed the vote of the educated woman to restore it to its past glory. "Kentucky men class women poetically and rhetorically with whiskey and horses, and politically and legally with criminals and idiots," said the speaker.

Representative John E. Raker of California, the only man speaking for the Suffragists, made an impassioned plea for justice and fair play, and said, "Women are bound to have, in a short time, a chance to help conditions."

Mrs. Mary Beard, wife of Professor Beard of Columbia, created a deep impression on the Committee. After pleading for a special committee in order that woman suffrage might be acted upon by a truly representative body, she told the Democratic majority of five members that a refusal to do this might endanger their party by bringing up the question of representation according to population. In the West, where the Republican, Progressive, and Socialist vote predominated, women were enfranchised and the representation in Congress had not been increased; in the Democratic South, where not only women, but some colored men were disfranchised, the representation had not been decreased. She also pointed out that five majority members of the Committee having the decision of this momentous question, were elected by the small total of 63,570 votes—less than the vote behind two of the minority members.

Mrs. Carrie Chapman Catt, the last speaker, gave a survey of the suffrage movement in foreign countries. When interrupted by a Representative with the question, "Are you not doing well with the State Legislatures?" Mrs. Catt showed how hard it is to teach not only the prejudiced native-born, but the foreigner, who does not know our language or the meaning of true democracy. She said that the United States offers the "most outrageously unfair process by which any unenfranchised class in any land are called upon to get the vote."

The routine of the afternoon session of the Convention was given a reminder of the morning's excitement when the following motion was enthusiastically passed:

> Since the President omitted all mention of woman suffrage in his message, and since he has announced that he will send several other messages to Congress outlining the measures that the Administration will support: I move that the Convention wait upon the President in order to lay before him the importance of the suffrage question and urge him to make it an Administration measure, and send immediately to Congress the recommendation that it proceed with this measure before any other.

Mrs. Medill McCormick and Mrs. Desha Breckenridge were appointed a committee of two to wait upon the President.

The Convention's evening meeting was turned over to the men and was presided over by Mr. James Lees Laidlaw, of New York, President of the Men's League for Woman Suffrage. Addresses were made by George Creel, Senators Charles S. Thomas of Colorado, Joseph L. Bristow of Kansas, Robert L. Owen of Oklahoma, and Representatives Frank W. Mondell of Wyoming, J. W. Bryan of Washington, Victor Murdock of Kansas, and other members of Congress.

December 4, after a lengthy and at times bitter debate, a new constitution for the N.A.W.S.A. was adopted, thus placing the organization on much firmer financial ground.

Dr. Shaw, who was opposed by Mrs. Harriet Taylor Upton, was able to overcome the opposition and, for the eighth consecutive term, was elected President.

There was some disappointment when the Committee of Two appointed to ask President Wilson to receive the Convention delegates, was told that he was too ill to see them. However, this disappointment was somewhat assuaged by information from Assistant Secretary Foster that the President, if he had sufficiently recovered, might be able to receive the delegates the following day. For this, the Convention, on motion from Miss Jane Addams, tendered the President a vote of thanks.

Where the next convention would be held was a question of doubt. Invitations poured in so fast that Dr. Shaw remarked, "How we are wanted! One of the hopeful signs of our popularity is the call from the South. Georgia wants us, and Senator Shields of Tennessee requests us to meet next year in Chattanooga."

Senator Clapp of Minnesota came in person to add weight to St. Paul's pressing invitation and said:

> I will promise you a most cordial reception. I do not know when we will get woman suffrage, but we will get it. God never designed that a nation, a race, or a sex should live in slavery. The only question is "When will this Government be a government by the people?"

Then Senator Clapp referred to President Wilson's failure to mention woman suffrage in his message and expressed disappointment over the omission. He added, however, that we should "deal kindly and generously with the President as with all others who have not seen the situation as we see it. It is a matter of growth—a matter of development." A rising vote of thanks was given the Senator for the invitation that he brought.

At the afternoon session, the formation of the $50,000 National Woman Suffrage Publishing Company was approved. The idea back of this move was the necessity to insure the continuous, adequate production of suffrage literature and supplies in as large a quantity and for as long a period as they might be needed for the several State campaigns, the national amendment campaign, and also for the publication of literature suited to the needs of the newly enfranchised women.

So certain was it that the company would be formed that more than $5,000 worth of stock was subscribed in advance of its formation. And after the Convention voted in its favor, it took only a few minutes to dispose of additional shares amounting to over $11,000. Among the Pennsylvanians that subscribed for stock were Mrs. Lawrence Lewis, Dean Reilly of Bryn Mawr, Miss Mary E. Garrett, and Miss Vida Hunt Francis.

The principal event of the last public session of the Convention on December 5th was the report made by Alice Paul, Chairman of the Congressional Committee of the National Association, and Chairman of the Congressional Union for Woman Suffrage. Some of the achievements recorded in this report were:

Three big parades; three Hearings before the national Congress; the presentation of a petition bearing 200,000 signatures that called forth twenty-two speeches on the floor of the Senate; two national conventions, one of which represented 4,000,000 women voters; three summer campaigns, one of which resulted in the formation of a Suffrage society in North Carolina that sent delegates to the 45th Convention; the opening of headquarters in Delaware; the maintenance of headquarters in Washington for nearly a year; the establishing of an important press department in the national capital that kept in touch with the press of the country; the formation of a Men's League for Woman Suffrage with Dr. Harvey W. Wiley as president, and many Congressmen as working members; eight crowded theatre meetings, and an average of five or six meetings in Washington every day. In addition, 1500 subscriptions had been secured for a weekly paper, that, though less than a month old, was, through its advertisements, self-supporting. And this stupendous work was accomplished at a cost of $25,000, $20,000 of which was raised in Washington and $4,000 in Philadelphia. The remaining $1,000 was subscribed by various Suffrage organizations throughout the country.

Mrs. Catt, in moving the adoption of the report, asked many questions. She wished especially to understand why a committee appointed by the National Association should be compelled to finance itself.

Miss Addams, a Vice-President of the National Association, replied in part:

I had the honor in Philadelphia of making a motion to form the Congressional Committee. They promised to pay their own expenses and have honorably filled their pledge. The committee is a brilliant and able one and we should be unwise to change it when such splendid work is being accomplished.

Before the session closed, a promise of financial help to the Congressional Committee from the National Association was made.

A committee of fifty-five women, representing every

State and every association in the organization, was appointed to wait upon President Wilson who, so far, on account of illness, had been unable to see the Suffragists.

The last afternoon of the Convention, representatives of the N.A.W.S.A. were given an opportunity to speak again before the Rules Committee of the House, this time in rebuttal of things said by the *opposition*. The anti-suffragists had had nine hours in which to present their reasons for not wanting to vote and for objecting to the granting of that privilege to other women who felt it a duty to vote.

Miss Alice Stone Blackwell, daughter of that great pioneer, Lucy Stone, was the first of a long list of speakers at the rebuttal proceedings, and she was a happy choice for that task. Among the other speakers representing all classes of women, were many Southern women, who seemed eager to refute the accusation that they were not interested in woman's enfranchisement. They took pains to emphasize the fact that they were not "lilies, roses, or moons" and were tired of being thought unlike other women. They wanted the rights and privileges of human beings and the opportunity to perform a human being's full duty.

And now a confession. Although I had had three years of experience in press work, I had had no training whatever for that work. Yet somehow I did not seem to realize, when asked to report the Convention, how unprepared I was to undertake a telegraphed story to a metropolitan newspaper. My newspaper contacts had been mainly with the City Desk and I just did not know about the machinery through which "copy" finally reached the reader. In consequence, my first instalment to the *Press* was a gruelling experience.

My avid interest in everything that took place at the Convention and my duties as a delegate had so absorbed my attention that I failed to realize the difference between writing a story at Suffrage Headquarters and working against the clock at the end of an exciting and busy day. When, fairly late in the evening, I sat down at the typewriter, I began to wonder just what a thousand words really meant! (My plan at the Pennsylvania Headquarters had been to garner every bit of news that I thought might interest the papers and to dress it up as attractively as I could, thinking only of the kind of words used, not their number). Mr. Beamish must, I thought, be saving a definite amount of space and I was expected to fill it exactly. I did not even know that a compositor could, if necessary, either crowd or spread the lines a little. The clock was ticking away and the "dead line" was not far off. I had to begin. I wrote the introduction and counted the words. I wrote the second paragraph, counted the words, and added them to the first one. At least I was "playing safe." This mathematical process naturally interfered with speed and consecutive thinking, but there was no way out. Finally the story was finished and I rang for a Western Union messenger. I was, I think, a little short of the thousand words, but I feared that that was as bad as going over the number. Tired and genuinely in need of rest, I went to bed, but I was too excited to sleep. I got up, called Mr. Beamish on long distance, and explained to him the difficulty I was facing. I told him I was used to weighing my words, but not to counting them. As usual, he was very kind and understanding, and that comforted me. But would the morning ever come!

Bright and early I was up and in quest of a copy of the *Press*. Feverishly I turned the pages until I reached the last one. Not a word on the Convention. My heart sank.

Perhaps, in my haste, I had overlooked the article and should start again and go more slowly. EUREKA! On the first page, a place I had, apparently, not even thought to look, in big, beautiful headlines, was our story. Mr. Beamish had even used my photograph as a "by-line."

Encouraged by Mr. Beamish's understanding of my predicament, and stimulated by the many interesting things to report on the Convention, I grew bolder as the days went by. Two out of the seven days of the Convention my stories ran up to about sixteen hundred words, but our good friend of the *Press* used them without rebuking me for thus over-reaching our verbal contract.

11

DR. SHAW FIGHTS UNJUST TAXATION
1913-1915

Dr. Anna Howard Shaw had the courage to fight not only for woman suffrage, but against unjust taxation. Standing out for a principle, she refused in the fall of 1913 to pay what she considered an unjust tax. When a tax assessor of Upper Providence Township in Delaware County, Pennsylvania, left at her Moylan home a legal paper requesting her to make out a statement of all her "personal property, mortgages, stocks, and bonds with minute details," her reply was that while she was illegally denied the right of participating in the Government of the State it was "heaping injury upon tyranny" to ask her to make out a list upon which taxes were to be levied. "In the spirit of 1776," she "declined to be a party to an act which violated the Constitution." She therefore returned the document unadorned. In doing this, she said she was not violating any law because the document itself stated that, if for any reason the list was not made out by the person to be taxed, the assessor should "learn the amount of the property and make out a reasonably fair statement." Did the baffled assessor do this? No indeed! Dr. Shaw said she had witnesses before whom the assessor boasted he would make the assessment so large she would be compelled to make out the statement. The amount of his assessment was $50,000.

Dr. Shaw did not pay the exaggerated tax on personal property she did not own, but she did change her legal address to New York, sending in first a personal notice, then a second witnessed by her attorney, and finally a third in registered letter to make sure of its reaching its destination. But no notice was taken of these three communications. Claiming New York as her legal residence and denying that Moylan was her legal abode, Dr. Shaw refused to pay taxes in two places and denied the right of the authorities in Pennsylvania to make her pay State taxes.

A sequel to these legal complications came nearly two years later. For many details of the following colorful story I am indebted to the New York *Times* because this paper ran *instalments* of it for several days.

June 29, 1915, friends and admirers of Dr. Shaw presented her with an automobile with the intriguing name, Eastern Victory. The car was painted a gay yellow, the color that Suffragists had adopted for all of their campaigns. In those days a yellow car was such a novelty that it attracted attention wherever it went, and, as was intended, advertised the suffrage movement. Dr. Shaw, then sixty-eight years of age, took her first two weeks' vacation in three years to learn to run the car herself.

But her joy in her new possession was soon to be marred. The Tax Assessor of Upper Providence Township, Delaware County, Pennsylvania, was again on her trail. One day, when only her little maid was at her Moylan home, the assessor took possession of Dr. Shaw's car to force payment of a tax that she had insisted was unjust when it was levied in 1913. And, before leaving, he told the maid that unless this tax were paid within five days the sale of the car would be advertised. Dr. Shaw's attorney instituted equity proceedings to enjoin the Delaware County authorities from selling the car at public auction to satisfy the tax assessment.

But, as scheduled, the Constable's sale took place July 24, 1915. Dr. Shaw, however, was not to lose out. The Woman Suffrage Society of Delaware County bought the car and presented it to her. Although the tax had amounted to only $126, two bidders against the Suffrage Society forced the redemption price to $230. This, the Suffrage Society no doubt thought a small price to pay in support of the stand Dr. Shaw had taken in defense of a principle.

But this "happy ending" does not close our story. The chauffeur sent Dr. Shaw a bill for $5.08 for instructing her to run the car. Through some inadvertence Dr. Shaw did not receive the bill when first sent out, and when she heard of it through the Constable, who presented it for collection, she immediately sent her check to the company. Not only was the check returned to the maker, but the following letter of apology from the company came with it:

> We have never before known any of our salesmen to do such a thing. This in itself was bad enough, but the fact that he placed a bill in the hands of a constable we consider an insult to this company. We apologize and beg to assure you that such a thing as this never happened before and we believe will never happen again. Mr. S———— [the name was written out] has been dismissed from the employ of this company.

12

EASTERN DISTRICT OF PENNSYLVANIA MOVES ITS HEADQUARTERS
1914

February 26, 1914, the Eastern District of Pennsylvania moved its Headquarters from the Hale Building at Juniper and Chestnut Streets, Philadelphia, to the second floor of 1723 Chestnut Street. By this time, the Woman Suffrage Party's lunch and tearoom at 1721 Chestnut Street, which had been started as a venture, had proved successful and the organization had also rented the second floor of 1723 Chestnut Street. Mrs. Anna M. Orme was still Chairman of the Woman Suffrage Party and Mrs. George A. Piersol had been appointed Chairman of the Campaign Committee.

Suffrage leaders in Philadelphia thought it would be well to have one central location for all suffrage organizations. 1721-23 Chestnut Street thus became headquarters not only for the Eastern District of Pennsylvania, and the Woman Suffrage Party, but for the Woman Suffrage Society of the County of Philadelphia, the Equal Franchise Society of Philadelphia, the Pennsylvania College Equal Suffrage League, the Pennsylvania Men's League for Woman Suffrage, and the Pennsylvania Limited Suffrage League.

As usual, Mr. Wilmer Atkinson was keeping an eye

on us to see where he might help. For two months, beginning March 16th, he paid the salary of a young woman whose special duties at the new headquarters of the Eastern District of Pennsylvania were to take charge of the Committee Room and to meet visitors. He also asked if he might buy a desk for me and soon a lovely one arrived.

Frances Lichten, then a struggling young artist, who was later to win prominence by writing a book on special phases of decorative art, helped us by painting needed wording on several of our doors.

But despite this auspicious beginning at the new suffrage center, complications soon developed, and it seemed plain the move we had made would not prove satisfactory. Theoretically, the plan of having all our organizations in one place appeared sound, but in practice it did not work out. The atmosphere of the place was entirely different from that at the Hale Building where we had spent nearly three and a half years working in harmony. The situation began to affect my health and at the end of three months I decided to take a rest and withdraw temporarily from the campaign. The rest, however, did not last long as the following chapter will show.

Here are some of the happenings and some of the work accomplished at the new Headquarters of the Eastern District of Pennsylvania between February 26 and the end of May, 1914:

The Philadelphia *North American,* which had supplied us with one of its clever suffrage cartoons for *The Suffragist* of February 21, gave us permission to use another of its cartoons for the *Woman's Journal* of April 11.

At the request of the Philadelphia *Evening Times,* I wrote an editorial on Woman Suffrage nearly two columns long, which was used in its issue of March 26.

The *Times-Leader* of Wilkesbarre used a special suffrage article that I wrote for its Woman Suffrage edition in March.

An opportunity was given Dr. Anna Howard Shaw to reply through Philadelphia papers to an attack made upon her by a prominent Philadelphia anti-Suffragist, Mrs. Violet Birdsall.

Arrangements were made with Philadelphia newspapers for an interview on Woman Suffrage with Mrs. Medill McCormick and Mrs. Crystal Eastman Benedict.

Permission was obtained from the State Headquarters in Harrisburg to accede to a request from the National Woman Suffrage Publishing Company, Inc., to use our *Farmers' Flyer* and print their name instead of ours on the leaflet. The N.A.W.S.A. considered it the best thing of the kind they had seen.

At the request of Mrs. R. C. Talbott-Perkins of New York, we inquired of Dr. Russell H. Conwell what his position was on woman suffrage. He not only assured us of his sympathy with the movement, but he kindly prepared a statement for publication.

We provided speakers to the A. M. Collins Mfg. Company; the West Philadelphia High School for Girls; the Young People's Society of Christian Endeavor of Temple Lutheran Church; the Lighthouse Women and Girls' Club; the 24th and 27th Ward Socialist Party; and the Business Men and Women's League for Woman Suffrage.

Three meetings were arranged to take advantage of a generous offer made by Mrs. Marion Booth Kelley, State Lecturer of the Massachusetts Woman Suffrage Association, who wrote us she should be in Philadelphia in June and should be glad to lend us a helping hand.

To arouse interest in our suffrage parade in Philadelphia May 2, 1914, we wrote letters to ministers in the city asking them to preach sermons on woman suffrage the

Sunday preceding the parade and received some beautiful replies.

A personal invitation to march in the parade was extended to social workers at their meeting April 22, and later 342 letters were sent to Philadelphia members of that group.

When the Congressional Union for Woman Suffrage had its suffrage parade in Washington, D. C., May 9, the Pennsylvania Railroad allotted the Pennsylvania delegation of about eighty persons a special coach and gave us reduced rates.

Headquarters responded to requests for information and help from nineteen towns and cities in Pennsylvania and New Jersey. Assistance was given Mrs. M. C. Cain in her suffrage work among Negroes; and material was supplied for a suffrage debate before the Delaware State Grange.

Prominent among the persons asking us for information were Professor Scott Nearing, of the Department of Economics at the University of Pennsylvania, who was preparing to speak on Woman Suffrage during the summer; Professor Thomas O'Bolger, also of the University of Pennsylvania, who wished to reply to Sir Almroth Wright's *An Unexpurgated Case of Woman Suffrage;* and Miss Mary H. Ingham, who needed material to be used in the new handbook of the Progressive Party.

May 14th, the Manager of Keith's Theatre sent us tickets for a box because moving pictures of our May 2nd parade were a part of the theatre's program. And the Evans Photographic Studio sent us complimentary photographs of the parade.

13

SOCIETY OF FRIENDS ENDORSES WOMAN SUFFRAGE . . . . CLERGYMEN AND EDUCATORS SPEAK IN ITS BEHALF . . . . AN ANTI-SUFFRAGE CLERGYMAN RAILS AGAINST IT
1914

All through the years in which I was active in suffrage campaigns, I realized how fortunate women were in having many outstanding men working side by side with them, and I also realized the special debt of gratitude they owed the Society of Friends for the many leaders, both men and women, that this fearless group gave to the woman suffrage movement. As far as I can recall, the Society of Friends were the only religious sect that gave endorsement as a body to the woman suffrage campaign. A resolution adopted by the Society of Friends at their Yearly Meeting in Philadelphia, May, 1914, was used by us as a part of our suffrage literature. Here is that resolution:

In view of the fact that the Society of Friends, by reason of its inheritance and present organization, gives evidence of the advantage which results to the home, to the meeting and the community, through a full recognition of the dignity of woman and her right to complete development, the Philadelphia Yearly Meeting of

HANNAH CLOTHIER HULL

ISAAC H. CLOTHIER   DR. WILLIAM I. HULL

Mrs. Hull, daughter and wife of Mr. Clothier and Dr. Hull, two of Pennsylvania's leading Suffragists.

With best wishes for woman
suffrage in Pennsylvania in
1915 M. Carey Thomas

the Religious Society of Friends records its indorsement of equal suffrage as a principle of justice to woman and an opportunity for more effective service. The Yearly Meeting recommends that monthly meetings be watchful for opportunities to influence equal suffrage legislation and encourage their members to give active interest in the accomplishment of this reform.

Individual leaders in other religious groups gave valiant support to the suffrage movement and won our sincerest gratitude. Outstanding among these leaders were Rev. Frederick R. Griffin, of the First Unitarian Church in Philadelphia; Dr. Joseph Krauskopf, of the Congregation Keneseth Israel, and his successor, Dr. W. H. Fineshriber; Rev. Carl E. Grammer, of St. Stephen's Episcopal Church; Dr. Stephen S. Wise, of Free Synagogue in New York; Rev. Arthur Hilton, of the Baptist church, and Rev. Irving S. Chenoweth.

Also from educational institutions in Pennsylvania we had fine support. Among the busy teachers that gave time to the suffrage campaign and spoke at many public meetings were Dr. William I. Hull, Dr. Jesse Holmes, and Dr. Robert Brooks all of Swarthmore College; and Dr. Scott Nearing and Dr. Thomas O'Bolger of the University of Pennsylvania. And Frank Stephens, of Single Tax fame, was another strong supporter of our campaign.

But occasionally even a representative of the church saw fit to attack us. One afternoon when I came home from our office, my next-door neighbor sitting on his porch said, with an amused smile, that he had seen my picture in the *Evening Times*. As we had had no meeting and, as far as I could recall, had done nothing to merit publicity, I hurried to get a copy of the *Times;* and this is what I saw. At the top of a page were two good-sized photographs placed in a friendly position side by side, but with this caption in large letters over them, AUTHOR AND SUF-FRAGETTE WHO ARE AT WAR OVER BUTTONS. The handsome author was the Rev. Dr. Cyrus Townsend Brady of the Episcopal Church, whose prolific pen produced numerous novels. His dignified photograph bore the credit line of Gutekunst, the photographer of the élite of that day. The picture of me was, I think, one that a *Times* photographer had some time in the past "snapped" at a meeting, and it certainly made me look as if I were ready for the fray.

Now, this is what had happened. A young woman reporter had visited our headquarters and asked me to reply to Dr. Brady who, according to the reporter, had said that because women followed the current style of buttoning their dresses up the back they certainly hadn't sense enough to vote. (As Dr. Brady's photograph showed him in a clerical vest, his criticism on buttoning clothes up the back had a peculiar flavor.) I told the reporter that while the minister's statement was as good an argument as any against the enfrachisement of women, it was too patently silly to merit a reply. However, so that I should not appear to the reporter to be uncoöperative by declining to be interviewed, I talked with her, as I explained, not for publicity, but just as woman to woman. My experience in the past had led me to believe that I could trust the reporters not to quote me without permission. It was easy to point out to her that the men of that day were not always sensible in the styles they followed. They sweltered in the hottest weather in woolen suits far too heavy for summer wear. They wore shirts with such stiffly starched fronts that these fronts sometimes crumpled long before the end of the evening; and high starched collars that added to the men's discomfort. And weren't men a bit slavish as to dates in regard to straw hats, not daring to wear them before May 15th and after September 15th, no matter what the thermometer registered? Yet in spite of this lack of good common sense, no attempt had been made to disfranchise male voters. Having thus, as I thought, ministered to our Cause by ignoring the learned divine's attempted stab in the back and, at the same time not having antagonized the press by refusing an interview, I went on my way rejoicing and forgot the whole affair. Not so the reporter. Tempted perhaps by the B's in Brady and Buttons, she indulged her fancy in an outburst of alliteration that evidently pleased her editor who allowed her space for a double column over twelve inches long. Above the body of the story, in big black letters was this quotation credited to *Suffragettes,* "BUTTONS ARE NO BAR TO BRAINS." But the alliteration and logic credited to Dr. Brady were rare indeed. Here are some quotations from the article—"Brains, brawn, and ballots will never belong to beauteous, belligerent belles so long as they button blouses behind." "Buttons up the back are foes to common sense and to liberty. And so long as women continue to wear them they certainly haven't sense enough to vote. Picture hats and hobble skirts are almost as bad—the latter look like a combination born of the Spanish Inquisition and an insane asylum, and they all show that women are men's inferior and certainly are not ready for the ballot."

With this and similar astute opposition in high places, wasn't it remarkable that women were ever enfranchised?

14

*AN ATTEMPT TO CLARIFY SUFFRAGE
SITUATION . . . EQUAL FRANCHISE
SOCIETY OF PHILADELPHIA OPENS
NEW HEADQUARTERS
1914*

In order to help the reader understand what might naturally appear to be, and perhaps was to some extent, a duplication of suffrage work in Philadelphia in 1914, I shall give some details about the situation at that time. In doing this, I must refer to some facts already told.

When the Pennsylvania Woman Suffrage Association opened Headquarters in the Hale Building in 1910, the oldest Philadelphia suffrage organization was the *Woman Suffrage Society of the County of Philadelphia.* In 1910, the *Equal Franchise Society of Philadelphia* was organized, and in the beginning planned to devote its efforts to propaganda only. Also, in 1910, the Pennsylvania Woman Suffrage Association, at its annual convention, authorized the formation of the *Woman Suffrage Party,* a non-partisan, non-dues-paying organization, membership in which was open to men as well as women. The organizing of the Woman Suffrage Party was an effort to break away from the *club* idea and to begin organizing Suffragists into Legislative Districts. So eager were we to make progress in our campaign that we welcomed the formation and assistance of any suffrage group that felt it could do its best work if its membership were bound by a special tie, such, for instance, as being all college women. When in February, 1914, 1721-23 Chestnut Street became the center of all suffrage activities in Philadelphia, seven organizations made that address their headquarters.

By this time, differences of opinion as to the best methods of securing woman suffrage nationally had arisen between the two national organizations—the *National American Woman Suffrage Association,* led by Dr. Anna Howard Shaw, and the newly formed *Congressional Union for Woman Suffrage,* led by Alice Paul. The former organization believed in the need to enfranchise women nationally, but devoted most of its strength to working for their enfranchisement through amendments to the State constitutions. The Congressional Union, on the other hand, while not opposing work for the passage of State constitutional amendments, felt the time had come for Suffragists to concentrate their efforts on amending the national constitution. By degrees, differences of opinion between these two national organizations became so marked that an actual split resulted.*

Members of the Pennsylvania Woman Suffrage Association began to take sides in this controversy, some bitterly opposing the aggressive campaign of the Congressional Union, and others just as strongly endorsing it. But as our State Association was an auxiliary of the National American Woman Suffrage Association there was no division of opinion about our allegiance to that body in our campaign to amend the Constitution of Pennsylvania. It was only in our work of trying to amend the Federal Constitution that a division in our ranks took place. By this time we must have begun to realize that women, like men, differed in their political thinking and had the courage to follow their convic-

---

* More details of this breach will be given in the third chapter of Part Two.

tions. However, for the good of the Cause, we soft-pedaled our differences and tried to emphasize the things on which we agreed wholeheartedly.

When I decided to take a needed rest, I had no idea that the Equal Franchise Society of Philadelphia was planning to have its own headquarters and that I should be asked to be its executive secretary. But the coincidence of these two things, plus the fact that the growth of the Congressional Union had made that organization feel it necessary to have a State Chairman in Pennsylvania and modest headquarters in Philadelphia,* quite naturally, I suppose, aroused some speculation in the city. This speculation intrigued a reporter on the Philadelphia *Press*, who saw here the possibility of a good story. Not being supplied with sufficient facts, the reporter fell back on his vivid fancy, and succeeded in giving Suffragists considerable trouble. In his long, first-page story, he made this comment:

> When it became known that the Equal Franchise Society was in sympathy with the Congressional Union and because of the strained relations between the two national organizations, it caused immediate dissension in the Philadelphia societies. . . . Members of the suffrage organizations despite their discord have consistently denied there was any trouble between them. They countered all questions by saying all of them were working for the same thing—equal suffrage.

In an effort to make clear the Equal Franchise Society's position in the campaign and its aims for future work, Miss Mary H. Ingham, a member of its Board of Directors,

---

* Mrs. Lawrence Lewis was the State Chairman and an office in her home at 1820 Pine Street, Philadelphia, served as Pennsylvania Headquarters.

prepared the following statement for the newspapers, May 27, 1914:

> The Board of the Equal Franchise Society held a meeting at the house of the President, Mrs. Wilfred Lewis, Haverford, Thursday, May 21st, when definite action was taken looking to an enlargement of the work of the Society and to greater co-operation with the other Suffrage Societies of Philadelphia, especially by the starting of a new center for suffrage work.
>
> The Equal Franchise Society was started purely for propaganda for suffrage and has not so far taken any part in political work. It has not taken up the duty of opposing or supporting candidates for the legislature or other office, and is entirely non-partisan in its character. Owing to the questions of some of the members of the Society as to whether the Board had taken any part as a Board in the activities of the Congressional Union, it seems advisable to draw the attention of the members of the Society and of the public to the fact that the Board of the Society and its Advisory Committee, count as members men and women prominent in all the political parties; among them being William Draper Lewis, Progressive candidate for Governor; Roland S. Morris, Chairman of the State Committee of the Democratic Party; Mr. J. Levering Jones, a prominent Republican; and among the women members Miss Mary A. Burnham, Chairman of the Good Government League; Miss Mary H. Ingham, Secretary of the Progressive League; and Mrs. Lawrence Lewis Jr., a member of the National Committee of the Congressional Union. It is, therefore, obvious that political action either for or against any of these political parties or associations is out of the power of the Equal Franchise Society. The Society is closely connected with the National Board as

Miss M. Carey Thomas of Bryn Mawr College is Vice President of the Society and is a member of the Official Board of the National American Woman Suffrage Association.

The opening of the new office will serve to aid the other organized societies, the Woman Suffrage Party, and the State Association in the joint work of furthering the passage of the amendment to the State Constitution in 1915. All of the State societies of which the Equal Franchise is one have the same aim and there should be no misunderstanding of their purpose.

And, as the Congressional Union will from this time on play an important part in the Pennsylvania campaign, I shall here interpolate a letter from Alice Paul to one of the State's most prominent Suffragists, Miss Mary A. Burnham. It relates to the formation of that young organization and the reasons for its existence:

> 1420 F Street, N. W.,
> Washington, D. C.,
> June 12, 1914

Miss Mary A. Burnham,
3401 Powelton Av.,
Philadelphia, Pa.

Dear Miss Burnham:

Mrs. [Lawrence] Lewis has asked me to send you some notes concerning the formation of the Congressional Union.

The Congressional Union for Woman Suffrage was formed last spring by the Congressional Committee of the National American Woman Suffrage Association.

It was formed for the purpose of aiding in the work for the passage of the federal suffrage amendment. Our congressional Committee felt that we could accomplish little as five women working alone. We were appointed as a committee of the N. A.* on the understanding that we would not receive any financial help from them. When we turned to the states for help, we were told frequently that they had already given to the national work by contributing directly to the National Association and therefore could not give to us also. We also found that the state associations were usually engrossed in their state campaigns so that we could not expect much from them in the way of personal service. When we turned to individuals for help we usually found that they were giving their time and service to the association of the state in which they lived. We found, therefore, there was almost no one outside of our group of five upon whom we could call for help in working for the federal amendment. We therefore formed the Congressional Union as an organization of women in various parts of the country who were interested in helping in the federal work.

Another reason for forming the Congressional Union was that it would be permanent and could continue to carry on the federal work as long as the necessity for so doing remained, while the life of a committee, of course, could be terminated at any time by the Association which it represented or its activities could be directed into other channels.

The Congressional Union was formed after Mrs. Lewis and I had discussed the matter at length in the New York headquarters of the National American Woman Suffrage Association with Dr. Shaw and Mrs. Dennett.† They both approved heartily of the plan and Mrs. Dennett was even responsible for the choice of the name. We had decided on the name, "Women's Political League." On March 31st, 1913, we received a

---

* National Association.

† Mrs. Mary Ware Dennett, Cor. Sec. of the National American Woman Suffrage Asso.

telegram from Mrs. Dennett saying, "How would Congressional Workers Union of the N.A.W.S.A. do?" This gave us the idea of the phrase, "Congressional Union," and we called ourselves "Congressional Union of the N.A.W.S.A." for some time. Dr. Shaw then informed us that she did not wish us to use the words "N.A.W.S.A.," so we changed our name in accordance with her desire and called ourselves "The Congressional Union for Woman Suffrage."

Later in the year when the Congressional Union applied for admission to the National Association as an auxiliary in accordance with the suggestion made to me by Mrs. Dennett, both Dr. Shaw and Mrs. Dennett aided in securing our admission as an auxiliary. We were finally admitted in November, 1913, (at least we were informed of our admittance at that time, and I presume the decision was made not long before we were notified of it).

The Congressional Committee appointed by the National last year consisted of Mrs. Mary Beard, Mrs. Crystal Eastman Benedict, Mrs. Lawrence Lewis, Miss Lucy Burns and myself. We are all still members of the Executive Committee of the Congressional Union and are entirely agreed upon every point which has been in dispute between the National and ourselves. Mrs. Lewis and Mrs. Benedict were not re-appointed upon the Congressional Committee. Mrs. Beard, Miss Burns and I were re-appointed but declined to serve under the conditions and circumstances involved.

I trust that this covers the points about which Mrs. Lewis wished me to write to you.

With appreciation of your constant co-operation, I am

Very sincerely yours,
Alice Paul,
Chairman Congressional Union for
Woman Suffrage.

Returning now to the unfortunate publicity in the *Press,* Miss M. Carey Thomas wrote to me, May 28, 1914, complaining of the misrepresentation by that newspaper of her personal connection with the State campaign.

Miss Thomas, Founder and President of the National College Equal Suffrage League, was said by the *Press* to be "Founder and President of the Woman Suffrage Society of the County of Philadelphia." This was a forgivable error. But when the *Press* said that "the Equal Franchise Society was in sympathy with the Congressional Union" and had decided to "align itself with the Congressional Union," it placed Miss Thomas in a very embarrassing position. She was a member of the Official Board of the National American Woman Suffrage Association whose opposition to the aggressive campaign of the Congressional Union for a federal suffrage amendment was very pronounced; and she was also a Vice-President of the Equal Franchise Society which was erroneously said by the *Press* to be aligned with and sympathetic to the Congressional Union.

I wrote Miss Thomas I was in no way responsible for the *Press* reporter's mistakes. Also I explained I had arranged to have Mrs. Wilfred Lewis, President of the Equal Franchise Society, give an interview to the *Press* and had been assured by the City Editor that space would be allotted to it. Mrs. Lewis was, of course, as eager as Miss Thomas for the public to understand that the Society was opening its own headquarters in order to intensify its work for the passage of a Woman Suffrage Amendment to the State Constitution, and was neither opposing nor endorsing the Congressional Union's campaign for a federal woman suffrage amendment.

Prompted by the recent inaccurate publicity we had had, the President of the Equal Franchise Society wrote to me

May 29, 1914, suggesting things she thought I should emphasize in answering queries about our organization when the Headquarters at 35 S. 9th Street were opened. Here is her letter:

> Dear Miss Katzenstein,
>
> . . . There are several points that I hope you will insist upon when people question you about this society.
> *First:* It has no connection with the Congressional Union and takes no stand for or against it except that it stands for fair play for everybody.
> *Second:* The C.U. will not have a desk in the new office of the E.F.S. but expects to maintain separate headquarters as at present.
> *Third:* The E.F.S. chose its colors as shown on its banner at least two years ago and selected purple and gold for purely decorative reasons.[1] It refuses to consider purple a militant color unless as an ecclesiastical color it stands for the Church Militant.
> I want to have a little talk with you and hope you can come out some afternoon. Would Friday be a convenient day for you? . . .
> Are you going away for your rest? If so, we can have our talk earlier. Tomorrow afternoon (Saturday) would suit me very well. . . .
>
> Sincerely yours,
Emily Sargent Lewis

The following corespondence between Dr. Anna Howard Shaw and me is further evidence that Suffragists were trying to understand one another and to work effectively together as difficult as this sometimes became. March 27, 1914, Dr. Shaw wrote me:

---

[1] The official colors of the Congressional Union were purple, white, and gold.

There is one other point I would like to speak to you about. Miss Anthony told me that you said to her, I think it was, that I said we would never win another Western State. She was amazed that I should have made such a statement, and I think she might well have been, for I certainly could not have made such a statement. If I made such a statement it was under certain conditions that we could not do it. There are qualifications for it. I have said that if the Congressional Union goes into the enfranchised States and seeks to defeat the Senators in Colorado, Oregon, Arizona, or any other of the enfranchised States, dividing up the Democratic women and antagonizing the Democratic men, we will not be able to win a single one of the Western States in which the amendment is now pending. Of course I do not pretend to be infallible in such cases, but it looks to me, and I should think it would to every one who has common sense, that the result of such interference with the States where women vote, would naturally make Democrats everywhere vote against our measure.

I have probably also said that we would never win another State as easily as we have won those in the past, and we certainly never will, and that now is the only time there is any hope for it in the immediate future, because now we are in a political upheaval and, if you study the history of the incoming of all the States where we have suffrage, you will find that every one came in at a time when there was a political upheaval, either in the State or in the nation.

Of course I believe we will win every Western State, in fact I believe we will win every State in the nation, but we are not going to do it unless some of the women who are in the work now, show more intelligence and political sagacity than they are showing at the present time in the Congressional Union. I think the attitude of the Union

this past winter has put us back at least ten years
and, if it keeps up, will keep us back as many years
as it keeps on the same sort of political unwisdom
which has been manifested during the past six
months.

In my reply to Dr. Shaw March 30, 1914, I wrote:

I am sorry that Miss Anthony repeated our
conversation of Saturday a week ago to you, as I
felt all the time we were talking that neither my
words nor the motives that prompted them were
fully understood by Miss Anthony. We discussed
the old and new amendments to the National Constitution—the two introduced by Bristow, and
Shafroth.* I said frankly that the old one seemed
more feasible to me as the new one would make
a referendum to the people necessary and the old
one need only be submitted to the legislative
bodies. Miss Anthony replied that there was really
no hope of having the Shafroth measure actually
carried but that agitation for it was good propaganda. The hopelessness of this set me to thinking and I turned over the leaves of my memory
to recall something that you said, or rather, something that I understood you to say one day when
we met on Chestnut Street. I hope you recall
the conversation. I think it was shortly after the
Wisconsin defeat. I understood you to say that the
liquor interests saw in Woman Suffrage such an
arch enemy that they determined to defeat us at
any cost. Their almost limitless funds concentrated on any campaign State or States would make
it impossible to win more States one by one . . .
If the liquor interests would prevent the passage
of more State amendments, and the National
Amendment were only for propaganda, things

* Senator Bristow introduced the Susan B. Anthony Amendment at
the request of the C.U. Senator Shafroth introduced the new amendment
sponsored by the N.A.W.S.A.

were certainly in a pretty hopeless condition!

Something else has troubled me. Miss Anthony complained that the Philadelphia papers have more news about the Congressional Union than about the National. I showed her a copy of my press notices for the day and also of what I had sent the day previous and told her that I discharged my duties as conscientiously and impartially as I knew how. I explained that the Union some weeks sends almost daily bulletins while the National sends once a week . . .

I have tried every scheme in my power to give a local touch to the National Press Bulletin or in some other way to make it usable by the Philadelphia papers. If you remember, I 'phoned to you at Moylan to ask if I might take advantage of your nearness to Philadelphia to make of the National Bulletin an interview. It happened to have that week either a survey of the past year or a prophecy of the new—something especially adaptable for an interview. When members of the Official Board went South, I wrote to Mrs. Dennett to try to arrange interviews when the party passed through Philadelphia. I sometimes take the foreign news and send it, under separate cover, to the Foreign Editor, etc., etc. On the other hand I must confess that I am not responsible for all the suffrage news in our papers. The enclosed clipping from this morning's *North American* came direct from Washington as is not infrequently the case. Either news from the Capital is of especial interest or some one there is a good publicity agent.

I believe you can hardly know how pained I am and have been all along over the difference of opinion between the National and the Union. As I wrote to Mrs. Dennett weeks ago, there are persons on both sides that I love and wish to assist. As my work is primarily local in character, this position seems a tenable one. The enclosed editorial from the *Woman's Journal* of March 28th strengthens me in this belief. Surely we are all striving for the same thing and we may, I hope, before long be able to pull together. This is my earnest prayer.

WILMER ATKINSON   JUDGE DIMNER BEEBER

Mr. Atkinson, founder of the *Farm Journal,* succeeded Judge Beeber as President of the Pennsylvania Men's League for Woman Suffrage.

15

PENNSYLVANIA MEN'S LEAGUE FOR WOMAN SUFFRAGE
1913-1916

All through the suffrage campaign in Pennsylvania, progressive men, working as individuals, had supported the movement. In 1913, believing the time had come to organize their efforts, they formed the Pennsylvania Men's League for Woman Suffrage, with Judge Dimner Beeber as its first President.

In 1915, Mr. Wilmer Atkinson was elected President of the League. He was then nearly seventy-five years of age and, as Editor of the *Farm Journal,* a position he had held since the publication was founded by him in 1877, was a busy man. However, as he had all his life been an ardent friend of woman suffrage, he felt he could not well refuse to serve at a time when help from the Men's League was sorely needed.

Mr. Atkinson lost no time in calling a special meeting of his organization in order to commit the members to joining in the Suffrage Parade already planned by the women for May first, 1915, just a few weeks off. So successful was this special meeting that the League was well represented in the parade which started in front of the *Farm Journal* office, Washington Square, and ended at the Metropolitan Opera House, Broad and Poplar Streets. There an immense meeting was held, with Dr. Anna Howard Shaw and Mrs. Antoinette Funk as speakers.

With only seven months in which to prepare for the referendum on the Woman Suffrage Amendment to the State Constitution, November 2nd, 1915, Mr. Atkinson set apart rooms at the *Farm Journal* building for the Men's League, employed a competent salaried working force, and set a number of printing presses in motion. He selected an energetic executive secretary with four assistants, including a stenographer.

Those directors of the Men's League unable to give time to the business of the organization were shifted to the list of vice-presidents, and some new directors were appointed. Also, a carefully selected campaign committee of energetic, earnest men, who could be depended upon to take an active part in the campaign until it closed, was chosen. This committee consisted of John W. Shrigley, George C. Small, Henry Johns Gibbons, John J. Ridgway, Ryerson W. Jennings, and Frederick H. Graser.

Perhaps the best tribute that can be paid to the leaders of the Men's League for their part in the 1915 campaign for the enfranchisement of women in Pennsylvania will be to quote from Mr. Atkinson's report read at the organization's Fourth Annual Meeting in March, 1916. Here are some excerpts from that report:

> Previous to March 31, 1915, the Pennsylvania Men's League for Woman Suffrage was not a going organization, and was not intended to be; now it must get to work.
>
> An appeal was sent to all men who had signed slips pledging their support to the cause by their influence and votes. At first there were about 5000 of these, but this number rapidly increased until just before election we had 48,175 all of whom were circularized.
>
> The actual membership of the League grew from 500 in May to 8683 on November 2nd,

omitting the Pittsburgh list, which, under the presidency of Julian Kennedy, numbered over 15,000.

Circular letters and literature were sent into every county, not only to men who had made pledges, but in thousands of cases to lists of voters which had been sent in by county leaders. Return postcards were used in many send-outs.

Letters and literature were sent to all granges in Pennsylvania with follow-ups; to all clergymen whose names appeared in the telephone book in and near Philadelphia; to all ministers of the Reformed Church in the state; to all members of the Republican and Democratic Committees, to city officials, and to all the trade unions in the city.

Urgent appeals were twice sent to men of prominence whose names appeared in the Blue Book, also in the county directories near Philadelphia. There were 16,000 of these persons appealed to, apparently with good effect.

In September, C. E. Wells, a young colored man, was employed to canvass and distribute suitable literature among the colored voters. He was kept busy all through the remainder of the campaign.

Thousands of free buttons were distributed, and for the parade, which was held in October, 2000 badges were given out, and 500 lanterns were bought so that every man who promised to march in the parade might have one to carry.

There was a great demand for the literature printed by the League, and large quantities of it were distributed by district leaders, campaign speakers, and by various headquarters. Much literature was sent by mail to women leaders all over the state. About 400,000 copies altogether were printed and distributed.

A letter, with state suffrage maps, was sent to all Senators and Repersentatives of Pennsylvania, urging them to vote for the National Woman

Suffrage Amendment when it should come up in Congress.

An elaborate analysis of the November vote was made, and a black and white map of the state was printed by the League . . . Many thousands of these maps were supplied free. The vote in the entire state was 385,348 for, and 441,034 against, making an adverse majority of 55,686, of which Philadelphia contributed 45,272.

The League printed a facsimile of the decoy ballot which was intended to defeat and which did defeat the suffrage amendment. The ignorant and 'kept' among the electorate united with the saloon interests and brought defeat at the polls.

It is unfortunate, indeed pitiful, that the women of Pennsylvania should have to spend one-third or one-half of their time and strength in collecting money to carry on their campaign for equal political privileges, while many men stand aloof, withholding requisite funds that they are amply able to provide, and which they should provide without solicitation.

The devotion of our women to their cause has never been surpassed in the whole history of the struggle for human rights since the nation was founded.

Although the Woman Suffrage Amendment was defeated in Pennsylvania in November, 1915, the Men's League continued to function throughout 1916. After that, again to quote its president, Mr. Atkinson said:

Since the legislature of Pennsylvania had refused the women of the state another chance to win suffrage through an amendment to the Constitution and since efforts were being concentrated upon Congress to secure the passage of the Susan B. Anthony Amendment, efforts of the Pennsylvania Men's League subsided, though my deter-

mination to stand by the women's just rights was
not in the least abated, and I am ready to answer
any call for future service.

16

PENNSYLVANIA DEFEATS STATE SUFFRAGE AMENDMENT
1914-1916

Although Suffragists differed in their ideas as to the best method of campaigning and sometimes even allowed bitterness to creep into their espousal of the plan that appealed to them most, there was deep sincerity in their convictions and an eagerness that the method they thought right should prevail.

This spirit of wanting to know the right thing to do was manifested in a letter from Mr. Henry Johns Gibbons one of the best friends the suffrage movement had. As he and I did not see the suffrage situation in quite the same light, the receipt of his letter, sent to my home during the short time of my retirement from the campaign, was appreciated. Here is his letter:

June 5, 1914

Dear Miss Katzenstein:—

I am sorry to learn that you found it necessary to resign your position as Executive Secretary at the Suffrage Headquarters. All the various organizations have profited a great deal by your intelligent and faithful performance of duties, that I know must have been at times quite irksome.

In yesterday's mail I received a letter from Miss Dulles stating that the Equal Franchise Society is going to increase its activities, open a separate office, "and engage the services of a competent executive secretary." Has there been any break among the organizations at 1721 Chestnut Street? This letter of Miss Dulles asks for contributions towards the expenses of new headquarters, and I do not desire to encourage any duplication along this line. I think that all headquarters should be at the same place, unless good reason is shown for the contrary. With your inside knowledge of conditions, you will, I know, advise me as to how I should stand in this matter.

I hope that you may have a good rest this summer and return to the work strengthened for the fall campaign.

Cordially yours,
Henry J. Gibbons

P. S.

I am against the Congressional Union's activities as futile and misdirected.

Soon the Equal Franchise Society was settled in its new Headquarters and busily at work campaigning for the passage of a Woman Suffrage Amendment to the Pennsylvania Constitution. The recent unpleasant publicity was now a thing of the past.

The selection of the Headquarters was a happy one. We had a large office on the street floor with a show window that made advertising the Cause an easy matter. Katherine Milhous, a young artist, who was later to become a prominent author and illustrator of children's books, helped to add beauty to our display by making attractive posters for the window. 35 S. 9th Street was in the heart of the business section of the city. We were just opposite the Central Post Office located in the Federal Building which had a moat on its Market, Chestnut, and 9th Street sides. This moat seemed to make the wide 9th Street pavement in front of the building look even wider than it was and afforded us an ideal spot for open-air meetings. It was practically our front yard which we used freely!

Also, we were almost within a stone's throw of the newspapers. The *Record* was on Chestnut Street just west of 9th; the *Press* at 7th and Chestnut; the *Public Ledger* at 6th and Chestnut; the *Evening Telegraph* near 7th and Chestnut; the *Inquirer* at 11th and Market; the *North American* in its own building at Broad and Sansom; and the *Evening Bulletin* at its present location, Filbert and Juniper.

And I should emphasize our nearness to Philadelphia's large department stores. One of the workers at Gimbel Brothers', Bertha Sapovits, became an enthusiastic Suffragist and volunteered to speak at our open-air meetings in the middle of the day. She had a remarkable voice that could rise above the noise on busy 9th Street and she loved to be heckled by the crowd. Her good humor and quick wit won us many friends. She was so generous in helping us and so free to come at different times of the day that her lunch hour seemed to be a movable feast. Or perhaps Mr. Gimbel was really interested in our campaign and was not too strict about his employee's time.

Unlike our other suffrage organizations, the Equal Franchise Society's official family was composed of men as well as women. The prominence of many of the officers, some of whose names were known not only locally but nationally, gave our letterhead real propaganda value. It was the Legislative Committee of this Society that drew up the Woman Suffrage Amendment submitted by the State Legislature to the voters November 2, 1915.

To glance a moment at the not-too-distant past, in 1885 the Pennsylvania Woman Suffrage Association proposed a similar Constitutional Amendment to the Legislature, which was passed by the House of Representatives, but was lost in the Senate by a vote of 13 to 19. That was the first concerted action of Pennsylvania Suffragists to influence legislation for women. And thirty years were to pass before the first referendum on Woman Suffrage was submitted to Pennsylvania voters.

In 1912, the Society published a 30-page pamphlet by Wendell Phillips, *Shall Women Have the Right to Vote.* This was either a part, or perhaps all, of a speech made by Mr. Phillips at Worcester, Mass., in 1851. As a very special gift to the Cause, Mr. Isaac H. Clothier, one of the founders of the Strawbridge and Clothier store, and a member of the Board of Directors of the Equal Franchise Society, kept us constantly supplied with this most convincing treatise in favor of the enfranchisement of women. It was sold locally, and to the National American Woman Suffrage Association for distribution through its own Literature Department.

The new Headquarters became a beehive of activity. There were open-air meetings, indoor meetings, dinners, luncheons, teas, parades, interviews with key politicians, etc. We finally decided to try to inject a little of the dramatic into the good old tried methods of campaigning, relying as always on the press as our main support in reaching the public. For instance, the example set us by political parties of placarding the highways and byways with posters during political campaigns had been adopted by us to the extent of placing VOTES FOR WOMEN posters not only in store windows but in the windows of private homes as well. As good as this was, it was not exciting and something was needed to add color to the poster campaign.

Only a few squares from 35 S. 9th Street was a sturdy old brick wall that had lots of color and was truly inviting as an ally to our scheme. Old Philadelphians will recall the spacious home at 1203 Walnut Street which was built by Nathaniel Burt, great-grandfather of Struthers Burt, and which was mentioned so interestingly in that author's book, *Along These Streets*. This high wall enclosed the Burt yard and extended for a considerable distance on both Walnut and 12th Streets. It really was an ideal place for advertising!

A "Poster Brigade" was formed of some of the older and socially prominent members of the Equal Franchise Society whose names had publicity value. I am sure Miss Mary A. Burnham was a member of the brigade and, if my memory serves me right, Mrs. Horatio Gates Lloyd and Mrs. Frank Miles Day made up the rest of the "team." With a large bucket of paste and plenty of brushes, we gathered at the "Burt" Wall to begin work. The newspapers had of course been invited to send reporters and photographers, and while I did not say that the dignified ladies were going to cover a large part of the city instead of the one spot, it was not my fault if the reporters jumped to that conclusion and thought they were seeing just the beginning of a hard day's work for women unaccustomed to such strenuous labor. The women had the spirit to do an unusual job and would, I have little doubt, have prolonged their activities if it had been necessary.

I happened to hear one of the bystanders call the attention of another onlooker to the way "those women" were "defacing private property." With a very polite, "Pardon me, Sir," I explained that the owners of the property were members of the Equal Franchise Society and were assisting us in this advertising of our campaign. At that time, 1203 Walnut Street was the home of two aunts of Struthers Burt, the Misses Edith and Theodora Burt, who had cheerfully given us permission to use their wall.

Another instance of injecting color into the campaign was the formation of an Uncle Sam section to one of the parades. We wore white skirts with vertical stripes of red sewed on, and our blouses were made of dark blue material on which were sewed or pasted many white stars systematically spaced. Despite the labor of this attempt to portray the flag, marchers cheerfully provided their costumes; and the section attracted much attention and drew admiration from the crowds watching the demonstration.

As the fateful 1915 Pennsylvania referendum on Woman Suffrage came nearer and nearer, we had many instances of the splendid support men were giving us. Conspicuous among these men was Judge Dimner Beeber. In the Philadelphia *Public Ledger* of September 12, 1915, there appeared the following:

Former Judge Dimner Beeber, honorary president of the Pennsylvania Men's League for Woman Suffrage, said yesterday:

"I do not agree with Mr. Taft when he suggests delaying the suffrage until women as a class shall be better prepared for the exercise of the franchise. It is not a privilege we are extending to women, but a right. If such an argument can be used against women, it would re-act against men. If ignorance in the electorate is the thing to be feared, it will mean that we should limit man suffrage.

"I think the outlook for the enfranchisement of the women of Pennsylvania on November 2 is particularly flattering. I am confident that we shall win. The antis' position is untenable. They say certain women may not have it because they do not want it. They need not use the ballot if they do not want to. There are men, too, who are 'too nice' to mix in and vote on questions that affect our Government, but we do not disfranchise them (though we ought to); so the women who are afraid of being spoiled by voting would not be alone in their position.

"In no logical way can the right to vote be a

matter of sex. If a woman owns property and pays taxes she should vote how that money should be spent. For every reason that can be given why a man should vote there is a corresponding one why women should.

"When it comes to the irresponsibility phase our boys of 21 are surely as irresponsible as our young women. And as for the majority of women having to want it, the answer is that the majority of men never wanted the franchise. It has always been extended by an active minority."

Judge Beeber was the first president of the Men's League in this State when it was organized three years ago. The organization was formed as an auxiliary body to show the women fighting so valiantly for the ballot that there were men with them in the fight. There were 500 members. Since Pennsylvania became a campaign State many thousands of men have signed the yellow membership blank which promises a "Square Deal for Women."

But the best efforts of Suffragists from all the various organizations in the State did not secure for us a majority vote on the Woman Suffrage Amendment. However, when some persons said we had lost, it was, I think, Dr. Shaw who replied that we had not lost because we had had nothing to lose! It was, of course, true that we were just what we had been before the referendum—an unenfranchised class. But the discouraging thing about the Pennsylvania situation was this. To amend the Constitution of the State, the law requires (Article 18, section 1) that a proposed Constitutional amendment be approved by two successively elected General Assemblies, which in our case had been the Legislatures of 1913 and 1915. However, the Constitution also states no amendment shall be submitted oftener than once every five years.

I wish I could remember the name of a prominent Socialist that came to 35 S. 9th Street that sad November 3rd, 1915, when we learned what the referendum had *not* brought us. He suggested that we at once arrange a big Mass Meeting at which we would announce that our campaign was still on and that we would fight until victory crowned our efforts. This dynamic suggestion was too good not to be acted on immediately. It was easy to telephone to Dr. Shaw at Media and to Miss M. Carey Thomas at Bryn Mawr College to secure two speakers that would be sure to draw a crowd. The officers of the Equal Franchise Society, whom I was able to reach quickly, were all in favor of going ahead with the plan, and, fortunately, the Academy of Music was available for that night.

In a few hours, the Mass Meeting was arranged and on the evening of November 3rd, from the stage of the Academy of Music we announced in no uncertain words that there would be no interregnum; the campaign would go right on. Thanks to the suggestion of our Socialist friend, we had shown such a spirit of confidence in the impossibility of defeat that our courage caught the imagination of both the press and the public. The *Public Ledger*, in its issue of November 4th, said:

> Accepting their defeat, but hailing it as a magnificent victory, 2500 suffragists held the most enthusiastic suffrage rally in Philadelphia's history last night at the Academy of Music. Dr. Anna Howard Shaw, the suffrage leader of the country, made a great speech. The meeting inaugurated a new campaign for suffrage victory.

And letters from two members of the Board of Directors of the Equal Franchise Society to Miss Mary H. Ingham, one of the Society's Vice-Presidents, give additional evidence that the Mass Meeting had not suffered because of the haste in which it had been planned, and that the campaign as a whole had been waged in a way to command both respect and admiration. Here are the letters:

> Ballytore,
> Wynnewood P. O., Pa.

My dear Miss Ingham,

How were the expenses of Wednesday evening's meeting met? Were funds provided in advance, or was there an unexpended surplus?

It was a great meeting. I felt so enthused that I almost felt like asking permission to say a few words myself at the close. But it was better not to mar a good thing.

> Always sincerely yours,
> Isaac H. Clothier

LAW OFFICES
704-707 Land Title Building
Philadelphia
November 4, 1915

Miss Mary H. Ingham,
35 S. 9th St.,
Phila., Pa.

My dear Miss Ingham:

Thank you for the tickets for the Mass Meeting. It was not possible, owing to professional engagements, to use them. I would have liked to have been there to cheer your great victory.

I think that the vote, on the first opportunity given men to vote on behalf of Woman Suffrage, was phenomenal and overwhelming. Personally recognizing the conservatism of men, naturally, upon this question, and the enormous feminine counter-influence against you, I am astounded at the favorable result. Never was any political campaign in this country conducted with better judgment, more steadiness of clear purpose, and with more energy, than this. You have created an organization that, from sheer force of momentum, apart from the great principles involved, must go on growing in strength.

Victory is inevitable. It is as certain as the courses of the stars.

"They cannot fail,
Whose courage never dies,
Such natures are immortal,
And, living on,
Contribute, by diffusion of their qualities,
To the greatness of all mankind."

Your courage will not fail. The Cause, of necessity, must remain, and your knowledge of the real, thorough patriotic relationship of women to future politics and future governments, be increased by delay in reaching the fruition of your purpose.

With my compliments, most heartily to you and your colleagues, for your great achievement, I beg to remain,

Yours very sincerely,

J. Levering Jones

Although Pennsylvania's voters had refused to enfranchise the women of the State, Pennsylvania's legislators had responded favorably to the appeal for a referendum to those voters. Here is a short summary of that legislative action:

In 1913, Bill No. 185 was introduced in the House by Mr. Frank H. Rockwell, Republican from Tioga County, and was passed, February 5th, by a vote of 131-70. In 1915, Bill No. 108 was introduced in the House by Mr. William H. Wilson, Republican, 5th District of Philadelphia County, and was passed, February 9th, by a vote of 130-71.

In 1913, Bill No. 231 was passed by the Senate, April 22nd, by a vote of 26-22. In 1915 Bill No. 186 passed the

Senate March 15th, by a vote of 37-11. (P. 663 of Senate Journal states a Mr. Wills, absent when vote was taken, wishes to be put on the record as being in favor of bill.)

As stated previously, the Amendment was defeated at the polls in the November elections of 1915 by a vote of 441,034 to 385,348.

Serious difficulties faced Pennsylvania Suffragists if they wished again to seek their enfranchisement through an amendment to the State Constitution. Under normal procedure, the bill proposing it again would first be introduced at the 1919 legislative session and again at the 1921 session and be voted on at the 1921 election.

It is, of course, true that had the amendment been proposed in 1917 and again in 1919 it might have been voted on in 1920 if a full five years had elapsed between the November election in 1915 and the November election in 1920.

Despite these difficulties, the Equal Franchise Society maintained its headquarters at 35 S. 9th Street for another year and tried in many ways to keep the question of VOTES FOR WOMEN in the public mind.

But although the State situation was discouraging from the standpoint of time—a sort of watchful-waiting period—conditions in the national field were entirely different. At the nation's Capital, a campaign for the passage of a Federal Woman Suffrage Amendment was being waged with vigor by the Congressional Union for Woman Suffrage and held out great hope for the enfranchisement of all the women of the United States.

I became a member of the Congressional Union when it began its work in 1913 because I firmly believed it was right in thinking the time had come to concentrate on the national enfranchisement of women. But as Pennsylvania was at that time waging an active campaign for its first referendum on woman suffrage, I could give comparatively little time to work in Washington, although I coöperated in every way possible when there was something Pennsylvania could do.

Toward the end of 1916, however, I began to feel it was almost a waste of valuable time to continue what was, to a great extent, an educational campaign in Pennsylvania, while the Congressional Union had opened the way for all of us to do constructive political work in the national campaign. Also, the Congressional Union needed our personal and financial help. I discussed this situation with the President of the Equal Franchise Society, Mrs. Henry Pemberton, and told her I should like to devote my whole time to the campaign that was being waged from the Washington Headquarters. Mrs. Pemberton agreed I was "quite right."

In a few weeks the headquarters at 35 S. 9th Street were closed, and many members of the Equal Franchise Society then transferred their allegiance whole-heartedly to the Congressional Union, the only organization that never wavered in its campaign for the passage of the federal amendment that Susan B. Anthony herself had helped to have introduced in Congress in 1878.

PART II

ALICE PAUL

Chairman of the National Woman's Party

1

WE NOW TURN TO THE NATIONAL CONSTITUTION

We have now reached that part of our story when the all-absorbing theme will be the campaign for the NATIONAL enfranchisement of women. No longer shall we consider amending State Constitutions, but shall focus our whole attention on so amending the United States Constitution as to obviate in the future any interpretation of it that might question woman's right to vote on equal terms with man.

And here again, as in Part One, we should acknowledge with gratitude the magnificent work of the pioneers. This time, however, we shall stress principally their claim that women, under the United States Constitution, were already entitled to the franchise and needed only to exercise that right in order to establish the fact that it belonged to them.

Before taking up the campaign of the National Woman's Party (previously called the Congressional Union) to secure federal woman suffrage, let us see how the pioneers tried to make that work unnecessary.

Susan B. Anthony led in the agitation to arouse women to claim their right to vote under the Fourteenth Amendment, passed by Congress June 16, 1866, and declared in force July 28, 1868. The Fourteenth Amendment read:

1. All persons born or naturalized in the United States, and subject to the jurisdiction

thereof, are citizens of the United States and of the State wherein they reside. No State shall make or enforce any law which shall abridge the privileges or immunities of citizens of the United States, nor shall any State deprive any person of life, liberty, or property without due process of law, nor deny to any person within its jurisdiction the equal protection of the laws . . . .

Acting upon a strong plea in the *Rochester Democrat and Chronicle* of Friday, November 1, 1872, that persons should register for the approaching election, Miss Anthony summoned her three faithful sisters, went to the registry office, and asked to be registered. Meeting some official hesitation in acceding to this request, Miss Anthony read to the election officials the Fourteenth Amendment and the article in the State Constitution in regard to taking the election oath, which contained no sex-qualification. At length their names were duly entered by the inspectors. Several other women in her ward followed Miss Anthony's example.

Immediately after registering, Miss Anthony went to a number of leading lawyers in Rochester for advice as to her right to vote the following Tuesday, but none would consider her case. Finally she found an attentive listener, who agreed to accept for examination the mass of documents she had brought. Also he promised to give her an answer the following Monday. The man making this promise was Henry R. Selden, a leading member of the bar and formerly judge of the Court of Appeals. After he and his brother Samuel had spent an entire day examining Miss Anthony's documents, they were convinced her claim to a right to vote under the Fourteenth Amendment was valid, and Mr. Selden said, "I will protect you in that right to the best of my ability."

Despite Miss Anthony's caution in trying to avoid trouble in her test of the Fourteenth Amendment, she and fourteen other women were indicted under the 19th Section of the Act of Congress of May 31, 1870, for "voting without having a lawful right to vote." Her trial opened June 17, 1873, in the lovely village of Canandaigua. Associate-Justice Ward Hunt was on the bench and U. S. District-Attorney Richard Crowley was the prosecutor. Mr. Henry R. Selden and Mr. John Van Voorhis were the lawyers for the defense. The courtroom was crowded, ex-President Fillmore being among the many prominent persons present.

Why was Canandaigua, in Ontario county, selected as the place to hold this famous trial although Miss Anthony lived in Rochester, Monroe county?

When Miss Anthony heard that her trial was set for the term of court beginning May 13, 1873, she decided to make a canvass of Monroe county, not to argue her own case, but to inform the people on the constitutional points involved in the trial. Beginning March 11, she spoke in twenty-nine post-office districts.

Informed that District-Attorney Crowley threatened to move her trial into another county because the jury would be prejudiced as a result of her addresses, she notified him she would see to it that the county he selected would also be well canvassed, and asked him whether she was prejudicing a jury by reading and explaining the Constitution of the United States. When the time for the trial came, District-Attorney Crowley, as promised, did obtain an order to remove the case to the United States Circuit Court at Canandaigua.

With only twenty-two days in which to canvass Ontario county, Miss Anthony asked Matilda Joslyn Gage to assist her. Miss Anthony spoke in twenty-one places on the question, "Is it a crime for a United States citizen to vote?" Mrs. Gage spoke in sixteen places on "The United States on trial, not Susan B. Anthony."

The trial began as scheduled. After a two-hour speech by the District-Attorney, Judge Hunt, without leaving the bench, delivered a *written opinion*. And at its conclusion *he directed the jury to bring in a verdict of guilty*.

When Miss Anthony's counsel insisted that the Court had no power to make such a direction in a criminal case and demanded that the jury be permitted to bring in its own verdict, the Judge made no reply except to order the clerk to take the verdict. Mr. Selden then demanded that the jury be polled. Judge Hunt not only refused, but at once discharged the jury without allowing them any consultation or asking whether they agreed upon a verdict. Not one of them had spoken a word. After being discharged, the jurymen talked freely and several declared they should have brought in a verdict of "not guilty."

The next day Mr. Selden argued the motion for a new trial on seven exceptions, but Judge Hunt denied this. When Miss Anthony attempted to reply to Judge Hunt's question, "Has the prisoner anything to say why sentence shall not be pronounced?" she began:

> Yes, your honor, I have many things to say; for in your ordered verdict of guilty you have trampled under foot every vital principle of our government. My natural rights, my civil rights, my political rights, my judicial rights, are all alike ignored. Robbed of the fundamental privilege of citizenship, I am degraded from the status of a citizen to that of a subject; and not only myself individually but all of my sex are, by your honor's verdict, doomed to political subjection under this so-called republican form of government.

But here and all through her several attempts to answer

Judge Hunt's question, Miss Anthony was constantly interrupted, and twice she was peremptorily ordered to sit down.

However, Miss Anthony had her day in Court after Judge Hunt made this pronouncement:

> The sentence of the Court is that you pay a fine of $100 and the costs of the prosecution.

This time, without interruption, Miss Anthony said:

> May it please your honor, I will never pay a dollar of your unjust penalty. All the stock in trade I possess is a debt of $10,000, incurred by publishing my paper—*The Revolutionist*—the sole object of which was to educate all women to do precisely as I have done, rebel against your man-made, unjust, unconstitutional forms of law, which tax, fine, imprison and hang women, while denying them the right of representation in the government; and I will work on with might and main to pay every dollar of that honest debt, but not a penny shall go to this unjust claim. And I shall earnestly and persistently continue to urge all women to the practical recognition of the old Revolutionary maxim, "Resistance to tyranny is obedience to God."

Judge Hunt—Madam, the Court will not order you to stand committed until the fine is paid.

Miss Anthony never paid this fine, nor did she go to prison for her refusal to pay it. Thus came to an end the great trial, "The United States of America *vs*. Susan B. Anthony." Henceforth woman suffrage was not a question of grievances, but one of Constitutional Law.

In her journal, Miss Anthony wrote:—"The greatest judicial outrage history ever recorded! No law, logic or demand of justice could change Judge Hunt's will. We were convicted before we had a hearing and the trial was a mere farce." Later, Mr. Selden, Miss Anthony's counsel, wrote her:—"I regard the ruling of the judge, and also his refusal to submit the case to the jury, as utterly indefensible." Mr. Selden had endeavored to have Judge Hall, of Buffalo, an interested spectator at the trial, try the case with Judge Hunt in order that, if necessary, it might go to the Supreme Court, but he refused to do this. With only one judge presiding, an appeal to the Supreme Court was not possible.

Scarcely a newspaper in the country sustained Judge Hunt's action, and reverberations of the trial continued. The arbitrary action of Judge Hunt in ordering a verdict of guilty, and his refusing the defendant's right to poll the jury were only some of these echoes that would not die. Finally Miss Anthony and her counsel decided to make an appeal to Congress for the remission of her fine, the granting of which would, in effect, be a declaration of the illegality of Judge Hunt's act, and would establish a precedent. (Sufficient authority for making this appeal had been found by both Mr. Selden and Mr. Van Voorhis.)

Early in 1874, this appeal was presented in the Senate by Aaron A. Sargent of California, and in the House by William Loughridge, of Iowa, and was referred to the Judiciary Committee of the two Houses, both of which made adverse reports.

Women, however, still maintained that the Fourteenth Amendment to the Constitution gave them the right to vote, and they did not relinquish this claim until all ground for it was destroyed by a decision of the United States Supreme Court in the case of Minor v. Happersett.

Mr. Francis Minor, a St. Louis lawyer, asserted that women were enfranchised by both the letter and the spirit of the Fourteenth Amendment, and had advised his wife to register in the Presidential election of 1872. Because of the refusal of the inspector to register Mrs. Minor (Virginia L.), she brought suit against him for the purpose of making a test case. Following an adverse decision by the lower Court, the case was carried to the Supreme Court of the United States. Despite the keen logic and impressive plea for justice made by Mr. Minor in his argument before this high tribunal in the October term of 1874, the Court denied the right of women to vote under the Fourteenth Amendment.

The decision of the Supreme Court in the Virginia L. Minor case made further efforts to obtain woman suffrage under the National Constitution useless until it should be amended for this special purpose.

Advocates of woman suffrage were therefore compelled to return to their former policy of demanding a Sixteenth Amendment which should prohibit disfranchisement on account of *sex* as the Fifteenth had done on account of *color*.

The first attempt to secure a woman suffrage amendment to the Federal Constitution had been made by Congressman George W. Julian, of Indiana, more than three years before Miss Anthony, in 1872, made her test of woman's right to vote under the Fourteenth Amendment. Mr. Julian's proposed "Joint Resolution" to Congress for a Sixteenth Amendment to enfranchise the women of the Republic was submitted March 15, 1869, and read:

> Art. 16. The Right of Suffrage in the United States shall be based on citizenship, and shall be regulated by Congress; and all citizens of the United States, whether native or naturalized, shall enjoy this right equally without any distinction or discrimination whatever founded on sex.

This action was hailed with enthusiasm by Miss Anthony as a momentous step forward, and in her paper, *The Revolutionist*, she promptly outlined a comprehensive program for Suffragists to follow in support of it. Congress, however, took no action on the Julian Amendment; and it was not re-introduced.

There followed more years of public lecturing and of arduous campaigning in States where Suffragists were attempting to amend State constitutions, although Miss Anthony's strong conviction that the enfranchisement of women should be obtained through a Federal Amendment had in no way abated.

However, a Sixteenth, a Seventeenth, and an Eighteenth Amendment were added to the United States Constitution before women, fifty-one years later, succeeded in 1920 in securing a Nineteenth Amendment enfranchising all the women of the country.

2

CONGRESSIONAL COMMITTEE OPENS WASHINGTON HEADQUARTERS . . . NATIONAL WOMAN SUFFRAGE BECOMES POLITICAL ISSUE 1913

Now let us review briefly the status of the proposed federal suffrage amendment when Alice Paul, newly appointed chairman of the Congressional Committee of the National American Woman Suffrage Association, and her Committee opened headquarters in Washington, D. C., January 2, 1913, in a basement room at 1420 F Street N. W., and let us note the early activities of this Committee.

This Amendment, first introduced in Congress, January 10, 1878, by the Hon. Aaron A. Sargent, and re-introduced every year thereafter until it was passed, had never progressed beyond the Committee stage except on one occasion, January 25, 1887. That vote was in the Senate where the amendment was defeated. There were 16 yeas and 34 nays with 4 of the absentees announced as favorable and 2 opposed.

Prior to the 1913 revival of interest in the national enfranchisement of women, the national amendment had not been actively pushed since Susan B. Anthony retired from the leadership of the movement—it had been considered only a means of propaganda. Suffragists all over the country were devoting most of their strength to securing amendments to State Constitutions.

The Chairman of the Congressional Committee immediately preceding Alice Paul was Mrs. William Kent of California, wife of a Congressman from that State. When Mrs. Kent was asked to assume that official position, she was told it would entail practically no work. She need only have the Amendment introduced, and hearings arranged before two Congressional Committees. There was no thought of putting the Amendment through Congress or of lobbying for it, no thought that it could be adopted. An expense account of $10 was allowed for this work and at the end of the year Mrs. Kent was able to return some change.

But when Alice Paul and her Committee began their work in Washington the passage of the Susan B. Anthony Amendment not only ceased to be just a means of propaganda, it became at once a piece of legislation that could and would be enacted into law—the only practical method of enfranchising all the women in the United States. It was this campaign that resulted in the great suffrage victory of 1920.

The new Headquarters seethed with activity. Not only was it necessary to build up a capable working force and to raise sufficient funds for a difficult campaign, but the need to take advantage of a great opportunity for publicity was immediate and imperative. March 4, 1913, Woodrow Wilson would be inaugurated President of the United States and a huge crowd from all over the country would be in Washington for the Inauguration festivities. Might not Suffragists share some of the limelight on that occasion?

A monster demonstration in the shape of a procession

was arranged for March 3rd, the day before the Inauguration. It was a procession of great beauty in which about
eight thousand women from far and near came to Washington to take part. From the Capitol the women marched
down Pennsylvania Avenue, past the White House, and
when they arrived at the Hall of the Daughters of the
American Revolution they held a great mass meeting,
with Dr. Anna Howard Shaw as one of the principal
speakers.

Despite the fact that a permit had been issued for the
procession, a permit that carried with it the right to the
street, the police, as it had been rumored they would,
failed to protect the marchers. Suffragists found Pennsylvania Avenue almost impassable. A tremendous crowd of
sightseers acted in the rowdiest manner and many of the
police seemed to decide not to see what was happening.
Such disgraceful things occurred that Secretary of War
Henry Lewis Stimson had finally to send to Fort Meyer
for troops. Later, a Committee of the Senate made an
investigation of the action of the police and some of the
testimony in that voluminous report (557 pages) was truly
shocking. The Chief of Police of the District of Columbia
was ultimately removed. The investigation served for
many weeks to keep the suffrage procession alive in the
public mind, robbing the Inauguration itself of much
publicity.

It was in this suffrage demonstration that a banner, which
later in a slightly modified form was to become known as
the Great Demand banner, was first carried. Until the
Susan B. Anthony Amendment was passed, this famous
banner had a conspicuous place in the history of the suffrage
movement. It read:

WE DEMAND AN AMENDMENT TO THE CON-
STITUTION OF THE UNITED STATES ENFRANCHIS-
ING THE WOMEN OF THE COUNTRY.

When, on March 3rd, Woodrow Wilson arrived in
Washington for the Inauguration and drove through practically empty streets on his way from the station to his
hotel, he asked, "Where are the people?" "Over on the
Avenue watching the Suffrage Parade," came the answer.
Although the President missed the crowd he had expected
to meet him on his arrival at the Capital and very naturally
had to inquire, "Where are the people?", he was never
thereafter forced to ask, "Where are the Suffragists?"

The publicity on the suffrage parade must have been
a sudden shock to the President's utter indifference to the
enfranchisement of women. The advantage thus gained
for the women's cause was followed up by every conceiv-
able method of education on the subject that a wide-awake
leader and her followers could devise.

Following the March 3rd demonstration that called
the President's attention to the demand for national woman
suffrage, the Congressional Committee of the N.A.W.S.A.
in a few short weeks, was ready with a second demonstration
—to impress upon Congress woman's insistent demand
to be enfranchised nationally.

On the first day of the opening of the special session
of the Sixty-third Congress, April 7, 1913, women from
each of the 435 Congressional districts of the United States
were in Washington with petitions from the folks back
home for favorable action on the national suffrage amendment.

Immediately after the presentation of these petitions,
the Susan B. Anthony Amendment was introduced in the
Lower House by Congressman Frank W. Mondell (Repub-

lican) of Wyoming, and in the Upper House by Senator George Earle Chamberlain (Democrat) of Oregon.*

But the strain of the first four months of work at the Washington Headquarters convinced the Congressional Committee of five members that they alone could not possibly conduct a national campaign such as had been planned. Therefore the Congressional Committee, with the approval of the president and the corresponding secretary of the N.A.W.S.A., formed the Congressional Union for Woman Suffrage, which described itself as "a group of women in all parts of the country who have joined together in the effort to secure the passage of an Amendment to the United States Constitution enfranchising women."

By July, 31, 1913, the Congressional Union for Woman Suffrage (for brevity called the Congressional Union) was sufficiently well organized to have State delegations converge upon Washington with petitions to the United States Senate urging favorable action on the pending national suffrage amendment. Preceding the mass presentation of these State petitions there was a picturesque parade large enough to attract the attention of the entire country.

The demonstration, planned to impress the Senate with the nationwide demand for the passage of the Susan B. Anthony Amendment, had drawn Suffragists from every State in the Union.

July 29th, 1913, an automobile party from New York City, which included Mrs. Mary Ware Dennett, Mrs. Frances Maule Bjorkman, Mrs. Rheta Childe Dorr, and Miss Helen Todd, visited the Philadelphia Headquarters of

* In 1914, the Susan B. Anthony Amendment was again introduced in the House by Congressman Frank W. Mondell. In the Upper House, it was sponsored by Senator Joseph L. Bristow (Republican) of Kansas. As it is customary for a Resolution to be named after those who introduce it, the Suffrage Amendment was then referred to as the Bristow-Mondell Amendment.

the Eastern District of Pennsylvania on their way to this Washington demonstration. In order to take advantage of the presence of these distinguished guests, we arranged open-air meetings giving them an opportunity to explain why they were bound for Washington. A morning and an afternoon meeting were held on City Hall Plaza, and another at Baldwin Locomotive Works. A newspaper man estimated that one of the City Hall meetings drew a crowd of fifteen hundred persons. The brightly decorated automobile of our guests, which stood for some time in front of our Headquarters, attracted so much attention that traffic at Chestnut and Juniper Streets was for a time almost blocked.

The following day, Pennsylvania's large delegation left for Washington to march in the parade and to present its petition to the Senate.

3

TWO PROPOSALS FOR A FEDERAL WOMAN SUFFRAGE AMENDMENT BEFORE CONGRESS 1914-1916

The Congressional Union for Woman Suffrage in the beginning was affiliated with the National American Woman Suffrage Association. In 1914, after the N.A.W.S.A. turned to a new federal amendment instead of the original suffrage amendment for which Susan B. Anthony and her followers had been working, the Congressional Union became an independent national organization.

In this chapter I shall give some details of the opposing positions taken by these two national organizations concerning the text of the Amendment to be pressed in Congress.

For the first time since the amendment was introduced in 1878, Congress was, early in 1914, presented by the Suffragists of the country with two proposed amendments. Senator John F. Shafroth of Colorado and Congressman A. Mitchell Palmer of Pennsylvania introduced an entirely new amendment reading as follows:

> Whenever any number of legal voters of any State, to a number exceeding ten percent of the number of legal voters voting at the last preceding election held in such State, shall petition for the submission to the legal voters of said State of the question whether women shall have equal rights

179

with men in respect to voting at all elections to be
held in such State, such question shall be so submitted and if, upon such submission, a majority of
the legal voters of the State voting on the question
shall vote in favor of granting to women such
equal rights, the same shall thereupon be deemed
established, anything in the constitution or laws of
such State to the contrary notwithstanding.

This new amendment was introduced at the request of
the National American Woman Suffrage Association
through its new Congressional Chairman, Mrs. Medill
McCormick, who at the beginning of 1914 had succeeded
Alice Paul in that position. The amendment was, from
the beginning, opposed by the Congressional Union.

The original suffrage amendment, which now came to
be known as the Susan B. Anthony Amendment, was introduced by Senator Joseph L. Bristow of Kansas and Congressman Frank W. Mondell of Wyoming in the same
Congress. It read:

ARTICLE—SEC. 1. The right of citizens of
the United States to vote shall not be denied or
abridged by the United States or by any State on
account of sex.
SEC. 2. Congress shall have power to enforce
this article by appropriate legislation.

The introduction of the Shafroth-Palmer Amendment
was a source of undisguised amazement to members of the
Congressional Union who could not understand why an
attempt should be made to offer a substitute for the original
amendment proposed by Susan B. Anthony and her colleagues and adhered to by the great body of Suffragists
for 36 years.

The *Suffragist,* official organ of the Congressional

Union, of March 21, 1914, pointed out that even if the new amendment were passed by Congress and ratified by three-fourths of the State Legislatures no woman would thereby be enfranchised.

Among the many other reasons why the Congressional Union opposed the new amendment, that same issue of the *Suffragist* emphasized the following:

> We oppose the amendment because, while it is innocuous in itself, it is harmful nevertheless in that it divides the suffragists of the country and thus weakens the forces that are working for the vote. Could Congress, or that part of it that is opposed to suffrage, ask for a better situation? With that amendment before Congress, no man would have to avow himself an anti-suffragist. He need only "voice his honest conviction" that he belonged in one camp or the other. This would give the caucus a splendid chance to apportion the sheep in two folds in about equal numbers, making it impossible to pass any kind of suffrage measure.
>
> We oppose it because it is a weak measure, whereas the present suffrage amendment is a strong one. . . .
>
> Certainly this proposed measure never can, to any thinking, self-respecting suffragist, be regarded as a possible substitute for a Federal Amendment removing the sex disability from the electoral system.

The following week, the *Suffragist* made this urgent appeal for support of the Susan B. Anthony Amendment:

> We now call upon the women suffragists of the Nation to refuse to be misled into taking a backward step when the cause of suffrage in Congress is on the eve of complete success. We call upon

them to rally to the support of the original amendment, which is the only direct road to nation-wide
enfranchisement.

Not only did the introduction of the Shafroth-Palmer
Amendment greatly disturb the Congressional Union, but
the National American Woman Suffrage Association had
difficulty in making its own membership understand why the
action was taken. Mrs. Ida Husted Harper, historian of
the N.A.W.S.A., wrote regarding the introduction of the
Shafroth-Palmer Amendment:

> Mrs. Mary Ware Dennett, corresponding sec-
> retary of the National American Association,
> wrote to the State presidents the first week in
> May, 1914: "Strange as it may seem, we find that
> quite a number of the members of our association
> have gotten the impression that the introduction
> of the *Shafroth amendment* means the abandoning
> of the old amendment which has been introduced
> into Congress for forty years or more, and which,
> as you know, has now been re-introduced and at
> this session will be called the Bristow-Mondell
> amendment. Nothing could be further from the
> truth. The reason for the introduction of the
> Shafroth amendment is to hasten the day when
> the passage of the Bristow-Mondell amendment
> will become a possibility. . . . Both Amendments
> are before Congress but only the new one stands
> any chance of being acted upon before adjourn-
> ment. We stand by the old one as a matter of
> principle; we push for the new one as a matter
> of immediate practical politics and to further the
> passage of the old one." Mrs. Dennett also vig-
> orously advocated the new amendment in the
> *Woman's Journal.**

---

* From the *HISTORY OF WOMAN SUFFRAGE*, edited by Ida
Husted Harper, Vol. V. National American Woman Suffrage Association.
Printed by J. J. Little and Ives Company, N. Y. 1922.

The Congressional Union, at that time only a very small group, had become a national organization entirely independent of the National American Woman Suffrage Association in 1914 in order that the campaign for the original federal suffrage Amendment might be continued. For two years, 1914 and 1915, the entire burden of the campaign for the original suffrage Amendment was borne by the Congressional Union while the N.A.W.S.A. worked for the substitute Shafroth-Palmer Amendment.

Finally, after advocating the new amendment for nearly two years, the N.A.W.S.A. at its national convention in 1915, returned to the original Amendment. Mrs. Harper described that decision as follows:

> At a morning session of the convention on December 18, [1915] a motion was passed that "last year's action in regard to the Shafroth Amendment be rescinded." The following motion was then carried:—"The National Amerian Woman Suffrage Association re-indorses the Susan B. Anthony Amendment to the U. S. Constitution, for which it has been working forty-five years, and no other amendment of the U. S. Constitution dealing with National Woman Suffrage shall be introduced by it during the coming year." . . . This was the end of the so-called Shafroth Amendment, which had threatened to carry the old association on the rocks.*

Thus for nearly two years Suffragists were divided in their work on Congress because two amendments were before that body. In 1916, all suffrage organizations united again in supporting the Susan B. Anthony Amendment, which passed Congress three years later.

---

* See footnote on page 182.

4

*PARTY IN POWER CONTINUES OPPOSITION . . .
CONGRESSIONAL UNION CAMPAIGNS AGAINST
IT . . . WOMEN VOTERS FORM INDEPENDENT
NATIONAL POLITICAL PARTY . . .
PENNSYLVANIA LENDS A HELPING HAND
1916*

October 13, 1916, Mrs. Lucretia M. B. Mitchell, Corresponding Secretary of the Pennsylvania Committee of the Congressional Union for Woman Suffrage, wrote me:

> At a meeting of the Pennsylvania Committee held Oct. 6, it was voted to ask you to take the office of Executive Secretary for the Congressional Union in Pennsylvania provided such arrangements could be made whereby you would feel free to accept the same.
>
> Since that meeting we learn that your resignation has been given to the Equal Franchise Society, thus leaving you open to take up the work of the Union in the Headquarters already established at 213 Hale Building.
>
> After your return from the West you will find a hearty welcome and all hands ready to make your burden as light as possible in consideration of the great work there is to do.

On the letterhead used by Mrs. Mitchell were the names of Alice Paul, National Chairman, Lucy Burns, National

Vice-Chairman, and the following prominent local Suffragists: Mrs. Anna Lowenburg, Miss Harriet Winslow Dulles, Mrs. Edwin C. Grice, Miss Elizabeth Elder, Miss Sarah Graham Tomkins, Miss Ellen Lane Leaf, Miss Rebecca D. Ernst, Miss Cornelia Greenough, Miss Alice Gibson Brock, Miss Ella Riegel, Miss M. Theodora Burt, Mrs. Charles Z. Klauder, Miss Fanny Travis Cochran, and Miss Florence Lucas Sanville.

In my letter of October 16th accepting the new position, I explained that I was that day leaving for Chicago to confer with Alice Paul and have "our thrilling campaign mapped out." But this visit developed into more than just a conference on what work our leader wished the Pennsylvania Branch to undertake in the immediate future. I did not return to Philadelphia until after the November elections.

In order to explain why Alice Paul was for the time being in Chicago instead of in Washington, it will be necessary to give a summary of special work done by the Congressional Union in preparation for the 1916 national elections.

For two years elaborate plans had been carried out to build up an organization in the western States where women were enfranchised, and by April, 1916, the Congressional Union was ready to undertake its most pretentious election campaign. Heretofore it had asked the women voters to aid the unenfranchised women of the East to secure the ballot. Now, the Congressional Union was sufficiently well organized to make an effective appeal to 4,000,000 women voters to organize themselves into an independent political group that could be a real factor in the November national elections.

To carry out this ambitious plan, the Congressional Union held a conference in Washington April 8 and 9, 1916.

Attending the Conference were national officers, State officers, and members of the Advisory Council representing 36 unenfranchised States. Brilliant speeches were made by Alice Paul, Lucy Burns, and Anne Martin.

Alice Paul pointed out that the two major Parties were about equal; that the Suffrage States were doubtful States and would, therefore, be eagerly sought by both Democrats and Republicans; that the history of national elections covering the last twenty years showed it would have required a change of only nine per cent of the total vote cast in the presidential elections in order to have thrown the election to the other Party. She then emphasized the advantages the political set-up in 1916 offered Suffragists to carry out the plan the Conference proposed:

> This gives us a position of wonderful power, a position that we have never held before and that we cannot hope to hold again for at least four years, and which we may not hold then.
>
> . . . We now have to demonstrate to the Administration, to the majority Party in Congress, that the organization in the Suffrage States does exist and that it is a power to be feared. There are many months still remaining, probably, before Congress will adjourn. If in these months we can build up so strong an organization there that it really will be dangerous to oppose it, and if we can show Congress that we have such an organization, then we will have the matter in our hands.
>
> We have sent a request to our branches in the East to select one or more representative women who will go out to the West and make a personal appeal to the women voters to stand by us even more loyally than they have before—to form a stronger organization than has ever before existed.
>
> Today we must consider what concrete plan we shall ask these envoys who go out to the West to

propose to the voting women. I do not think it will do very much good to go through the voting States and simply strengthen our Suffrage organizations. That will not be enough to terrify the men in Congress. Suffrage organizations, unfortunately, have come to stand for feebleness of action and supineness of spirit. What I want to propose is that when we go to these women voters we ask them to begin to organize an independent political Party that will be ready for the elections in November. They may not have to go into these elections. If they prepare diligently enough for the elections they won't have to go into them. The threat will be enough. We want to propose to you that we ask the women voters to come together in Chicago at the time that the Progresives and Republicans meet there in June, to decide how they will use these four million votes that women have, in the next election.

Now, if women who are Republicans simply help the Republican Party, and if women who are Democrats help the Democratic Party, women's votes will not count for much. But if the political Parties see before them a group of independent women voters who are standing together to use their vote to promote Suffrage, it will make Suffrage an issue— the women voters at once become a group which counts; whose votes are wanted. The Parties will inevitably have to go to the women voters if the latter stand aloof and do not go to the existing political Parties. The political Parties will have to offer them the thing which will win their votes. To count in an election you do not have to be the biggest Party; you have to be simply an independent Party that will stand for one object and that cannot be diverted from that object.

What I would like to propose, in short, is that we go to the women voters and ask them to hold a convention in Chicago the first week in June, and that we spend these next two months in preparation. We could not have a better opportunity for preparation than this trip of the envoys through every one of the Suffrage States, calling the women together to meet in Chicago, the place where the eyes of the whole country will be turned in June.

The Conference decided unanimously to send an appeal to all members in the Suffrage States to meet June 5, 6, and 7 in Chicago to form a *Woman's Party.*

Branches of the Congressional Union in the East had selected twenty-three envoys who, as spokesmen of their States, were to carry this appeal to the West. Organizers were sent ahead of the envoys to advertise their arrival and to arouse interest in their coming. The envoys were:

> Mrs. W. D. Ascough, Harriot Stanton Blatch, Abby Scott Baker, Lucy Burns, Agnes Campbell, Mrs. A. R. Colvin, Anna Constable, Edith Goode, Jane Goode, Florence Bayard Hilles, Julia Hurlbut, Caroline Katzenstein, Winifred Mallon, Mrs. Cyrus Mead, Agnes Morey, Katharine Morey, Gertrude B. Newell, Mrs. Percy Read, Ella Riegel, Mrs. John Rogers, Mrs. Townsend Scott, Helen Todd, and Mrs. Nelson Whittemore.

Two of these twenty-three envoys were Pennsylvanians, Ella Riegel and I. Miss Riegel, Chairman of the Congressional Committee of the Pennsylvania Branch of the Congressional Union, filled the important post of Business Manager of the *Suffrage Special.* She had to see that our well-filled coach, which served as hotel and train, never failed to make the proper connection with the various railroad lines that carried us across the continent. So well did she perform this task that we never failed to arrive on time at our various destinations. She had had exceptional training in a great institution of learning under a brilliant teacher and knew how to apply this training in business affairs.

From 1885, when Bryn Mawr College first opened its doors, to 1888, Woodrow Wilson taught history and political science to eager young women in that institution. Ella Riegel, who was graduated in the class of 1889, had majored in the two subjects Professor Wilson taught. But in those happy, carefree years, she had no idea that she should one day be campaigning against President Woodrow Wilson and members of his political Party because he, as leader of that Party, had failed to get a passing mark in his test on Democracy—an easy test, which he should have passed, and later did.

In order that I might help with publicity work on the *Suffrage Special,* the Equal Franchise Society of Philadelphia gave me leave of absence for the duration of the western campaign. (At that time I was the Society's Executive Secretary.)

Miss Rebecca D. Ernst, Chairman of Literature for the Pennsylvania Branch of the Congressional Union, who did not feel physically able to take part in the campaign, made generous donations toward its heavy expenses.

April 9th, automobiles flying the purple, white, and gold tri-color took the envoys to Union Station in Washington, where five thousand persons had gathered to bid them farewell. The Naval Gun Factory Band greeted them with the Marseillaise, and in the half-hour before the train pulled out of the station it continued to play martial music. The crowd broke into song when *Onward Christian Soldiers* and *America* were played.

From April 9th to May 16th, the *Suffrage Special* was the crowded but happy home of the envoys as they wound their way across the country covering principal cities in all the

Suffrage States—Wyoming, Colorado, Utah, Idaho, Washington, California, Kansas, Oregon, Arizona, Montana, Nevada, (listed chronologically) and Illinois, where women had Presidential, not full suffrage.

The drawing-room of the *Suffrage Special*, crowded with piles of mimeographed press material prepared at Washington Headquarters, a typewriter and office supplies, served as sleeping quarters for Abby Scott Baker and me. We handled the publicity. So well had the newspapers of the country been alerted that reporters were on hand at train-stops of only a few minutes and were given, in addition to "canned" copy, as colorful a story as we had been able to prepare. When time permitted, Mrs. Baker and I made personal calls on editors—"lobbied" for the Cause! The campaign was so picturesque, its purpose so dynamic, it made a good story, and the newspapers of the country gave it abundant space.

The work of the organizers who preceded the *Suffrage Special*, the usual excellent publicity from headquarters in Washington, and the fact that Lucy Burns was at the helm, combined to make the trip more of a "triumphal march" than a gruelling campaign. High public officials, leading women's clubs, Chambers of Commerce welcomed the women and showed them beautiful courtesies.

At Sacramento, California, they were given a reception and luncheon by the Chamber of Commerce.

At Seattle, Washington, the station was decorated with Congressional Union banners, national colors, and hanging baskets of flowers. A big crowd, including the Acting Mayor, had gathered to welcome the visitors.

When the envoys went in to breakfast on the stretch between Maricopa and Tucson, Arizona, they found the tables in the dining car had been decorated by the railway management with Congressional Union colors—sweet peas and laburnums. At Tucson, Eugene Debs was with the crowd that came to meet them. And so the hospitality continued.

A Convention at Salt Lake City, May 11, was the last official meeting of the envoys on their way back to the East and brought the tour to the pinnacle of its success.

The Convention passed resolutions demanding favorable action on the Suffrage Amendment in the current session of Congress, and elected three women voters to take these resolutions to Congress.

When the *Suffrage Special* arrived at the Union Station in Washington, the campaigners were welcomed at a luncheon in the Station. Then in brightly decorated automobiles they drove through streets lined with posters that invited the public to COME TO THE CAPITOL where a simple but impressive pageant had been arranged.

Two buglers stationed on the broad platforms at the top of the wide stairway of the Capitol alternatively sounded a note of triumphant welcome to the approaching group. A large chorus of women in white sang *America*. Through an aisle formed on the Capitol steps by ribbons held in the hands of other women in white, the envoys ascended the steps into the rotunda where they formed a semi-circle that faced another semi-circle of nearly one hundred Senators and Representatives. The Senate had taken a recess especially to meet the returning campaigners.

The three women voters elected at the Salt Lake City Convention then presented the assembled members of Congress with the resolutions passed at that Convention, and speeches followed.

While the envoys were arousing the West, the Congressional Union was trying to get declarations of support from political leaders to influence the approaching National Political Conventions. One of the deputations sent on this important mission, Mary Beard, Elizabeth Gerberling, Alice Carpenter, and Mrs. Evan Evans, succeeded in getting from Theodore Roosevelt, long a convert to the principle of suffrage for women, a statement that he favored the Federal Amendment and a promise of his active support in the campaign for its enactment.

Soon another plan outlined at the Congressional Union's Conference in Washington, D. C., April 8 and 9, 1916, was successfully carried out. Western women voters responded favorably to the appeal of the twenty-three envoys on the *Suffrage Special* to meet in Chicago, June 5, 6, and 7, 1916, to form a new political party—the Woman's Party. Chicago would be an ideal place for this dramatic step because the annual conventions of the Republican and Progressive Parties would be held there June 7-10, and the eyes of the nation would be focused on the Windy City.

A few weeks later, July fifth, the Woman's Party was officially launched at the Blackstone Theatre in Chicago. Helena Hill Weed, Chairman of the Credentials Committee, in presenting her report, explained that the gathering was not a delegated body, but was a mass convention of all members of the Congressional Union, the enfranchised and the unenfranchised. The former had the right to speak and to vote; the latter might speak from the floor, but might not vote. More than fifteen hundred delegates were registered.

Maude Younger, temporary Chairman of the Convention and keynote speaker, said in part:

> A new force marches on to the political field. For the first time in a Presidential election women are a factor to be reckoned with. Four years ago, women voted in six States—today in twelve, including Illinois. These States with their four million women constitute nearly one-fourth of the

LEADERS OF PENNSYLVANIA BRANCH,
NATIONAL WOMAN'S PARTY

Left to right, top row: Mary E. Bakewell, Katharine G. Halligan. *Middle row:* Mrs. Lawrence Lewis, Mrs. J. Sharon McDonald, Mrs. Edwin C. Grice. *Bottom row:* Mabel Cronise Jones, Mary A. Burnham.

LEADERS OF PENNSYLVANIA BRANCH,
NATIONAL WOMAN'S PARTY

Left to right, top row: Ella Riegel, Rebecca D. Ernst. *Middle row:* Mary H. Ingham, Fanny Travis Cochran, Martha Davis. *Bottom row:* Anna Lowenburg, Florence L. Sanville.

electoral college and more than one-third of the
votes necessary to elect a President. With enough
women organized in each State to hold the balance
of power, the women's votes may determine the
Presidency of the United States. The Woman's
Party has no candidates and but one plank, enfranchisement of the women of America through a
Federal Amendment.

Anne Martin was chosen permanent Chairman of the
Woman's Party; Phoebe A. Hearst and Judge Mary A.
Bartelme, Vice-Chairmen; Mabel Vernon, Secretary.

The Party's platform, adopted unanimously amid cheers,
closed with this significant paragraph:

The National* Woman's Party, convinced that
the enfranchisement of women is the paramount
issue, pledges itself to use its united vote to secure
the passage of the Susan B. Anthony Amendment,
irrespective of the interests of any national political Party, and pledges its unceasing opposition to
all who oppose this Amendment.

Ida M. Tarbell, describing the Woman's Party in the
New York World of June 7 and 8, 1916, said:

The new Woman's Party had permitted representation of five different political Parties to
appear before them and briefly present their
various claims to the Suffrage of women. "We do
not ask you here to tell us what we can do for
your Parties, but what your Parties can do for us,"
Miss Martin told the speakers in a tone of exultant
sweetness which sent a cheer from shore to shore

---

* The National Woman's Party was the name adopted when the Congressional Union for Woman Suffrage and the Woman's Party combined
March 2, 1917. The word *National* was here used to indicate that the new
organization was national in scope.

of the human sea that filled the house. . . .
. . . The one and only thing they wanted to
know, so the women told the men after they had
gone through their ordeals, was whether or no
they proposed to support the Susan B. Anthony
Amendment. That was the only possible interest
they had in what the gentlemen could say. Was it
yes or no?

The Convention of the newly-formed Woman's Party,
which ended the day the Republican and Progressive Conventions began, sent delegates to speak before the Resolutions Committee of each of these Conventions. The Progressives came out immediately for national woman suffrage,
thus becoming the first national political Party ever to
endorse the Federal Suffrage Amendment. The disappoint-
ing plank of the Republicans read:

> The Republican Party favors the extension of
> the suffrage to women, but recognizes the right
> of each State to settle this question for itself.

Later, members of the Woman's Party went to St.
Louis when the Democratic Convention was held in that
city. But there they were met by the continued opposition
of President Wilson. He had favored the plank in the
Democratic platform that recommended the question of
woman suffrage should be confined to the States. It read:

> We recommend the extension of the franchise
> to the women of the country by the States upon
> the same terms as to men.

Although the Resolutions Committee of the Republican
Party at its Convention in Chicago had failed to follow the
example set by the Progressive Party in endorsing the

national enfranchisement of women, there was still hope
that the Republican candidate, Charles Evans Hughes,
might himself declare his support of the measure. To accomplish this a nation-wide and vigorous campaign was
begun. Telegrams were sent all over the United States asking various persons to urge Mr. Hughes to take this step.
Many women went to plead with him; and some went to
Theodore Roosevelt and other leading Progressives and
Republicans to ask their support in obtaining favorable
action by Mr. Hughes. The Republican members of Congress were asked to write to their candidate or to see him;
and Mr. Hughes was beseiged by newspaper editorials. I
doubt, however, if any argument used was more convincing
or more simply stated than Alice Paul's when she went to
see Mr. Hughes. She said:

> Your Party consists of two factions, the old
> stand-pat Republicans and the Progressives. Now
> if you put a Suffrage plank in your platform, you
> will not alienate the Progressives, because the
> Progressives have a Suffrage plank and the old
> stand-pat Republicans will not vote for a Demo-
> crat, no matter what you put in your platform.

The Congressional Union did not have long to wait.
August 1, 1916, in a telegram to Senator Sutherland of
Utah, Mr. Hughes declared himself in favor of the Federal
Woman Suffrage Amendment. For the first time a Presidential candidate of one of the two major political Parties
had publicly declared the Federal Woman Suffrage Amendment a part of his policy.

The Democratic Party vigorously and bitterly opposed
the Congressional Union's 1916 western campaign, and this
opposition reached its climax in Chicago when, October 19th,
about one hundred members of the Woman's Party, some of

whom carried inscribed banners, stationed themselves in front of the Auditorium where President Wilson was to speak, and quietly held aloft those banners as a silent protest against the President's continued blocking of the Federal Amendment.

The effectiveness of this attempt of the Congressional Union and the Woman's Party to emphasize the President's opposition was shown by the publicity received the following day. October 20, the demonstration "stole" from the President headlines, position, and space in the press.

In Philadelphia's five morning papers, the suffrage publicity was remarkable. All of them gave us first-page stories with big headlines. Even the *Record*, a Democratic paper, which allotted the President nearly three columns of space, gave the demonstration almost three-quarters of a column.

The *Public Ledger*, considered a very conservative paper, had these headlines:

ANTI-WILSON WOMEN MOBBED IN CHICAGO. BANNERS SEIZED. SUFFRAGISTS IN "SILENT DEMONSTRATION" CHARGED, MANY KNOCKED DOWN— PRESIDENT SEES START OF NEAR RIOT

The story began:

An attempted "silent demonstration" by members of the National Woman's Party in front of the Auditorium late this afternoon developed into a near-riot, in which the banners opposing Wilson were torn from the demonstrators and trampled and the women were roughly handled. President Wilson on his way to the Auditorium to address an audience of women, was seated in an automobile a few hundred feet away when the demonstration started, but passed into the building and was not a witness to the scene that followed.

(Seven paragraphs follow. And then the paper quoted the following comment by Alice Paul.)

> Miss Alice Paul, national chairman of the Congressional Union, characterized it as an attack by Democrats. "The violent attack by Democrats upon the demonstration shows the seriousness with which they take our campaign," she said. "Evidently they feel keenly the weakness of President Wilson's Suffrage position when they resort to such violence to prevent his hostility to national woman suffrage being revealed to the people of Chicago."

The story on President Wilson's speech was relegated to an inconspicuous place on the 7th page! And not much space was allotted it.

The *Inquirer*, the *North American*, and the *Press* had stories similar to the *Public Ledger's*. Their headlines were: The *Inquirer*:

WOMEN ILL-TREATED BY WILSON RIOTERS WITH CHICAGO MOB
MANY KNOCKED DOWN, THEIR CLOTHING TORN, BANNERS TRAMPLED
PRESIDENT URGES THEIR GREATER PARTICIPATION IN NATIONAL AFFAIRS AFTER DEMONSTRATION

The *North American*:

ANTI-WILSON WOMEN MOBBED IN CHICAGO AS PRESIDENT VISITS
BANNERS TORN FROM THEM AND TRAMPLED IN STREET

Then followed smaller headlines on President Wilson's speech to a New Citizens' meeting and the cordial reception given him.

The *Press*:

CROWD SMASHES ANTI-WILSON FLAGS
SUFFRAGE DEMONSTRATION AGAINST PRESIDENT IN CHICAGO ENDS IN RIOTOUS OUTBREAK

In all the suffrage States, women worked to defeat President Wilson and the candidates of the Democratic Party for the Senate and the House of Representatives because of the non-passage of the Federal Suffrage Amendment. They did this to make the Suffrage Amendment a live political issue; and in this they succeeded. Wilson's claim to have "kept us out of war" had made an especial appeal to women. Our job was to keep the Democratic Party on the defensive and to make them realize they had to get rid of the Suffrage Amendment before the 1920 elections. And again in this we succeeded. To look ahead, in 1919 both the Senate and the House passed the Susan B. Anthony Amendment, and in 1920 it was ratified and women voted that year throughout the United States. Suffrage leaders felt convinced that victory could not have been won in 1920 if we had been quiescent in the 1916 national elections.

Alice Paul was in the midst of this exciting campaign when I, as newly-appointed Executive Secretary of the Pennsylvania Branch of the Congressional Union, left Philadelphia October 16th to confer with her about the special work she wished us to undertake in Pennsylvania. After a few days in Chicago, I was given the unexpected assignment of handling the publicity of the Woman's Party in the State of Montana, a task that troubled me because I felt unprepared for it and also was campaign-weary.

But Montana's cordial reception of us was characteristic of the welcome given by women voters to the Congressional Union's appeal. I found I did not really need to know in any detail the political situation in the State. The Congressional Union had a convincing story to tell and a receptive audience. Western women, it seemed certain, were sufficiently interested in promoting the cause of justice and in elevating the status of women to place these ideals for a time above Party allegiance. And so sure was the Congressional Union of our being on the home stretch that we could tell the women voters we believed their willingness to forgo Party allegiance need be of only short duration.

The following letter, sent to the editors of all Republican, Progressive, and Independent dailies in the State, will indicate our method of presenting the Congressional Union's campaign to the press:

> I am enclosing another appeal to western women to vote against President Wilson and other Democratic candidates because of their continued opposition to national woman suffrage, and hope that you will see the timeliness of this.
>
> The Democratic campaign managers are evidently doing their best to make capital of the fact that *Mr.* Wilson, a private citizen, voted in favor of the proposed woman suffrage amendment to the Constitution of his own State. The fact, however, is that we are concerned with *President* Wilson, the nation's head, and it is on his record as our national leader that he should ask for support November 7th.

The Montana publicity seems to have been satisfactory because Alice Paul, in a letter to me dated January 22, 1917, closed with this paragraph:

> May I take this opportunity, now that we are settling up the campaign account, to thank you again for the splendid help that you gave us in Montana. I hardly know how we would have gotten through that campaign without having you come for the last few weeks.

March 2, 1917, there was a merger of the *Congressional Union* and the women voters, recently banded together under the name *Woman's Party*, to assist in the passage of the Susan B. Anthony Amendment. As the name adopted by these two organizations, when they joined, was *National Woman's Party*, I shall in future, when referring to the organization led by Alice Paul, call it by the new name. Occasionally, I may use only the initials N.W.P.

The merger was to bring about a unity in organization that would prevent duplication and divergence of method. Also it would make for unity of spirit in the whole suffrage movement. Voters and non-voters would be integral parts of the whole.

The tragic fate of one of our most beloved members cast a gloom over the closing months of 1916.

In the stirring campaign of that year, beautiful Inez Milholland was chosen as a special flying envoy to the twelve equal suffrage States of the West to carry an appeal for help from the unenfranchised women of the East.

Forgetful of self and filled with ardor and enthusiasm for her mission, she underestimated the strain of her arduous trip. Speaking at a large Los Angeles mass meeting in October, and recalling President Wilson's words, "The tide is rising to meet the moon; you will not have long to wait," she asked, "How long must women wait for liberty?" On the fateful word *liberty*, she fell to the floor in a faint. In a few short weeks, Inez Milholland was dead.

5

PICKETING CAMPAIGN BEGINS . . .
PENNSYLVANIA ACTIVELY SUPPORTS IT
1917

When, in October, 1916, the Pennsylvania Branch of the National Woman's Party opened headquarters in the Hale Building,* S. W. Corner of Chestnut and Juniper Streets, Pennsylvania members of the organization were galvanized into action. No longer were they faced with a double allegiance—to a State and to a national campaign—as was the case in 1913 when the N.W.P (then the Congressional Union) began its Washington campaign.

However, even when Pennsylvania Suffragists worked for two campaigns at one time, Pennsylvania was the banner State in supporting the campaign of the N.W.P., and it held that enviable position until the national amendment was ratified.

In substantiation of this claim, I hope I may be pardoned for emphasizing here just a few of Pennsylvania's outstanding contributions to the national campaign, some of which have already been mentioned.

From the opening of the Washington Headquarters, Pennsylvania women were in the vanguard. Mrs. Lawrence Lewis of Philadelphia was a member of the Congressional Committee of the National American Woman Suffrage

---

* By coincidence, the same building in which Pennsylvania's first suffrage headquarters were opened in 1910.

Association which began to function early in 1913, and later she became a member of the Executive Committee of the Congressional Union for Woman Suffrage, a position held throughout the campaign. After the Susan B. Anthony Amendment was passed by Congress, Mrs. Lewis was appointed National Chairman of the Ratification Committee, supervising that work from Washington Headquarters and taking a personal part in the ratification campaigns in Maine and Delaware. Also she was chairman of Pennsylvania's Ratification Committee.

Another invaluable worker from the Keystone State was Lavinia L. Dock of Fayetteville. Though frail in body and no longer young, Miss Dock spoke at open-air meetings, took an active part in the picketing campaign, and served three prison sentences in the District Jail and at Occoquan Workhouse for these activities. A nurse by profession, an author of many text books on nursing, Miss Dock assisted in relief work during the Johnstown flood and during the Florida yellow fever epidemic. In the Spanish-American War she was an army nurse. Her professional and humanitarian work made her internationally known and her name a real publicity asset to the campaign.

Mrs. Anna Lowenburg, a leader in both State and national suffrage work, made frequent visits to Washington, taking part in many of the demonstrations. Also she gave generous financial support to the campaign and was helpful as a speaker at meetings.

Miss Mary A. Burnham's long years of association with worthwhile movements in Philadelphia and her knowledge of political affairs made her advice eagerly sought. Also, she was Pennsylvania's outstanding financial supporter of the national suffrage campaign.

When the validity of Ohio's ratification of the Susan B. Anthony Amendment was attacked by anti-Suffragists, three Philadelphia lawyers, George Wharton Pepper, William Draper Lewis, and Shippen Lewis represented the N.W.P. in contesting the suit, and succeeded in having the validity of the ratification sustained.

In the first issue of the *Suffragist*, November 15, 1913, all financial contributions received up to that time toward a $25,000 fund for the federal suffrage campaign were listed. Pennsylvania contributed the first six of them:

Mrs. Lucretia M. B. Mitchell $25.00
Mrs. Edith W. Carter 10.00
Miss Alice Paul (collected) * 84.00
Mrs. Lawrence Lewis 50.00
Phila. Equal Franchise Society 100.00
Pennsylvania General Suffrage Fund (per
Mrs. Lawrence Lewis) 75.00

Wood from a tree in Philadelphia's Independence Square was used to start the first of the Watchfires for Freedom that burned in front of the White House, and one-eighth of all the pickets serving prison terms for helping to keep these Watchfires burning, and for helping in other suffrage demonstrations in Washington were Pennsylvanians.

In seeking the passage of the federal suffrage amendment, the National Woman's Party had at first attempted to work through individual members of Congress, and congressional committees. But individual Congressmen declared they had to stand by their political Party, and committees gave different excuses for failing to act. For instance, Chairman Henry of the powerful Rules Committee wrote to Alice Paul in 1915 frankly explaining that the blame for his failure to report the Suffrage Resolution was due to the Democratic Caucus which he said, "has tied my

---

* The amount left over from fund Alice Paul had collected for Philadelphia's first open-air campaign.

hands." On another occasion Chairman Henry declared, "Without definite instructions from my Party, I shall do nothing." And as it was acknowledged that President Wilson, during his Administration, dictated the policies of his Party, it became plain that the President held in his hands the fate of the national enfranchisement of women. Also it should be remembered that President Wilson himself had a large measure of responsibility for the unsatisfactory Woman Suffrage plank in the Democratic platform of 1916.

For years, the National Woman's Party had struggled valiantly, but without success, to have Congress pass the Susan B. Anthony Amendment. Huge petitions had been presented to the President and to Congress; deputation after deputation had marched to the White House to prove by their numbers that women in every walk of life wanted to be free; parades and pageants had been arranged. At hearings before different committees facts and irrefutable arguments had been presented. In short, the ingenuity of women had been taxed to the uttermost to prove the obvious—that women under a democratic form of government are entitled to the franchise.

Just what could the National Woman's Party do to move the President to use his great power in obtaining justice for women? President Wilson had said definitely that he would receive no more deputations from the N.W.P. And when he lightly shifted to his Party the responsibility for getting results on the question of woman suffrage, he had advised the women to devote their attention to "concerting public opinion." But the N.W.P. well knew there was no hope of getting the Federal Amendment through Congress without the support of the President as leader of the Party in control. They decided to take the President's advice and started out to "concert public opinion."

Since deputations from the N.W.P. were now denied the

privilege of entering the White House to present their case to the President, it seemed that the best way to "concert public opinion" sufficiently to force the President to act was to have a constant, direct, and public appeal made at a place where the President and the public could not fail to *see* it. The N.W.P. therefore placed Silent Sentinels at the White House gates where, with their backs to the wall, they held aloft banners that spoke eloquently for them—banners with poignant messages, banners that, as time went on, related news events of international interest. On a number of the banners were quotations from President Wilson, whose vanity might have been aroused by this deference to his beautiful use of words.

On January 10, 1917, Alice Paul led the first line of Silent Sentinels to the White House gates and thus injected into the aggressive campaign that she and Lucy Burns had begun in 1913, something so dramatic that it made either bitter critics or ardent supporters. Four of the Silent Sentinels carried only the purple, white, and gold banners of the N.W.P.; two of them carried lettered banners that read:

MR. PRESIDENT, WHAT WILL YOU DO FOR WOMAN SUFFRAGE? HOW LONG MUST WOMEN WAIT FOR LIBERTY?

For more than five months these Silent Sentinels, soon to be known as Pickets, were permitted to stand in peace. When war broke out in April, 1917, it was decided to continue picketing to express women's demand that they be included in the world democracy for which the war was to be waged, and because the need of giving women the vote in war time had been attested in every great European nation, and had been found a practical step in the midst of war.

But after peaceful picketing had been permitted for nearly half a year, the policy of the police of the District of Columbia was changed and, June 23, 1917, they warned the Suffragists that they would be arrested. However, as picketing in the District was legal, as there was no law against holding a banner at the gate of the White House, and as the United States Constitution guaranteed to all American citizens the right of peaceful petition, the National Woman's Party refused to withdraw the pickets at the order of the police.

During this campaign, every State in the Union was represented on the picket line. Scores of women were arrested but not brought to trial; many others were convicted and their sentences suspended or appealed. More than 500 were arrested during the agitation, and of these 168 served prison terms, some of them several terms. Of the 168, 21 came from Pensylvania, the Keystone State thus providing one-eighth of the group. Here is that roll of honor arranged alphabetically. Where no city is mentioned, Philadelphia may be understood:

> Jennie Bronenberg; Mrs. William Chisolm, Huntingdon; Cora Crawford; Lavinia L. Dock, Fayetteville; Mrs. Mary Carroll Dowell; Mrs. Edmund C. Evans, Ardmore; Mrs. Rose Gratz Fishstein; Rose Fishstein; Reba Gomborov; Kate Heffelfinger, Shamokin; Mary H. Ingham; Marie Ernst Kennedy; Mrs. Lawrence Lewis; Kathryn Lincoln; Dr. Sarah H. Lockrey; Elizabeth Mc Shane; Martha W. Moore; Mrs. Martha Reed Shoemaker; Dr. Caroline Spencer; Ellen Winsor, Haverford; and Mary Winsor, Haverford.

While I had, of course, picketed many times before the arrests began, that was an easy thing to do. But never,

I think, in my life had I dreaded anything more than the thought of going to prison for picketing and never before had a duty faced me that I felt more keenly I should perform. My fellow-workers were making the sacrifice, why not I? And I seemed to be haunted by a reply that Alice Paul had made to a suggestion of mine when, on a visit to Washington, I had said to her that it seemed to me she was too much needed as leader of the campaign to risk imprisonment. She said simply, "I cannot ask others to do what I am not willing to do myself."

A part of my job as Executive Secretary of the Pennsylvania Branch of the National Woman's Party was to get recruits for the picket line. I was thus asking others to do what I had not done and what I was not absolutely sure I could do. But Alice Paul and the Philadelphia member of the Executive Board of the National Woman's Party, Mrs. Lawrence Lewis, continued to say that I was more needed at the Pennsylvania Headquarters than in prison. At the time, the four things for which I seemed to be especially needed in Pennsylvania were to raise campaign funds, to get recruits for picket duty, to prevent disaffection among our members as our campaign became progressively intensified, and, as Chairman of Publicity, not only to keep the newspapers informed, but to try to make their reactions to our campaign as favorable as possible.

As late as August 9, 1918, Alice Paul wrote me:

> . . . Thank you for the list of people you sent for Monday. You did not mention Dr. Butt. Will she return? Please let us know the address of Miss Martha Moore, so that we may communicate with her directly if we need to. May we also have your home address and telephone number, so that we may reach you when you are not at the office.
> . . . You have been a tremendous strength

to us in getting up this demonstration, as all others, and I am sure you know how we appreciate it. You are so valuable on the outside that I am always glad to have you there, rather than in jail, though, of course, we hope that you will be with us in a demonstration if we have to go on with them. I am sure that you will.

I hope that she was right in feeling certain I would, if needed, *serve time*, but the test never came and I cannot be sure.

June 20, 1917, at a meeting in the home of Mrs. James D. Winsor of Haverford, Mrs. Frederic C. Howe, wife of the Commissioner of Immigration of New York City, described with such force and clarity the effect this new method of campaigning was having on the suffrage movement that she should, I think, be quoted at some length. As a Vice-President of the New York State Woman Suffrage Association and as Leader of the 25th Assembly District of the Woman Suffrage Party of New York, Mrs. Howe had had experience in the more conservative suffrage organizations. Also, as an ordained minister who had served for ten years as pastor of the First Unitarian Church of Des Moines, Iowa, she had learned how to reach people. In part, Mrs. Howe said:

The National Woman's Party, formerly the Congressional Union for Woman Suffrage, has experienced a brief, but brilliant career. Four years ago, a great idea lay buried in a committee. The average suffragist had never heard of the federal suffrage amendment. To the general public, it was totally unknown. Four years ago, a group of women, or shall I say two women, brought that great idea out into the light. They made it a matter of vital discussion. Time went on. They made it a matter of violent discussion.

PHILADELPHIANS AT WORK AT WOMAN'S PARTY
CONVENTION HEADQUARTERS, CHICAGO, JUNE, 1916

Left to right: Marie Ernst Kennedy, Elizabeth Elder, Caroline Katzenstein,
Harriet W. Dulles.

NATIONAL WOMAN'S PARTY WORKS TO
DEFEAT DEMOCRATS IN MONTANA, 1916

Left to right: Mrs. Charles S. Haire, Edith B. Barringer, Mrs. G. Kelly,
Caroline Katzenstein.

They made it a political issue. They pushed it out from Washington into New York, Massachusetts, New Jersey, Pennsylvania, across into Ohio and Illinois, across the Mississippi into the middle west, across to the far west and the Pacific Coast, to California and Washington State. From Washington to Washington, from a committee to a political issue—one would say it could not be done; the National Woman's Party did it!

The National Woman's Party did more than this. It created a new spirit. Before Alice Paul had graduated from college,—we had a suffrage spirit in those days too—we used to be so anxious to please, so pleasant and ineffective, so frightened and smiling. Oh, the good old days when Alice Paul was still in college! Where is the anxious fear we used to see at every legislative hearing? Has it disappeared off the face of the earth? Not at all. You see it still at every legislative hearing, only now that fear is on the faces of the legislators.

If you could gather up Alice Paul, Lucy Burns, Anne Martin, Mrs. Belmont and send them all to Siberia, the National Woman's Party would live on in all of us who are here today, in thousands of women who are not here. This new attitude of the woman who respects herself and her cause is unquenchable.

The National Woman's Party did this. It did much more than this. It created a new method. The remarkable thing about this method is the way it retards suffrage. When the pickets stood before the White House, the first thing I heard,— even before I read about them in the newspapers —I heard, "the National Woman's Party has put back suffrage twenty years." And when the women let down their banner in Congress, in that quiet lady-like way to which no reasonable person could really object, again I heard the same comment, "the National Woman's Party had put back suffrage twenty years." And when we introduced the partisan method into our politics, it was prophesied that we had put back suffrage fifty years.

Fifty, plus twenty, plus twenty equals ninety. If we believe our critics, the suffrage movement, by these methods, has been pushed back to the days of Susan B. Anthony. Now, I ask you frankly, are we back to the days before Miss Anthony? Shall we believe our critics or our own eyes? For we plainly see that in the lifetime of the National Woman's Party suffrage has gone forward by leaps and bounds; every dramatic act has accelerated its progress.

Do not be influenced by our critics. They stand with their backs to the future looking to the past for a precedent, and standing so, they cannot read the signs of the times. Turn them right about face. Convert them, every one of them. It can be done. The National Woman's Party is doing it.

That the press in Pennsylvania continued to give us generous space was emphasized in a letter from our national headquarters when Alice Paul wrote me May 3, 1917:

Thank you for the clippings about the hearing. I feel that if we had someone like you in each big city to manage the publicity, it would do more than almost any other thing to advance the federal amendment campaign. I think the publicity which you obtain is better than any which comes from any other city in the country.

In response to an inquiry from the Philadelphia *Evening Bulletin* as to what I thought would be the effect of the picketing campaign on the public, I wrote, June 27, 1917:

I am grieved to think that cultured, high-minded women must suffer because of the refusal of our government to grant them a right that no democracy should withhold. On the other hand, I am proud to know women that care enough about freedom to risk their all in its defense. With every fibre of my being I love courage and freedom and naturally applaud a display of the one for the other.

A prophetic eye is not needed to see that the suffering and sacrifice of these women will fire the women of America as almost nothing else could. What woman can placidly enjoy ease and comfort while other women are imprisoned that she may be free? What man that values his own liberty can see women trampled upon because they demand the freedom he has?

There is strong evidence of the weakness of the government's position when it considers it necessary to attempt to silence a dignified protest that has been voiced for six long months by representative women from all sections of the United States and from several foreign countries. But the spirit of freedom is abroad and no government, not even that of the United States, can crush it.

Again, after the enfranchisement of the women of the country had been achieved—a goal for which the picketing campaign was aimed—the Philadelphia *Evening Bulletin* seemed interested to know if I thought the use of the ballot by women might not affect adversely the social relations between men and women, and perhaps influence men to show women fewer courtesies than before. Here is my reply:

To me, the courtesies that men show women are among the beautiful things of life that make it easier and more worth while. It is not because a woman is not able to pick up her handkerchief, to place a chair for herself, or to open a door that I like these and similar attentions shown her. It is because it helps to make the relations between men and women more attractive.

The winning of the ballot for women should not in the slightest alter her social relations with men. An injustice has been removed. That is all. When she was able to overcome the blind prejudice that denied her a college education, men did not forget that they were gentlemen. We hear today of the "sweet girl graduate" and shower her with flowers and gifts when she leaves college just as if her entrance into learned institutions had not stirred up a veritable nest of hornets and had not been accompanied with dire prophesies that a higher education would kill in her all interest in founding a home of her own and in being the mother of children. Man was, apparently, so modest that he felt only the ignorant woman could love him! Today he realizes that his charm is compelling even to the woman that reads, thinks, and combines intellectuality with grace.

A sensible woman does not, of course, expect all of the attentions that she receives in her drawing room to be extended to her during the rush hours of business. She knows that she must take her place in line when she goes to the bank, buys a theatre or a train ticket, etc. All else being equal, she would not have a tired working man give her his seat on the car. There are, however, numerous little courtesies that even the business man can show to the woman who, like him, earns her daily bread, and these attentions go a long way toward smoothing out the cares of the day.

If to be free intellectually, politically, and otherwise meant to be denied the gallantries of men, I should sorrowfully take my freedom. But, since the two blessings do not clash, I hope and expect to enjoy both.

As effective as the picketing campaign was, it proved an expensive phase of our work. Large amounts of pennants, posters, and other things needed to add color to this spectacular appeal were ruthlessly destroyed by street mobs whom the Washington police made little or no attempt to control. In consequence, our *peaceful ammunition* had constantly to be replaced. Fortunately, an unusual opportunity to raise funds had recently presented itself to Philadelphians. As this makes a cheerful interlude here, I am glad to report it and shall simply call it a *Rummage Sale* and tell how it was managed.

A RUMMAGE SALE

While women, in being denied the vote, were the persons directly aggrieved, it seemed to me that all fair-minded persons in a democracy should feel it a duty to help in removing this injustice. This strong belief stirred me sometimes to ask unusual favors when special needs arose. And such needs did arise several times when we were preparing for our most successful Rummage Sale. The nucleus of this sale was the breaking up of her Germantown home by Mrs. Henry Pemberton, formerly President of the Equal Franchise Society of Philadelphia. As not infrequently happens when one moves from a large and spacious place to smaller quarters, Mrs. Pemberton found many things to give away. These she offered to the Pennsylvania Branch of the National Woman's Party and named a day when I might call at her home to collect them. As usual, we were in need of funds, and this gift naturally suggested a Rummage Sale. And since it was not possible to store the gifts at our Headquarters, I asked the real estate firm of Mastbaum Brothers and Fleisher to lend us a vacant shop for that purpose. Soon a courteous young representative of that firm, Jack Solis-Cohen, Jr., located a shop on Sansom Street conveniently near our Headquarters and placed it at our disposal until we could contact members for additional contributions for the sale. I hired a truck and went out to Mrs. Pemberton's, but little did I realize the number of things she had to give us. Night overtook us before the two haulers and I arrived at the Sansom Street address, but fortunately our storage shop was a second story front room and the street lights helped us to see how to place the things. As the haulers were provided with a strong search light, we were able to climb the narrow steps with safety.

As many of our Main Line members promised contributions of clothes and other things, the question of transportation arose. I asked an important man in one of Philadelphia's large department stores (I think it was Lit Brothers) whether he could arrange to have the store trucks pick up packages for us on their regular Main Line trips. A list of names, addresses, and dates for making these calls was supplied the store and the major part of our transportation problem was thus settled! The store was also kind enough to lend us some display racks on which the better to show our beautiful dresses. Then began our hunt for a large vacant store on Chestnut Street for our rummage sale, and again it was Jack Solis-Cohen, Jr., who came to our rescue with a rent-free store at 1024 Chestnut Street. We were now almost ready for business. Just one more hurdle had to be leaped. As we had been given a number of lovely pieces of art that our Rummage Sale Committee did not feel competent to evaluate, I asked the Bailey, Banks & Biddle Co. if they would help us by having one of their experts appraise our art pieces. Again the answer was a kindly "yes."

In asking help from these various business groups we

were, I think, making friends as we went along. When a person accedes to a request for help, it is likely to stimulate in him an interest in the cause he helps. And when he receives a cordial letter of appreciation for his assistance, the little flame of interest is gently fanned! This might be classified as subtle propaganda or, perhaps, the psychological approach; but we genuinely needed everything we asked for, and the propaganda was simply a campaign by-product.

The sale cleared for us, I think, two thousand dollars, as there was practically no expense attached to it; and we shared our *fortune* with the Headquarters of the National Woman's Party in Washington. Although I cannot find an official record of the yield from our sale, the amount was at that time so outstanding that I feel sure I recall it with accuracy. Anyway, as proof of its success, I received this letter from Alice Paul, dated May 20, 1917:

> I want to thank the Pennsylvania Branch for the $500.00 from the Rummage sale, which reached here while I was in the South. I believe the Treasurer has already sent you a letter of acknowledgment, but I want in addition to express to you my own deep appreciation of this help. I had no idea that a rummage sale could be so profitable.
>
> This gift has lightened our hearts. Please convey our thanks to the Pennsylvania Committee.

Despite the government's attempt to silence the women's demand for justice by imprisoning the pickets on such a trumped-up charge as "obstructing traffic," the campaign progressed with increased vigor.

Persons who, while not opposed to the picketing, had not previously been sufficiently sure of the effectiveness of this new method of publicity to feel impelled to take part in it, now began to see the necessity of becoming active participants in the campaign. Conspicuous among these new recruits for picketing was one of Philadelphia's grandest women, Miss Mary H. Ingham. I believe that Miss Ingham truly wrestled with her soul for three days and nights before she was sure that it was her duty to follow where Alice Paul, Lucy Burns, and Mrs. Lawrence Lewis had led the way into prison itself. And surely no one knowing Miss Ingham could have questioned either her courage, or her devotion to political equality for women. What I wish to emphasize is Miss Ingham's eagerness to know the right and her dedication to it when once she had seen it.

Miss Ingham was a graduate of Bryn Mawr College. She had spent two years at the Woman's Medical College of Pennsylvania; had for three years been an instructor in the History of Art at Miss Irwin's School; had served as Secretary of the National Progressive League in 1912; been a member of the Board of Corporators of the Woman's Medical College of Pennsylvania; a member of the Board of Directors of the Bureau of Municipal Research; and, in addition to her various other activities, she had worked as a leader in both the State and national suffrage campaigns. After Pennsylvania voters defeated the Suffrage Amendment in 1915, her great strength became a vital factor in the achievements of the National Woman's Party, with which she worked until the campaign ended.

July 14, 1917, Miss Ingham was one of sixteen pickets at the White House gates. Among them were Mrs. John Winters Brannan, of New York City, daughter of Charles A. Dana, Founder and Editor of the New York *Sun,* and wife of Dr. Brannan, President of the Board of Trustees of Bellevue Hospital; Mrs. Gilson Gardner, of Washington, D. C., daughter of Frederick Hall, for many years

Editor of the Chicago *Tribune,* and wife of the Washington representative of the Scripps papers; Mrs. Florence Bayard Hilles, of Newcastle, Delaware, whose father, Thomas F. Bayard, was the first American Ambassador to Great Britain, and Secretary of State under President Cleveland; Mrs. J. A. H. Hopkins, of Morristown, N. J., whose husband was a leader of the Progressive Party, and later served on the Democratic National Campaign Committee in 1916; Miss Anne Martin, of Reno, Nevada, a graduate of Leland Stanford University, and Professor of History at the University of Nevada; Mrs. Betsy Reyneau, wife of Paul Reyneau, portrait painter; Mrs. John Rogers, Jr., of New York City, wife of a celebrated physician, and a descendant of Roger Sherman, one of the signers of the Declaration of Independence; and Miss Doris Stevens, graduate of Oberlin College, social worker and teacher. All of the 16 women were arrested, tried, and convicted. A sentence of 60 days in prison was imposed. But this time they had a friend at court!

Dudley Field Malone was one of a group of prominent men attending the trial; and his presence made possible one of the brightest pages in the history of the woman suffrage movement. Mr. Malone, Collector of the Port of New York, was not only a friend of President Wilson's and a supporter of the President's political career from its beginning, but he was also an ardent Suffragist. So greatly was he stirred by the trial and the outrageous sentence meted out to the women, that he went from the court directly to the White House and told the President he had come to resign his office of Collector of the Port of New York. A lengthy but very unsatisfactory discussion followed. However, at Mr. Wilson's earnest request, Mr. Malone consented to delay taking this step until the President had had an opportunity to investigate the facts that

Mr. Malone had presented to him. What followed will be told in the next chapter.

Not only did Mr. Malone dedicate himself with magnificent courage and unselfishness to the work carried on at the Headquarters of the N.W.P. in Washington, but he took time to advise us in Pennsylvania of ways by which we could give effective support to the national campaign. In a letter dated September 11, 1917, he wrote me:

> Will you not make the situation emphatic by getting every man and woman you know to send individual telegrams to the President, their Senators and Congressman, urging immediate passage of the Federal Suffrage Amendment as a war measure and a measure of justice?

The urgent need to work for the Federal Suffrage Amendment was also emphasized by Mrs. Ida Husted Harper when a few days later, October 31st, 1917, she wrote giving me details of recent work in a number of States where women had campaigned for different forms of partial suffrage—some of the legislation successful, and some of it declared unconstitutional by the Supreme Court. She closed her letter with this interesting comment:

> All of these partial suffrage victories are good for agitation, for rousing the women and educating public sentiment, but of course they are merely stepping-stones to the Federal Amendment, and after November 6th no *real* believer in woman suffrage will ever again voice an objection to this Amendment.

The effectiveness of the picketing campaign was noted in the Call to the third Annual Convention of the Pennsylvania Branch of the N.W.P. This convention was held in Philadelphia November 19, 1917, when Miss Mary H. Ingham was the State's Acting Chairman. The Call read:

> Since we last met in Convention, great strides have been made in the progress of the federal suffrage amendment. Our "Silent Sentinels" have held the freedom of 20,000,000 American women constantly before the public at a time when this necessary reform might otherwise have been overshadowed by a world war. An unfriendly Administration has been forced to grant small concessions and a "War Congress" has taken favorable action in both the Senate and the House. The Susan B. Anthony Amendment, after a burial of six months, has been reported out of the Senate Suffrage Committee to a place on the calendar of the Senate, and a resolution creating a Committee on Woman Suffrage in the House of Representatives has been passed by a vote of 181 to 147, a significant suffrage majority.
>
> For the first time in our history, American women have been sent to prison for asking to be free. One hundred and fourteen suffragists have been arrested for peacefully picketing the White House, and sixty-six of them have been sentenced to serve from three days to seven months in Occoquan Workhouse, and the national jail in Washington. Today, Alice Paul, Lucy Burns and fifteen other members of the National Woman's Party are behind prison bars, many of them in solitary confinement. Their courage and devotion to a principle have paved the way for an early victory.
>
> Every political party has endorsed woman suffrage, and the *National Party,* newly formed in Chicago by a union of several political parties, has made the demand for the national suffrage amendment one of the strongest planks in its platform. It has invited the National Woman's

Party to join forces with it, either by completely merging into one political organization or by coöperating in the next Congressional election.

We ask you to meet with us on the eve of the opening of Congress to plan how we may best use this strategic situation, so that suffrage may be made a war measure and the long struggle for woman's freedom be brought to an end.

Our one-day convention gave added proof that the picketing campaign had done more than have a wholesome effect upon Congress and the Wilson Administration. It had won many new friends and increased financial support for the passage of the Susan B. Anthony Amendment. At the evening meeting in the Ball Room of the Bellevue Stratford, Dudley Field Malone made a stirring speech. He aroused so much enthusiasm that when an appeal for campaign funds was made the audience responded by pledging more than $2,200 in sums ranging from $1 to $100.

Although Mr. Malone had refused to charge any fee for his legal services to the National Woman's Party, the organization's leaders in Washington realized that his continued professional help simply could not be accepted without some compensation. In giving up his position as Collector of the Port of New York, he had already made a great financial sacrifice, which Suffragists could never repay. Mrs. Lawrence Lewis telephoned us from Washington to ask our help in raising a $5,000 fee for Mr. Malone. A little telephoning from our Headquarters brought gifts of $750 from Miss Fanny Travis Cochran, and $250 from Miss Mary A. Burnham.

Mr. Abraham Sussman, whose excellent article on Woman Suffrage had been copied in the *Suffragist,* kindly offered to give us two columns of space a week in the

PENNSYLVANIA PICKETS THAT SERVED PRISON TERMS

Left to right, top row: Elizabeth McShane, Martha Reed Shoemaker, Rose G. Fishstein, Kate C. Heffelfinger. *Middle row:* Mary H. Ingham, Mrs. Lawrence Lewis, Mrs. William W. Chisolm. *Bottom row:* Kathryn Lincoln, Mary Carroll Dowell, Cora Crawford, Reba Gomborov.

PENNSYLVANIA PICKETS THAT SERVED PRISON TERMS

Left to right, top row: Ellen Winsor, Rebecca Winsor Evans, Mary Winsor. *Middle row:* Dr. Caroline E. Spencer, Lavinia L. Dock, Dr. Sarah H. Lockrey, Rose Fishstein. *Bottom row:* Jennie Bronenberg, Marie Ernst Kennedy, Martha W. Moore.

Jewish World. By the middle of December, the first two instalments had been sent him.

November 17, Martha Davis invited Lucy G. Branham and me to meet Mrs. Imogen Oakley, Mrs. Edward Biddle, Miss Constance Biddle, Mrs. Walter Cope, and Mrs. Harrison Morris at her home, 1822 Pine Street, to talk over the conditions at Occoquan Workhouse and the District Jail. Lucy Branham was an ideal person to arouse the interest of her audience. She looked more like a pretty débutante than the holder of an M.A. from Johns Hopkins, the winner of a Carnegie hero medal for rescuing a man and woman from drowning at St. Petersburg, Florida, and a picket with a sentence of 60 days in Occoquan and the District Jail to her credit. So successful was she in painting the horror of confinement in the two penal institutions that Mrs. Cope planned immediately to make some kind of public protest. In consequence, Lucy Branham and Mrs. Helena Hill Weed were asked to speak at the annual meeting of the Prison Reform League at the College Club in Philadelphia, December 11th. At this meeting, a resolution was passed to support the Congressional investigation of the prison conditions the pickets had had to face.

6

THE ADMINISTRATION'S OPPOSITION CONTINUES . . . DUDLEY FIELD MALONE RESIGNS . . . THE COURT EXONERATES PICKETS 1917-1918

When Dudley Field Malone had his interview with President Wilson on the suffrage situation July 14, 1917, he explained that he had come to place in the President's hands his resignation as Collector of the Port of New York. Although the President "earnestly urged" Mr. Malone "not to resign" and said, "If the situation is as you describe it, it is shocking," the arrest and imprisonment of the pickets on trumped-up charges continued, and there seemed to be no disposition on the part of the Administration to relax its opposition to the passage of the suffrage amendment.

After waiting nearly two months, Mr. Malone, September 7th, formally resigned. As he saw the suffrage situation, his pledge to the women voters of the West when he was campaigning for President Wilson's re-election in 1916, a pledge which the President "had approved," left no other course open to him. He acted with the courage and determination his character demanded.

Mr. Malone's letter:

September 7, 1917.

The President,
The White House,
Washington, D. C.
Dear Mr. President:

Last autumn, as the representative of your Administration, I went into the woman suffrage states to urge your re-election. The most difficult argument to meet among the seven million voters was the failure of the Democratic party, throughout four years of power, to pass the federal suffrage amendment looking toward the enfranchisement of all the women of the country. Throughout those states, and particularly in California, which ultimately decided the election by the votes of women, the women voters were urged to support you, even though Judge Hughes had already declared for the federal suffrage amendment, because you and your party, through liberal leadership, were more likely nationally to enfranchise the rest of the women of the country than were your opponents.

And if the women of the West voted to re-elect you, I promised them that I would spend all my energy, at any sacrifice to myself, to get the present Democratic Administration to pass the federal suffrage amendment.

But the present policy of the Administration, in permitting splendid American women to be sent to jail in Washington, not for carrying offensive banners, not for picketing, but on the technical charge of obstructing traffic, is a denial even of their constitutional right to petition for, and demand the passage of, the federal suffrage amendment. It, therefore, now becomes my profound obligation actively to keep my promise to the women of the West.

In more than twenty states it is a practical impossibility to amend the state constitutions; so the women of those States can only be enfranchised by the passage of the federal suffrage amendment. Since England and Russia, in the midst of the great war, have assured the national enfranchisement of their women, should we not be jealous to maintain our democratic leadership in the world by the speedy national enfranchisement of American women?

To me, Mr. President, as I urged upon you in Washington two months ago, this is not only a measure of justice and democracy, it is also an urgent war measure. The women of the nation are, and always will be, loyal to the country, and the passage of the suffrage amendment is only the first step toward their national emancipation. But unless the government takes at least this first step toward their enfranchisement, how can the government ask millions of American women, educated in our schools and colleges, and millions of American women in our homes, or toiling for economic independence in every line of industry, to give up by conscription their men and happiness to a war for democracy in Europe, while these women citizens are denied the right to vote on the policies of the government which demands of them such sacrifice?

For this reason many of your most ardent friends and supporters feel that the passage of the federal suffrage amendment is a war measure which could appropriately be urged by you at this session of Congress. It is true that this amendment would have to come from Congress, but the present Congress shows no earnest desire to enact this legislation for the simple reason that you, as the leader of the party in power, have not yet suggested it.

For the whole country gladly acknowledges, Mr. President, that no vital piece of legislation has come through Congress these five years except by your extraordinary and brilliant leadership. And what millions of men and women today hope

INEZ MILHOLLAND

PRESIDENT WOODROW WILSON PASSES SILENT
SUFFRAGE PICKETS AT WHITE HOUSE GATES

is that you will give the federal suffrage amendment to the women of the country by the valor
of your leadership now. It will hearten the
mothers of the nation, eliminate a just grievance,
and turn the devoted energies of brilliant women
to a more hearty support of the Government in
this crisis.

As you well know, in dozens of speeches in
many states I have advocated your policies and
the war. I was the first man of your Administration, nearly five years ago, to publicly advocate preparedness, and helped to found the first
Plattsburg training camp. And if, with our troops
mobilizing in France, you will give American
women this measure for their political freedom,
they will support with greater enthusiasm your
hope and the hope of America for world freedom.

I have not approved all the methods recently
adopted by women in pursuit of their political
liberty; yet, Mr. President, the Committee on
Suffrage of the United States Senate was formed
in 1883, when I was one year old; this same federal suffrage amendment was first introduced in
Congress in 1878; brave women like Susan B.
Anthony were petitioning Congress for the suffrage before the Civil War, and at the time of
the Civil War men like William Lloyd Garrison,
Horace Greeley, and Wendell Phillips assured the
suffrage leaders that if they abandoned their fight
for suffrage, when the war was ended the men
of the nation, "out of gratitude" would enfranchise the women of the country!

And if the men of this country had been
peacefully demanding for over half a century
the political right or privilege to vote, and had
been continuously ignored or met with evasion
by successive Congresses, as have the women,
you, Mr. President, as a lover of liberty, would
be the first to comprehend and forgive their inevitable impatience and righteous indignation.

Will not this Administration, re-elected to power by the hope and faith of the women of the West, handsomely reward that faith by taking action now for the passage of the federal suffrage amendment?

In the Port of New York, during the last four years, billions of dollars in the export and import trade of the country have been handled by the men of the customs service; their treatment of the traveling public has radically changed, their vigilance supplied the evidence of the Lusitania note; the neutrality was rigidly maintained; the great German fleet guarded, captured, and repaired—substantial economies and reforms have been concluded and my ardent industry has been given to this great office of your appointment.

But now I wish to leave these finished tasks, to return to my profession of the law, and to give all my leisure time to fight as hard for the political freedom of women as I have always fought for your liberal leadership.

It seems a long seven years, Mr. President, since I first campaigned with you when you were running for Governor of New Jersey. In every circumstance throughout those years I have served you with the most respectful affection and unshadowed devotion. It is no small sacrifice now for me, as a member of your Administration, to sever our political relationship. But I think it is high time that men in this generation, at some cost to themselves, stood up to battle for the national enfranchisement of American women. So in order effectively to keep my promise made in the West and more freely to go into this larger field of democratic effort, I hereby resign my office as Collector of the Port of New York, to take effect at once, or at your earliest convenience.

Yours respectfully,
Dudley Field Malone.

The President replied:

U.S.S. Mayflower,
12 September, 1917.

The White House
Washington
My dear Mr. Collector:

Your letter of September 7th reached me just before I left home and I have, I am sorry to say, been unable to reply to it sooner.

I must frankly say that I cannot regard your reasons for resigning your position as Collector of Customs as convincing, but it is so evidently your wish to be relieved from the duties of the office that I do not feel at liberty to withhold my acceptance of your resignation. Indeed, I judge from your letter that any discussion of the reasons would not be acceptable to you and that it is your desire to be free of the restraints of public office. I, therefore, accept your resignation, to take effect as you have wished.

I need not say that our long association in public affairs makes me regret the action you have taken most sincerely.

Very truly yours,
Woodrow Wilson.

Hon. Dudley Field Malone,
Collector of Customs,
New York City.

Mr. Malone sent the following reply:

New York, N. Y.,
September 15, 1917.

The President,
The White House,
Washington, D. C.
Dear Mr. President:

Thank you sincerely for your courtesy, for I knew you were on a well-earned holiday and I did not expect an earlier reply to my letter of September 7th, 1917.

After a most careful re-reading of my letter, I am unable to understand how you could judge that any discussion by you of my reasons for resigning would not be acceptable to me since my letter was an appeal to you on specific grounds for action now by the Administration on the Federal Suffrage amendment.

However, I am profoundly grateful to you for your prompt acceptance of my resignation.

Yours respectfully,
Dudley Field Malone.

Knowing what a drawing card Mr. Malone would be at an important meeting of the National Woman's Party in Philadelphia, September 19, we asked if he could accept an engagement with us for that date. He replied September 17, 1917:

Treasury Department
United States Customs Service
New York
September 17, 1917.

Miss Caroline Katzenstein,
213 Hale Building,
Philadelphia, Pa.
Dear Miss Katzenstein:

I am deeply sorry that I cannot come to Philadelphia on Wednesday evening, for my time is completely occupied in moving myself from public to private life; but I do wish you would say to those in attendance at your meeting that while I have been heartily in favor of the war and deem it the duty of every good citizen loyally and conscientiously to support the Government, we should also have the ambition not only "to make the world safe for democracy," but also to make America safe for democracy, and to make

that brand of democracy safe for both America
and the world, and this cannot be done until by
the passage of the Federal Suffrage amendment
the franchise has been given to the women of
this country.

Yours faithfully,
Dudley Field Malone.

Another friend among the many that spoke out in
behalf of the pickets was Gilson Gardner, the distinguished
journalist, who went to Africa to meet Theodore Roosevelt
and was with him on his return to America. In writing to
his friend, Raymond Pullman, Chief of Police in Washington, D. C., Mr. Gardner pointed out the inconsistencies
of the Police Chief in giving the Suffragists adequate protection while they picketed the White House for five
months both before and after the war, and then in having
them sent to jail and workhouse, in permitting the crowds
to mob them, and his own officers forcibly to take the
women's banners from them.

Mr. Gardner reminded Mr. Pullman of the efficient
protection the police were allowed to give a thousand
Suffragists when they marched around the White House
March third, 1917, and he suggested that if persons in
authority over Mr. Pullman were not willing to let him
continue to do his duty, it was up to him to resign. Being
forced, wrote Mr. Gardner, to "yield your judgment to
the District Commissioners who have yielded their judgment to the White House" makes "being Chief of Police
under such circumstances hardly worth while."

Not only were individuals in high places now coming
to the support of the pickets, but leading newspapers were
aiding the suffrage campaign by emphasizing the Administra-
ion's responsibility for the harsh and unjustifiable treatment of the pickets. Also, they were critical of the Wash-

ington police for failing to protect the women from hood-
lums in and out of the government service. The courage
and determination of the women in demanding the franchise had won the respect and admiration of this portion
of the press, even if not every detail of the picketing campaign was endorsed by it.

Two fine editorials should be especially mentioned, one
in the Washington, D. C., *Herald* of August 19, 1917, and
one in the Boston *Journal* the following day. The latter
was written by Herbert N. Pinkham, Jr., who in closing
his editorial gave this summary of the situation:

> All this suffrage shouting in Washington has
> as its single object the attainment of President
> Wilson's material support for equal suffrage. . . .
> President Wilson's word would carry the ques-
> tion into Congress. . . .
> Would there be any harm in letting Congress
> vote on a suffrage resolution? That would end
> the disturbance and it would make our shield of
> national justice somewhat brighter.
> It looks like President Wilson's move.

The "move" made by the Administration was one of
such intensified brutality as to be almost unbelievable. But
this renewed attempt to conquer the spirit of the Suffragists failed.

It is to emphasize the fact that President Wilson
simply forced the women to resort to extreme measures
in order to bring about his final capitulation that I have
interrupted the activities of the pickets to let the reader
see some of the public's reaction to the Administration's
stand.

Also I am eager to have everyone who feels as I do,
that the patience of Suffragists had been taxed to the

uttermost, admire to the full the courage, heroism, and unwavering determination of the pickets to win their fight for freedom no matter what price they had to pay or what personal sacrifice it required. And, too, I should like, if I can, to lessen the antagonism of others, who have in the past been critical of the pickets and whose opposition may have been based not only on an ultra conservative attitude toward them, but on incomplete information at the time they formed their adverse opinion.

October 6th, 1917, saw the last picketing of the Emergency War Session of the Sixty-fifth Congress, the date on which Congress adjourned. Ten of the eleven women in the picket line carried the purple, white, and gold pennants of their organization. Their leader, Alice Paul, carried a white banner on which was inscribed:

MR. PRESIDENT, WHAT WILL YOU DO FOR WOMAN SUFFRAGE?

Looking neither to the right nor left, the women marched from their Headquarters in Cameron House, diagonally across from the White House, toward the Executive Mansion. Before they could reach the White House gates, a sailor attacked them. Several pennants were torn from the pickets' hands, thrown to the ground, and trampled upon. Without saying a word, the women stooped and recovered their pennants, and soon the eleven, standing a few feet apart, with their backs to the fence, were stationed on both sides of the gates. Although the passing crowd had had an opportunity to read the message on the leader's banner, and the press had been able to broadcast it to the country, when Alice Paul reached the White House gates, she had only her bare staff left.

Soon the clang of the patrol was heard and the eleven women disappeared from the front of one government building into the inside of another. At the police station they were charged with "obstructing traffic," but the crowds watching the World Series returns that same day in Washington—crowds so dense that mounted police had to clear a space for the cars—were not considered a menace to the peace and calm of the nation's Capital.

Released on bail, the women were ordered to appear the following Monday, October 8th, for trial. At the trial they would not recognize the Court. They refused to be sworn, to question witnesses, or to speak in their own behalf. As quoted in the *Suffragist,* Alice Paul said:

> We do not wish to make any plea before this Court. We do not consider ourselves subject to this Court since, as an unenfranchised class, we have nothing to do with the making of the laws which have put us in this position.

To the surprise of the women, the Judge suspended sentence, and restored the bail they had furnished October 6th. No reason was given for this action. The charge, however, was not dismissed.

October 15th, four of the women under this suspended sentence picketed again, and were again arrested. This time Judge Mullowny offered them the choice of a $25.00 fine or six months in the District Workhouse. As usual, the fine was refused. In court, Rose Winslow, one of the four, said:

> . . . You can send us to jail, but you know that we have broken no law. You know that we have not even committed the technical offense on which we were arrested. You know that we are guiltless.

October 20, 1917, four other pickets stood at the West gate of the White House. Alice Paul's banner had a quotation from President Wilson, one that had recently been used on the 1917 posters for the Second Liberty Bond Loan:

THE TIME HAS COME TO CONQUER OR SUBMIT. FOR US THERE CAN BE BUT ONE CHOICE. WE HAVE MADE IT.

Dr. Caroline Spencer, of Philadelphia, carried a banner with a message that was a heritage from 1776:

RESISTANCE TO TYRANNY IS OBEDIENCE TO GOD.

As soon as the police had allowed a large enough crowd to assemble, they arrested the women and took them to the district jail. Alice Paul and Dr. Spencer, who had carried the banners, were sentenced to seven months in jail. The other pickets were given the choice of a five dollar fine or thirty days in jail and, as usual, they refused to pay a fine.

At this same time, the four women, arrested on both October 6 and 15, came up for further sentence. Rose Winslow, one of the four, spoke of the confusion of the Suffragists, and admitted that they were not more nonplussed than Judge Mullowny admitted the Court was. She said:

> You sentence us to jail for a few days, then you sentence us to the workhouse for thirty days, then sixty, and then you suspend sentence. Sometimes we are accused of carrying seditious banners, then of obstructing traffic. How do you expect us to see any consistency in the law, or in your sentence?

The Court smiled. In pronouncing the sentence, an additional thirty days was given the pickets: "First, you will serve six months, and then you will serve one month more."

During Alice Paul's imprisonment in the District Jail, I obtained permission to see her a few minutes. Knowing that I should be allowed only a brief visit and that she would wish above all things to have news about the campaign, I put some press clippings up my sleeve and hoped to be able to slip them to her when I leaned over to kiss her while she was in bed. But the heat of my body must have taken all the crispness from the clippings and they just would not tumble down! Also, I was conscious of being watched and did not dare do anything that might make it more difficult for some one else to visit our leader. I hurriedly told her as much as I could.

But the thing that stands out most clearly in my memory was Alice Paul's absolute fearlessness although she was behind prison bars. She seemed determined to let the official standing near realize that his severe treatment of them would be known to the outside world. She raised her voice so that he might hear, and began to tell me the unnecessary restrictions he had imposed upon them. "He will not let us"—one thing after another she listed. And in the listing she gave full vent to her righteous indignation.

When I left, I felt I had seen a miscarriage of justice that just did not seem possible in a democratic country like ours. Like thousands of others, I realized what Alice Paul's imprisonment in defense of a principle would do for the promotion of that principle. A short-sighted Administration had unintentionally stirred the followers of a great leader to re-dedicate themselves to the Cause, which she and they held dear.

The frightful conditions in the District Jail that Rose Winslow was able to make public through her smuggled notes to friends must have given penologists food for thought. Let us hope they shamed the authorities responsible for them. Here are extracts from those notes:

The women are all so magnificent, so beautiful. Alice Paul is as thin as ever, pale and large-eyed. We have been in solitary for five weeks. There is nothing to tell but that the days go by somehow. I have felt quite feeble the last few days—faint, so that I could hardly get my hair combed, my arms ached so. But today I am well again. Alice Paul and I talk back and forth though we are at opposite ends of the building and a hall door also shuts us apart. But occasionally—thrills—we escape from behind our iron-barred doors and visit. Great laughter and rejoicing! . . .

I told about a syphilitic woman with one leg. The other one was cut off, having rotted so that it was alive with maggots when she came in. The remaining one is now getting as bad. They are so short of nurses that a little colored girl of twelve, who is here waiting to have her tonsils removed, waits on her. This child and two others share a ward with a syphilitic child of three or four years, whose mother refused to have it at home. It makes you absolutely ill to see it. I am going to break all three windows as a protest against their boarding Alice Paul with these!

Dr. Gannon is chief of a hospital. Yet Alice Paul and I found we had been taking baths in one of the tubs here, in which this syphilitic child, an incurable, who has his eyes bandaged all the time, is also bathed. He has been here a year. Into the room where he lives came yesterday two children to be operated on for tonsilitis. They also bathed in the same tub. The syphilitic woman has been in that room seven months. Cheerful mixing, isn't it? The place is alive with roaches, crawling all over the walls everywhere. I found one in my bed the other day . . . .

Women from far and near rallied to the picket campaign when the news reached them that Alice Paul, October

20, 1917, had been sent to prison to begin serving her sentence of seven months. Plans were made for a demonstration November 10 with forty-one women on the picket line as a protest against their leader's imprisonment.

The night before the demonstration, the forty-one women and other friends of the cause went to the jail to try to communicate with Alice Paul. Katherine Morey led the delegation. She and Catherine Flanagan rang the door bell of Warden Zinkhan's house which was near the wing of the prison where Alice Paul was confined. They were told that the warden was ill and unable to see them. By a pre-arranged signal the two leaders notified the silent, waiting crowd of pickets and friends behind them and the whole group ran quickly and stood under Alice Paul's window. Before the prison guard could push them out of the yard, they were able to give the prisoner their names, announce the large amount of money received that day by the National Woman's Party, and tell her that forty-one women would be on the picket line the next day.

Almost immediately the whole group was arrested, and two days later, November 12th, they were tried. Again the charge was "obstructing traffic" and again the women pleaded "Not Guilty."

Among the witnesses that refuted absolutely the testimony offered by police sergeants and plain-clothes men, was Miss Mary H. Ingham of Philadelphia.

Mrs. John Winters Brannan said:

> The responsibility for an agitation like ours against injustice rests with those who deny justice, not those who demand it. Whatever may be the verdict of this Court, we shall continue our agitation until the grievance of American women is redressed.

Mrs. Harvey W. Wiley said:

> I want to state that we took this action with
> great consecration of spirit. We took this action
> with willingness to sacrifice our personal liberty in
> order to focus the attention of the nation on the
> injustice of our disfranchisement, that we might
> thereby win political liberty for all the women of
> the country. The Constitution says that Congress
> shall not in any way abridge the right of citizens
> peacefully to assemble and petition. That is ex-
> actly what we did. We peacefully assembled and
> then proceeded with our petition to the President
> for the redress of our grievance of disfranchise-
> ment . . . .

Judge Mullowny complained, "The trouble of the situation is that the Court has not been given the power to meet
it. It is very, very puzzling." Without imposing sentence,
he dismissed the pickets and said he would take the case
under advisement.

One hour later, twenty-seven of the women, just tried,
left Headquarters with four other pickets and, after walk-
ing twice up and down in front of the White House, the
thirty-one pickets stationed themselves at the White House
gates.

The police were taken by surprise, but they arrested the
women and took them in commandeered cars to police headquarters where they were ordered to appear in court
November 14. Kept waiting all morning, the women were
told by Judge Mullowny to come back November 16.

November 13, thirty-one pickets went out again and this
time they found the crowd friendly. Suddenly the same uni-
formed yeoman who, on August 15, had dragged Alice Paul
over thirty feet of pavement, began to destroy the banners,
but the pickets continued on their way carrying the bare

poles. When the friendly crowd showed its disapproval, the yeoman was arrested. By this time, he had destroyed six banners.

The long line of pickets that stretched from gate to gate were allowed to stand so long a time that they began to think the Administration had changed its attitude toward them. Suddenly, however, the patrol wagon appeared and all of the pickets were arrested. As the bail furnished by many of them the previous day had not been refunded, they refused to give more. They were kept in the house of detention over night and as that institution had only two rooms with eight beds in each room some of the women slept on the floor. The next day they were tried and sentenced. Three were given fifteen days, twenty-four were given thirty days, and the aged Mrs. Nolan's sentence was for six days. The three most heavily penalized pickets were Mrs. Lawrence Lewis and Mrs. John Winters Brannan, each of whom was given sixty days, and Lucy Burns, whose sentence was six months.

These women went through the *Night of Terror* which will be described in another chapter.

November 17th, Mrs. Harvey W. Wiley, Mrs. William Kent, and Elizabeth McShane of Philadelphia were given sentences of fifteen days on the November 10th charges.

Toward the end of November, a curious thing happened. At nine o'clock one evening, when all the prisoners were supposed to be in bed, a stranger entered Alice Paul's room. The visitor, a newspaperman known to be closely associated with the Administration, turned out to be David Lawrence. For two hours, Alice Paul talked over the situation with him and, although he did not say that he had come from the Administration, his visit spoke for itself. I shall report this incident as Maud Younger told it on many platforms:

> He asked Miss Paul how long she and the
> other pickets would give the Administration be-

fore they began picketing again. She said it would depend upon the attitude the Administration and Congress seemed to be taking toward the Federal Amendment. He said he believed the prohibition amendment would be brought up and passed, and after that was out of the way the suffrage amendment would be taken up.

He asked if we would be content to have it go through one House this session and wait till the next session for it to pass the other House. Miss Paul said that if the amendment did not go through both Houses this session, the Woman's Party would not be satisfied.

Then the man said he believed that the President would not mention Suffrage in his message at the opening of Congress, but would make it known to the leaders of Congress that he wanted it passed and would see that it passed.

He said in effect: Now the great difficulty is for these hunger-strikers to be recognized as political prisoners. Every day you hunger-strike, you advertise the idea of political prisoners throughout the country. It would be the easiest thing in the world for the Administration to treat you as political prisoners; to put you in a fine house in Washington; give you the best of food; take the best of care of you; but if we treat you as political prisoners, we would have to treat other groups which might arise in opposition to the war program as political prisoners too, and that would throw a bomb in our war program. It would never do. It would be easier to give you the Suffrage Amendment than to treat you as political prisoners.

November 27 and 28, just a few days after David Lawrence's visit to Alice Paul, the government, without giving any reason, released all of the suffrage prisoners.

The story of this visit to Alice Paul's cell was of course

given wide publicity by speakers of the National Woman's Party and it finally appeared in the *Milwaukee Leader* and in the *San Francisco Bulletin,* in an article by John D. Barry. At once, the National Association Opposed to Woman Suffrage questioned the truth of the incident.

As prophesied by David Lawrence, President Wilson did not mention suffrage in his message to Congress when it convened December 3, 1917, but, on January 9, 1918, the evening before the victorious vote in the House, the President came out in favor of the National Suffrage Amendment.

Immediately, the General Secretary of the National Association Opposed to Woman Suffrage, Minnie Bronson, sent a letter of apology to Alice Paul for questioning the truth of her statement. In her letter she also repeated Maud Younger's statement on David Lawrence's visit and said:

> The inference contained in this article that the President of the United States would under cover assist a proposition which he had publicly and unqualifiedly repudiated, seemed to us unworthy of his high office, and we felt justified in defending him from what seemed an unwarranted and unbelievable accusation.
>
> However, the President's subsequent public support of the Federal Suffrage Amendment, his announcement coming on the eve of the vote in the House of Representatives, indicates the truth of your original assertion, and we therefore deem it incumbent upon ourselves to apologize for having questioned Miss Younger's statement.
>
> We are sending a copy of this letter to the President and members of Congress.

When the picketing campaign first began, even some of the members of the National Woman's Party found it too radical a measure for their endorsement and some of them

MRS. FREDERIC C. HOWE   LUCY BURNS

LUCY G. BRANHAM

Mrs. Howe was a member of the Advisory Council, Miss Burns a Founder and Vice-Chairman, and Miss Branham an organizer of the National Woman's Party.

PICKETS ARRESTED ON CHARGE OF OBSTRUCTING
TRAFFIC IN FRONT OF THE WHITE HOUSE

resigned. On the other hand, the courage of the National Woman's Party and its insistent demand for simple justice not in some distant tomorrow but in the immediate today won the organization large numbers of new members. And the effectiveness of the picketing became so evident as time went on that the majority of those members that had withdrawn their support came back into the organization. Also, the picketing and its results unloosed purse strings in an amazing way. At times receipts doubled what they had been in corresponding months of the year before picketing began. And once they rose to six times the normal amount.

It has been emphasized many times that the pickets, at their trials, were puzzled by the diversity of charges brought against them for the same "offense," and by the widely different decisions handed down by the presiding Judges at these trials. It, therefore, seems fitting to close this chapter on picketing by giving a few details of damage suits filed by some of the women subjected to the greatest abuse during the "night of terror" at the workhouse. These suits, it should be explained, were not brought in a spirit of revenge, but to prevent the Administration's forgetting its record of brutality unless it made amends by passing the suffrage amendment.

After Judge Edmund Waddill had handed down a decision that the commitment of the pickets to Occoquan was illegal, sixteen suits for damage were filed by the pickets. Eight of these suits were filed in the United States Court for the Western District of Virginia at Richmond and were brought against Superintendent Whittaker, of the Workhouse at Occoquan, and his assistant, Captain Reams, because of their brutal treatment of the women while they were at Occoquan. The other eight suits were filed in the Supreme Court of the District of Columbia at Washington, and were against the Commissioners of the District of Columbia and

Superintendent Zinkhan of the District Jail for the unlawful transfer of the pickets to Occoquan Workhouse.

It was before Chief Justice Smyth, and Justices Robb and Van Orsdel in the District of Columbia Court of Appeals, January 8, 1918, that the appeals in the cases of two groups of women arrested August 23 and 28 came up. Representing the Suffragists were Matthew O'Brien, of Washington, and Dudley Field Malone, of New York. The case for the Government was conducted by Corporation Counsel Stevens.

"Suppose," suggested Justice Robb, "some upholders of Billy Sunday should go out on the streets with banners on which were painted some of Billy's catch phrases, and should stand with their backs to the fence, and a curious crowd gathered, some of whom created disorder and threw stones at the carriers of the banners. Who should be arrested, those who created the disorder, or the banner carriers?"

Mr. Stevens gave it as his opinion that both parties should be arrested.

"Did I make myself clear that the banner carriers were perfectly peaceful?" Justice Robb asked.

"When it is commonly known there is a fortyfoot sidewalk there?" Justice Van Orsdel reinforced him.

"Well, then," observed Attorney O'Brien, when he answered Mr. Stevens in his argument, "the honorable Justices obstruct traffic, according to learned counsel's definition, when court adjourns, and they walk down the street together."

In the opinion handed down by Judge Van Orsdel, March 4, and concurred in by the other two judges of the Court, it was stated that in the case of those pickets that appealed, no information had been filed that justified their arrest and sentence. As the offense of all the other pickets arrested was the same as that of these twelve women that appealed their case, they were all illegally arrested, illegally convicted, and illegally imprisoned. The decision of the District Police Court was thus reversed by the Appellate Court. Also the Apellate Court ordered the cases dismissed and it was decided that all of the costs involved in the cases should be paid by the Court of the District of Columbia, for which an appropriation would have to be made by Congressional enactment.

Later, Dr. Harvey W. Wiley appealed his wife's case. She had been one of the more than forty women that picketed the President in November, 1917, in the last demonstration on the picket line and her sentence had been to serve fifteen days in the District Jail. The Court's decision, early in April, 1918, that no information had been filed justifying Mrs. Wiley's arrest showed that she, too, had been illegally arrested, convicted, and imprisoned.

7

PRISON EXPERIENCES WITH EMPHASIS ON THE NIGHT OF TERROR
1917

> A fast is the sincerest form of prayer. It does not mean coercion of anyone. It does of course exercise pressure on individuals, even on Government, but this is a natural and moral result of an act of sacrifice. It stirs up sluggish consciences and inspires loving hearts to act. Those who have to bring about radical changes in human conditions and surroundings cannot do it without raising a ferment in society.*—*Mahatma Gandhi.*

We have now arrived at one of the blackest pages in the history of the United States—the treatment of the suffrage pickets in the several prisons to which they were committed.

It is impossible to believe that the Administration did not know what was happening to the women confined in the District Jail, Occoquan Workhouse, and, later, in the abandoned Workhouse. The National Woman's Party, through its excellent publicity department, had told the story to the whole country and the press had given much space to it. Also, the three Commissioners, who governed the District of Columbia, the police court judges, the Chief of Police, the warden of the jail, and the superintendent of Occoquan Workhouse were all directly or indirectly answerable to the President.

---

*From "The Women in Gandhi's Life," by Eleanor Morton.

The jail in which the pickets were first imprisoned was unspeakably dirty and was infested with vermin and rats. Julia Emory said the rats were so large and strong that prisoners at night could actually hear the light cell-chairs being moved by them. One night, she beat three of the rats ,one after another off her bed.

The constant complaints of the prisoners finally brought action, but no results. The poison used by the prison officials did not decrease the rats, and the dog that was brought in seemed afraid of them.

But as bad as things were at the District Jail, they were much worse in the Workhouse at Occoquan. Occoquan is beautifully situated in picturesque country and its group of white buildings, its cultivated fields, and other attractive outside features tended to give the impression that it was a model institution. But its exterior belied its interior and the place left a sense of horror in the pickets confined in it. Even Lucy Burns, who seemed not to know fear, confessed that while there she suffered nameless and inexplicable terrors.

The women's ward was a long, clean, sunny room with two rows of beds, but those beds served a very mixed group of white and colored prisoners, and often the blankets on them had not been changed since used by the previous occupants. Indeed, the matron, who handled the bedclothes, was compelled to wear rubber gloves, while the Suffragists, even when they were put to painting the lavatories, had no such protection. There seemed to be a premeditated plan to humiliate the Suffragists who were all made to undress in the same bathroom and, without any privacy, to take shower baths one after another.

The punishment cells, situated in another building, were tiny brick rooms with tiny windows very high up. A young relative of one of the jail officials, wearing the uniform of an officer of the United States Army, would come into this building at night and look through the undraped grating of these cells. One time he unlocked the door and entered a room where two young pickets were sleeping. One of the pickets thought quickly enough to ask, "Are you a physician?" When the man said he was not, she covered her head with the bedclothes. He soon left.

In September, 1917, Lucy Burns filed charges with Commissioner Brownlow of the District of Columbia about conditions in the Workhouse. In that complaint, she said:

> The hygienic conditions have been improved at Occoquan since a group of Suffragists were imprisoned there. But they are still bad. The water they drink is kept in an open pail, from which it is ladled into a drinking cup. The prisoners frequently dip the drinking cup directly into the pail.
>
> The same piece of soap is used for every prisoner. As the prisoners in Occoquan are sometimes negligent.
> afflicted with disease, this practice is appallingly

In September, 1917, Mrs. Virginia Bovee, an officer of the Occoquan Workhouse, was discharged. I shall quote from Mrs. Bovee's affidavit:

> The blankets now being used in the prison have been in use since December without being washed or cleaned. Blankets are washed once a year. Officers are warned not to touch any of the bedding. The one officer who has to handle it is compelled by the regulations to wear rubber gloves while she does so. The sheets for the ordinary prisoners are not changed completely, even when one has gone and another takes her bed. Instead, the top sheet is put on the bottom, and one fresh sheet given

them. I was not there when the Suffragists arrived, so I do not know how their bedding was arranged. I doubt whether the authorities would have dared to give them one soiled sheet.

The prisoners with diseases are not always isolated, by any means. In the colored dormitory there are now two women in advanced stages of consumption. Women suffering from syphilis, who have open sores, are put in the hospital. But those whose sores are temporarily healed are put in the same dormitory with the others. There have been several such in my dormitory.

When the prisoners come, they must undress and take a shower bath. For this they take a piece of soap from a bucket in the storeroom. When they have finished, they throw the soap back into the bucket. The Suffragists are permitted three showers a week, and have only these pieces of soap which are common to all inmates. There is no soap at all in the washrooms.

The beans, hominy, rice, cornmeal (which is exceedingly coarse, like chicken feed), and cereal have all had worms in them. Sometimes the worms float on top of the soup. Often they are found in the corn bread. The first Suffragists sent the worms to Whittaker on a spoon. On the farm is a fine herd of Holsteins. The cream is made into butter, and sold to the tuberculosis hospital in Washington. At the officers' table we have very good milk. The prisoners do not have any butter, or sugar, and no milk except by order of the doctor.

When the Superintendent of Occoquan told Katherine Rolston Fisher that no person under punishment—that is, in solitary confinement—was allowed to see legal counsel, she asked him, "Is that the law of the District of Columbia?" He replied, "It is the law here because it is the rule I make." In Miss Fisher's "From the Log of a Suffrage

Picket," in the *Suffragist* of October 13, 1917, she tells more of her experiences and of what she saw while confined in Occoquan:

> We learned what it is to live under a one-man law . . . Our Counsel after one visit was forbidden, upon a pretext, to come again.
>
> On Tuesday, September 18, we were made to exchange our new gingham uniforms for old spotted gray gowns covered with patches upon patches; were taken to a shed to get pails of paint and brushes, and were set to painting the dormitory lavatories and toilets. By this time we were all hungry and more or less weak from lack of food. A large brush wet with white paint weighs at least two pounds. Much of the work required our standing on a table or stepladder and reaching above our heads. I think the wiser of us rested at every opportunity, but we did not refuse to work.
>
> All this time we had been without Counsel for eight days . . . .
>
> The food, which had been a little better, about the middle of the month reached its zenith of rancidity and putridity. We tried to make a sport of the worm hunt, each table announcing its score of weevils and worms. When one prisoner reached the score of fifteen worms during one meal, it spoiled our zest for the game . . . .
>
> We had protested from the beginning against doing any manual labor upon such bad and scanty food as we received . . . .
>
> Mrs. Kendall, who was the most emphatic in her refusal, was promptly locked up on bread and water. The punishment makes a story to be told by itself. It clouded our days constantly while it lasted and we knew not half of what she suffered . . . .
>
> All this time—five days—Mrs. Kendall was locked up, her pallid face visible through the windows to those few Suffragists who had opportunity

and ventured to go to her window for a moment
at the risk of sharing her fate.

The imprisoned Suffragists managed to have samples of
their food smuggled out to the well-known food expert, Dr.
Harvey W. Wiley. Dr. Wiley, aroused by these samples,
asked the Board of Charities to let him make an investigation of the food. "A Diet of Worms won one revolution,
and I expect it will win another," said he.

It was, however, to the group of pickets arrested November 14, 1917, and sentenced to Occoquan, that the most outrageous things happened. They went through an experience
that was rightly called *The Night of Terror*. Sixteen of
these Suffragists, immediately upon their arrival at the
Workhouse, began a hunger-strike as a protest against the
Government's refusal to treat them as political offenders.
They demanded the privilege of exercising, receiving mail
and visitors, buying food and reading matter.

When these prisoners arrived at the Workhouse, Superintendent Whittaker was away; and they were kept in the
office of one of the small cottages. Because the Suffragists
were still making their demand to be treated as political
prisoners, Mrs. Lawrence Lewis, acting as spokesman for
the group, refused to answer the usual questions put to
them by Mrs. Herndon, the woman at the desk, saying that
she would wait and talk to Mr. Whittaker.

"You will sit here all night then," said Mrs. Herndon.
After the Suffragists had waited for hours, Mrs. Herndon
tried again to get them to register, but they made no reply.
Soon several men entered the room.

"You had better answer up, or it will be the worse for
you," said one man. Another man said, "I will handle you
so you'll be sorry you made me." Still there was no reply.

Suddenly the door was flung open and Superintendent

Whittaker rushed in followed by a number of other men. It was later discovered that he had just left a conference of the District of Columbia Commissioners at the White House. The Suffragists had been sitting or lying on the floor. Mrs. Lawrence Lewis rose and began to speak, saying, "We demand to be treated as political pris—" when the Superintendent interrupted with, "You shut up! I have men here glad to handle you!" "Seize her!"

Mrs. Lewis was seized by two men and dragged away from the other Suffragists. Another man sprang at Mrs. Mary A. Nolan, a frail, lame woman over seventy years of age. In describing this experience, Mrs. Nolan said:

> I am used to being careful of my bad foot, and I remember saying: "I will come with you; do not drag me. I have a lame foot." But I was dragged down the steps and away into the dark. I did not have my feet on the ground. I guess that saved me.

All that Mrs. Nolan recalls of the black outside was the approach to a low, dark building from which flew a brilliantly lighted American flag. As she entered the hall, a man wearing the uniform of Occoquan, branished a stick and called out, "Damn you! Get in there!" Before Mrs. Nolan was shot through the hall, Dorothy Day, a very slight, delicate girl, was brought in by two men who were twisting her arms above her head. She was suddenly lifted by her captors and her body was brought down twice over the back of an iron bench. "The damned Suffrager! My mother ain't no Suffrager! I will put you through hell!" called out one of the men handling Dorothy Day. Then Mrs. Nolan was pulled down a corridor and pushed through a door.

Back of Mrs. Nolan, and dragged along as she had

been, came Mrs. Cosu. Mrs. Nolan's fall was broken by
the bed, but Mrs. Cosu hit the wall. In a few minutes, Mrs.
Lewis, all doubled over, was thrown into the same room.
Her head struck the iron bed and she fell senseless to the
floor. Mrs. Nolan and Mrs. Cosu, thinking that Mrs.
Lewis was dead, began to weep, but they finally revived her.
Later, Mrs. Cosu was seized with a heart attack and was
desperately ill the rest of the night. Despite the women's
repeated calls for medical help, no attention was paid to
them by either the woman or the man guard in the corridor.
Provided with only two mattresses and two blankets, the
prisoners shivered all through the night.

But iron bars did not prevent Lucy Burns from taking
charge of the situation as she always did when arrested. In
order to find out if all the pickets were alive and there, she
began in her clear, beautiful voice to call the roll. To the
guard's order to "Shut up!" she paid not the slightest attention. "Where is Mrs. Lewis?" she demanded. Mrs. Cosu
replied, "They have just thrown her in here." The guard
yelled that he would put them in strait-jackets if they spoke
again. This so frightened Mrs. Nolan and Mrs. Cosu that
for a time they kept still. Lucy Burns, however, continued
to call the roll, and, when at the guard's order she refused
to stop, her wrists were handcuffed and the handcuffs were
fastened above her head to the cell door. Also she was
threatened with a buckle gag. Although little Julia Emory,
in her cell opposite Lucy Burns', could do nothing to help,
she made a sympathetic protest by putting her hands above
her head exactly as Lucy Burns' hands were bound and
stood before her door until Lucy Burns was released. The
handcuffs were worn by Lucy Burns all night.

In an effort to lower Lucy Burns' morale, the authorities
took her clothes away from her. When Mr. O'Brien, the
N.W.P. lawyer, visited her, she was lying on a cot in a

dark cell, wrapped in blankets. On his return to Headquarters, he was full of admiration for her remarkable spirit and said that she was as much herself as if they had been talking in the drawing room at Headquarters. Also news from Occoquan reached Headquarters through Mrs. Nolan after her release at the end of her six-day sentence. It was these things that made the Suffragists decide on habeas corpus proceedings. Mr. O'Brien applied to the United States District Court at Richmond for this writ. It was granted returnable on November 27. Fearing, however, that the women might by that time have collapsed from harsh treatment and starvation, Mr. O'Brien made a second journey to see Judge Waddill and succeeded in having the date of the hearing advanced to the 23rd of November.

In order to serve the writ on Superintendent Whittaker, Mr. O'Brien had to resort to a ruse. When, on the night of November 21, he called at Mr. Whittaker's home and was told the superintendent was not there, he left and telephoned from a nearby point that he would not return until the morning. Instead, he returned immediately, found Mr. Whittaker at home, and served the papers.

For some reason unknown to the others, Mrs. Henry Butterworth was taken away from the other Suffragists and put in a prison where there were only men.

Mrs. Paula Jakobi gave further details of the Night of Terror and of the days that followed it. Three Suffragists were thrust into each of the cold, unventilated cells that contained a single bed and a mattress on the floor. Both floor and blankets were "filthy." No facilities for washing in the morning were provided, and no food was offered although the women had had nothing to eat since noon of the previous day. Faint and exhausted by the treatment they had received, the women, at eight in the morning, were ordered before the superintendent for questioning.

The Rights of Political Prisoners being denied them, the Suffragists began a hunger strike. The first day's fasting did not make Mrs. Jakobi ill, only weak. The second day brought slight nausea and headache; the third day, fever and dizziness, the fever remaining and causing very dry, peeling skin and swollen lips. By this time, she was both weaker and more nervous and she showed symptoms of aphasia. She could remember no names and found it impossible to read.

The women, she said, were summoned so often and so suddenly from their rooms to see Mr. Whittaker or to be transferred to other rooms that they were never sure when they should be searched and when their few remaining treasures would be taken from them. Conspicuous among these *treasures* were stubs of pencils and bits of writing paper for exchanging messages inside the prison or for smuggling them outside to friends and relatives. Everything in prison seems conducive to concealment, and Mrs. Jakobi was especially ingenious in avoiding discovery. With woman's main tool, a hairpin, she ripped a small hole in the ticking of her pillow and hid stubs of pencils in this innocent-looking object. Her paper she hid behind steam radiator pipes. Dimes and nickels for the trusty she placed in a row over the sill of her door.

One evening a great commotion was heard in the corridor. Doors that did not lock were held, and there were rapid footsteps to and fro. Disturbing sounds came from the adjoining room. Lucy Burns was being forcibly fed. There were more hurried footsteps and the men went to Mrs. Lewis' room. Fifteen minutes later the two women were hurried into an ambulance and taken away—where, neither Mrs. Jakobi nor the other pickets were told. "We had," continued Mrs. Jakobi, "visions of being separated, hurried out of sight to oblivion, somewhere away from everyone we knew."

A note from Lucy Burns, smuggled out of the Washington District Jail to which she and Mrs. Lewis had been transferred, proved that the anxiety expressed by Mrs. Jakobi over their sudden disappearance from Occoquan was justified. As usual, neither of the women was told why they were sent to Washington, but they were simply told that they must go. When they refused to be examined by Dr. Gannon, the District Jail physician, they were dragged through the halls by force, their clothing partly removed by force, and an examination was made—heart tested, blood pressure and pulse taken.

When the pickets from Occoquan arrived at the Alexandria Court House, they learned the reason for the sudden disappearance of Lucy Burns and Mrs. Lewis to "parts unknown." It was to prevent their appearance at Court, despite the pleading of Counsel for the National Woman's Party that they be present at the trial. But Dudley Field Malone cleverly outwitted the authorities. The following day both Lucy Burns and Mrs. Lewis were at the trial.

From all over the country protests were sent to Washington. This public reaction, plus the prospect of forcibly feeding such a large number of women, seems to have had a direct influence on the Government, because three days later all of the imprisoned pickets were released.

Early in December a mass meeting in honor of the released pickets was held in Washington. The Belasco Theatre was crowded, and, despite the bitter cold, an overflow meeting of four thousand stood outside to listen to an address by Elsie Hill. And this time there was ample police protection. The police reserves, who had often in the past arrested the pickets, were on hand to keep order among the thousands of persons gathered in honor of these same Suffragists.

Eighty-one pickets that had served prison sentences marched down the aisles of the Theatre, carrying purple, white, and gold banners, and also banners with messages inscribed on them. They took their places on the stage. Each of these "prisoners of freedom" was presented with a silver pin that was a small replica of the cell doors they had so often faced. The speakers were Maud Younger, Mrs. O. H. P. Belmont, Dudley Field Malone, Mrs. Thomas Hepburn, and Mrs. William Kent.

Eighty-six thousand, three hundred and eighty-six dollars was raised in honor of the pickets that night. This sum included two contributions of thirty cents and fifty cents, which deeply touched the women. These two contributions from Occoquan, sent "because the Suffragettes helped us so much down there," were accepted on behalf of the pickets by Mrs. John Rogers, Jr., who gave "tenderest thanks for this help from our comrades in the Workhouse."

While the Suffragists had done much to improve conditions for their fellow-prisoners, much remained undone. Over and over again, the other prisoners asked whether things might not be improved for them if they, too, should go on a hunger-strike. But the Suffragists had to explain that such a protest would be useless to persons having no organization back of them. In every way open to the Suffragists, however, they tried to lend a helping hand to these unfortunates.

8

THE GOVERNMENT ATTEMPTS TO
DISCREDIT ALICE PAUL BY IMPRISONMENT
IN PSYCHOPATHIC WARD
1917

On leaving the court room, October 20, 1917, after she had been sentenced to seven months in jail for carrying a banner on which was inscribed a quotation from President Wilson that had appeared on the posters for the Second Liberty Bond Loan of 1917, Alice Paul said to the reporters:

> We are being imprisoned, not because we obstructed traffic, but because we pointed out to the President the fact that he was obstructing the cause of democracy at home, while Americans were fighting for it abroad.

Arriving at the District Jail late in the afternoon of October 20, 1917, Alice Paul found the Suffragists that had preceded her locked in cells. Every window was closed. Into this hopeless spot there were crowded approximately eighty white and Negro prisoners tier upon tier, frequently two in a cell.

In order to relieve the distress of the prisoners, who were suffering from lack of fresh air, Alice Paul tried to open one of the windows. She was immediately seized by a prison guard and thrown into a cell.

DUDLEY FIELD MALONE

As both Alice Paul and Lucy Burns were at this time serving long prison sentences, it became necessary for some one to consult with them if possible at the jail. But Warden Zinkhan peremptorily refused permission that this be done. Later, however, with the assistance of a faithful and most helpful charwoman, daily contact between N. W. P. Headquarters and the jail was established, and Alice Paul was thus able to direct the campaign despite the Administration's earnest efforts to prevent it.

The Suffragists, determined if possible to preserve health, started a fresh-air campaign. With two sets of iron bars between them and the windows, which were about twenty feet from their cells, they were forced to plan an attack on those closed windows with the available *weapons* at their command—tin drinking cups, electric bulbs, and even the copy of Browning's poems that Alice Paul had managed to take into her cell. With that improvised supply of ammunition, a simultaneous attack from every cell was made and one window broke under the barrage. The fresh fall air rushed in and that broken window proved an ally not only to all Suffragists then in jail but to all others who followed later.

When at the end of two weeks those prisoners that had completed their sentences were released, there were left in the jail only seven members of the N.W.P., five of whom were serving sentences of seven months and two of whom had been given sentences of one month.

Believing, apparently, that they could handle this reduced number of rebels without much trouble, the prison authorities removed some of the rigors previously imposed. The seven women were no longer kept in solitary confinement and denied all exercise. The cell doors were unlocked and they were permitted to go out in the yard. Rose Winslow fainted as soon as she reached the open air and had to be carried back to her cell. That night she and Alice Paul were taken on stretchers to the hospital. Placed in the same ward for the night, the two decided to use the last and strongest weapon in their armory—the hunger strike.

Although not generally known, the refusal of food in order to obtain something most earnestly desired has been in practice for centuries. As a form of "direct action," it has been resorted to when there was no legislative machinery to enforce justice.

When news of the hunger strike reached those in authority, they instituted a campaign of their own to try to prevent its use. In an effort to intimidate Alice Paul, the leader, she was threatened with removal to a "very unpleasant place" if she hunger-struck. It was vaguely hinted that she might be put in the psychopathic ward, or might even be sent to St. Elizabeth, the Government's insane asylum. Her reply was perfect silence, and a continued strike.

In a few days, Dr. White, the head of St. Elizabeth, entered Alice Paul's room announcing that he had been asked by District Commissioner Gardner to make an investigation. When Dr. White turned to a nearby attendant and asked, "Does this case talk?" Alice Paul quickly answered, "Why wouldn't I talk?" Still regarding her as a *specimen,* Dr. White said, "Oh, these cases frequently will not talk, you know."

Not suspecting Commissioner Gardner's requested examination was to be a test of her sanity, and not knowing that her caller was Dr. William A. White, the eminent alienist, Alice Paul said brightly, "I will be glad to talk. We talk to anyone on earth who is willing to listen to our suffrage speeches."

Dr. White was apparently pleased at her fine spirit of co-operation. He not only invited her to talk, but specifically requested that she tell him about woman suffrage, about the campaign she was leading, why she picketed, what she hoped to accomplish by picketing and, what was perhaps his most telling inquiry, why she had opposed the President. Wishing, apparently, to encourage his "case" to be completely relaxed and thus to enable him to plumb the secret recesses of her supposedly disturbed mind, he said, "Just talk freely."

With this alluring invitation, and with a ready-made audience apparently keenly interested, she prepared to do her best for the Cause. Propping herself up comfortably in bed, she made what she hoped was a good presentation of the suffrage cause. As nearly as possible, she related the long history of the suffrage movement from its beginning down to the immediate present. She knew that she was also speaking to an unseen audience because the stenographer, who came with Dr. White, was taking down everything in shorthand. Not only did she give the history of the suffrage movement, but she carefully explained the political theory that lay behind the activities of the N.W.P.

Dr. White was a delightful and stimulating audience, and interrupted the speaker only occasionally. He asked, "But, has not President Wilson treated you women very badly?" Still not realizing she was having a sanity test, she explained President Wilson's political situation and the difficulties that confronted him. She further explained why we felt he had the power to enfranchise us. She spoke of the President's extraordinary power, his great influence with his Party, and his undisputed leadership in the country, all the while making it plain that we did not oppose *Mr.* Wilson but *President* Wilson, the head of the Government.

Not until Dr. White took out a small light and held it up to her eyes did it suddenly dawn upon her that she was being personally examined, and that Dr. White's apparent interest in the suffrage movement and in the jail conditions was only a means of getting her reaction to these things. Still finding it hard to believe that an attempt was being made to investigate her sanity, she continued to talk until she realized with a sudden shock that Dr. White was trying to discover in her symptoms of the persecution mania— trying to see whether she might have an obsession on the subject of President Wilson.

The following day, when Dr. White returned, he was accompanied by District Commissioner Gardner, and Alice Paul was asked to repeat her suffrage story of the previous day. When she reached that part of it that dealt with the President's responsibility for obstructing the passage of the suffrage amendment, Dr. White turned to Commissioner Gardner and said, "Note the reaction."

Dr. Hickling, an alienist attached to the psychopathic ward of the District Jail, now joined the conference and made renewed threats of what would happen if the hunger strike were continued. There seemed no doubt the authorities were attempting to discredit the leader of a campaign that was proving troublesome to the Administration—discredit her by casting doubt on her sanity.

Later Commissioner Gardner, with whom she had previously discussed the Suffragists' demand to be treated as political prisoners, made another visit. He admitted that the charges she brought against the prison management were serious and might be true, but he, a "new Commissioner," did not know, and the jail gave an exactly opposite account of them. He promised, if she would discontinue the hunger strike, that he would immediately start an investigation to see which report was true. But when he definitely refused to treat the women as political prisoners, she told him the strike would continue.

She was then taken on a stretcher to the psychopathic

ward. Dr. Gannon immediately ordered that one of the two windows in the room be nailed from top to bottom, and that the door leading into the hallway be removed and an iron-barred door be put in its place. His command to the nurse was, "Observe her."

Faithfully following Dr. Gannon's directions, a nurse came once every hour during the day to "observe"; and once every hour through the night an electric light was flashed in Alice Paul's face. This meant that if sleep came at all it was only for a few minutes between the flashes. Dr. Hickling also came often to "observe" the patient, and Commissioner Gardner and others came to peer through the barred door. Over Alice Paul's mild protest to a young interne that it was unnecessary to make a blood test, he ignored her wishes and said: "You know you're not mentally competent to decide such things."

Surrounded, as she was, by persons on their way to an insane asylum, some waiting for their commitment papers, some having just got them, everything possible was attempted to make her feel that she, too, was a mental case.

Not content with inflicting such inhuman cruelty, the authorities now seemed bent on depriving her of light and air sufficient for ordinary comfort. One of her two windows was completely boarded up. The only light that then came into her room was through the upper half of the other window; also only a little fresh air came in.

But light of another sort reached her and brought with it something to cheer her spirits. The old man that had been assigned the job of nailing boards across the outside of one of her windows was both friendly and kind. Standing on top of a ladder, he discontinued the hammering of nails long enough to say a few gentle words to the prisoner and to advise her to be of good cheer. Though, he confided to her, he had been in prison many times for drinking, he believed he had never seen anything so inhuman as this thing he was now forced to do.

Somehow, the long dreary days in the psychopathic ward went by. Mental patients in the ward peered through the door. All through the day and night there were terrifying shrieks and moans from patients. One of these moans kept up "with the regularity of a heart beat" and made Alice Paul wonder how she could stand it.

The nurses, she said, could not have been more beautiful in spirit or kinder in their treatment of her. From them she learned the customary procedure of sending a patient to St. Elizabeth. A patient in a psychopathic ward must be examined by two alienists, an order admitting the patient must be signed, and at the end of one week the patient is sent to the insane asylum. There is no counsel, there is no trial, there is no protest from the outside world.

Not being permitted to see newspapers, counsel, her family, or friends, Alice Paul could only wonder whether she, too, might be railroaded to St. Elizabeth. She began to dread the visits of Dr. Gannon, the jail physician.

But, after nearly a week in the psychopathic ward, relief came. Dudley Field Malone, by appealing to court officials, finally succeeded in forcing his entrance into the jail. His vigorous protest against her continued confinement in the ward brought results. He demanded that the boards be removed from the window and they were. Again there appeared at the window the kindly old man. In taking down the boards, he said simply he did not believe when he put them up that America would let them stay long.

After Mr. Malone threatened court proceedings the sixth day of Alice Paul's confinement in the psychopathic ward, the attendants next day appeared with a stretcher. Was she being sent to the insane asylum or back to the jail hospital? She did not know. She had learned from experience that a prison does not confide to prisoners what it plans to do. As it happened, she was returned to the hospital.

After another week in the hospital, which she spent on a hunger strike, suddenly the jail doors were opened for the release of all the suffrage prisoners. Alice Paul's sentence of seven months thus came to an end in five weeks, and the Administration's attempt to intimidate the pickets had failed utterly.

Dr. White, it seems, in his capacity as an alienist, made no allegation that warranted Alice Paul's removal to the psychopathic ward. On the contrary, he later visited the National Woman's Party Headquarters and praised the admirable, logical, forceful, and most humorous way she had, while in the psychopathic ward, discussed with him the purpose of the N.W.P. campaign.

9

PRESIDENT WILSON ENDORSES FEDERAL
WOMAN SUFFRAGE . . . AMENDMENT
PASSES HOUSE . . . FAILS IN SENATE
1918

1918 brought the capitulation of President Wilson. His long five-year stand of determined opposition to the passage of the Federal Woman Suffrage Amendment was abandoned. A brief review of the position the President maintained over that period of time will throw light on the need for the aggressive campaign waged by the National Woman's Party to overcome his opposition and to win his powerful support.

There are, perhaps, some men congenitally unable to see in woman an equal of man. She may fill such rôles as "the sweetest thing in life," "the fairest of creation," "last and best of all God's work,"—but never his equal.

But that an historian, a contemporary of Miss Jane Addams, Dr. Anna Howard Shaw, Mrs. Carrie Chapman Catt, and Miss M. Carey Thomas, a former president of a leading University, a former governor of an important State, and President of the greatest democracy in the world—that such a man could, March 17, 1913, say to a deputation of four N.W.P. members that woman suffrage had never been brought to his attention, that it was entirely new, and that he did not know his position on it, is so remarkable as to seem almost incredible.

If, prior to his entry into the White House, President Wilson had somehow managed to be immune to a subject that had been agitated since 1648,* one might have thought that March 3, 1913, the day preceding his Inauguration, he could hardly have overlooked a woman suffrage demonstration in the nation's capital that proved to be a serious rival for the first-page space in the country's press the following day.

But the President, after stating his ignorance on the subject, did express to the four-woman deputation a wish for all possible information on it. And the N.W.P. certainly tried to see that his wish was generously fulfilled. However, no amount of information could move President Wilson in the beginning to assist the Federal Woman Suffrage Amendment. Instead, he declared his personal opposition to the Amendment on various changing pretexts, and, in the beginning, influenced opinion within his Party heavily against it.

In a number of contradictory statements on woman suffrage, the President attempted to defend his opposition to the Federal Amendment. At one time, he declared his "passion" was for "local self-government" and said that suffrage was a matter for settlement *only by the States.*

As the Founding Fathers had, in framing the Constitution of the United States, agreed upon a provision for amending that great instrument, and as the N.W.P., in its campaign for the passage of the Federal Suffrage Amendment, was only asking Congress to use the power clearly

---

* In the 28th chapter of his AUTOBIOGRAPHY, which is titled *Genesis of the Woman's Rights Movement,* Wilmer Atkinson refers to George Fox's activities in 1648, when he espoused women's right to "be meet-helps unto the men in the service of Truth, as they are in civil and temporal things" in these words: "Here we have the germ of the movement for woman's equality of rights with men, . . ."

granted it by the Constitution, President Wilson's position was surely untenable.

For nearly half a century Suffragists had been working for the passage of amendments to State Constitutions, but, between the years 1869 and 1912, when Mr. Wilson was elected President of the United States, only six of the forty-eight States had granted suffrage to women. If that rate of progress had been maintained, it would have required three hundred and forty-four years to accomplish the task that President Wilson cheerfully selected in the beginning of his contest with the Suffragists as the only course open to them.

But the N.W.P. knew that it was both legally and practically possible to secure a Federal Suffrage Amendment, and felt the time had come to dedicate its efforts to that end and thus to enfranchise all the women in the country. To pass an Amendment to the Federal Constitution requires a two-thirds majority vote in both Houses of Congress and its ratification by the Legislatures of three-fourths of the States—a difficult task to achieve and one requiring the approval of a large enough percentage of the people's elected representatives in both the State and the national governments to make it a truly democratic procedure.

President Wilson's declared objection to the Federal Amendment was that three-fourths of the States ought not to "force" suffrage on one-fourth of them.

Again, and still trying to condemn Suffragists to the difficult and, in some cases, practically impossible method of enfranchising all the women of the United States through the passage of State amendments, President Wilson said that women should first win thirty-six States separately; they could then "force" it on the remaining twelve! This was his reasoning December 10, 1914, to Miss Anne Martin of Nevada, who had just led the women of her State to a suffrage victory.

His opposition to the Federal Amendment because it enabled three-fourths of the State Legislatures to "force" their opinion on the other one-fourth had been expressed June 30, 1914, more than five months earlier. The three-quarter fraction was democratically wrong and it was democratically right! The President's arithmetic and his "passion for local self-government" seemed a difficult problem to adjust.

By 1918, the N.W.P. had emphasized so effectively the principle of Party responsibility, and had so clearly shown that the Democrats, the Party then in power, were responsible for the failure of the passage of the Susan B. Anthony Amendment, that leading Democrats were becoming aware of the political disadvantage in which their Party had been placed. And the Republicans, by emphasizing their Party's support of the Amendment, were benefiting by the situation. One Party was thus pitted against the other, and both Parties were anxious not to antagonize the millions of women voters in the West whose enthusiastic interest in aiding their disfranchised sisters in the East had been stimulated by the N.W.P.'s brilliantly planned and carefully executed western campaign in 1916.

Political pressure was winning where logic had failed, and President Wilson himself began to see the national enfranchisement of women in the light of political expediency.

Toward the end of December, 1917, Representative Mondell of Wyoming, Republican, had declared that the Republican side of the House would give more than the needed two-thirds majority of its members to pass the Amendment. He said, "It is up to our friends on the Democratic side to see that the Amendment is not defeated

through hostility or indifference on their side." And the
N.W.P. was, of course, making every effort to get the
President to secure sufficient additional Democratic votes
to insure the passage of the Amendment. Finally, on
the eve of the vote in the House, President Wilson made
his first declaration in support of the Amendment to a
committee of Democratic Congressmen.

During the House debate on the Amendment that memorable January 10, 1918, Representative Cantrill, Democrat from Kentucky, reported the good news in the House.
In part he said:

> It was my privilege yesterday afternoon to
> be one of a committee of twelve to ask the Presi-
> dent for advice and counsel on this important
> measure (prolonged laughter and jeers). Mr.
> Speaker, in answer to the sentiment expressed by
> part of the House, I desire to say that at no time
> and upon no occasion am I ever ashamed to confer
> with Woodrow Wilson upon any important ques-
> tion (laughter, applause, and jeers) and that part
> of the House that has jeered that statement be-
> fore it adjourns today will follow absolutely the
> advice which he gave this committee yesterday
> afternoon. (Laughter and applause.) After con-
> ference with the President yesterday afternoon
> he wrote with his own hands the words which I
> now read to you, and each member of the Com-
> mittee was authorized by the President to give
> full publicity to the following:
> "*The Committee found that the President
> had not felt at liberty to volunteer his advice to
> members of Congress in this important matter,
> but when we sought his advice (laughter) he very
> frankly and earnestly advised us to vote for the
> Amendment as an act of right and justice to the
> women of the country and of the world.*"

Then Representative Cantrill urged his "Democratic brethren" to stand by the President and vote for the Amendment "as an act of right and justice to the women of the country and of the world." He also said, "No one thing connected with the war is of more importance at this time than meeting the reasonable demand of millions of patriotic and Christian women of the Nation that the Amendment for Woman Suffrage be submitted to the States. . . ." Representative Cantrill had prefaced his speech, which caused so much merriment among the opposition, by announcing that he was not willing to risk another election, with the women of the West voting and the Amendment still unpassed.

All during the varied, sometimes bitter, long-drawn-out debate in the House, before the vote was taken, the main theme was *political expediency*. Mr. Lenroot of Wisconsin, Republican, won instant applause from his side when he said, "May I suggest that there is a distinction between the Democratic members of the Committee on Rules and the Republican members, in this, that all of the Republican members are for this proposition?" And Mr. Lenroot also made this pertinent comment: "From a Republican standpoint—from a partisan standpoint, it would be an advantage to Republicans to go before the people in the next election and say that this resolution was defeated by southern Democrats."

And Mr. Clark of Florida, despite his seeming fear of dire consequences if women were permitted to vote, made this unusually frank admission in referring to the President's sudden reversal of his stand on the Federal Suffrage Amendment:

> I was amused at my friend from Oklahoma, Mr. Ferris, who wants us to stand with the

President. God knows I want to stand with him. I am a Democrat, and I want to follow the leader of my Party, and I am a pretty good lightning-change artist myself sometimes (laughter); but God knows I cannot keep up with his performance. (Laughter.)

Wishing, apparently, to make clear how difficult he found it to "keep up" with the President's "performance," Mr. Clark then quoted a number of statements in defense of states' rights as recorded in President Wilson's early writings.

Did the dramatic campaign of the pickets have a hand in changing the President's mind? Representative Gordon of Ohio, Democrat, thought not, and he said so in these bitter words:

We are threatened by these militant Suffragettes with a direct and lawless invasion by the Congress of the United States of the rights of those States which have refused to confer upon their women the privilege of voting. This attitude on the part of some of the Suffrage members of this House is on an exact equality with the acts of these women militants who have spent the last summer and fall, while they were not in the district jail or workhouse, in coaxing, teasing, and nagging the President of the United States for the purpose of inducing him, by coercion, to club Congress into adopting this joint resolution.

But the Ohioan's oratory was interrupted by shouts from all sides of the House of "Well, they got him!" and "They got it!" and these shouts were followed by prolonged laughter and jeers.

In contrast to Mr. Gordon, Mr. Mays, of Utah, was one Democrat that placed the responsibility for *militancy* not on the Suffragists, but where it truly belonged. He said:

> Some say today that they are ashamed of the
> action of the militants in picketing the Capitol.
> . . . But we should be more ashamed of the un-
> reasonable stubbornness on the part of the men
> who refused them the justice they have so long
> and patiently asked.

And when some of the members of Congress wandered
off the main subject under discussion into fields of speculation, Mr. Little of Kansas, Republican, tried to recall his
colleagues to a moderate view of the situation by saying:

> It seems to me, gentlemen, that it is time
> for us to learn that woman is neither a slave
> nor an angel, but a human being, entitled to be
> treated with ordinary common sense in the ad-
> justment of human affairs. . . .

But, however the House members viewed the President's declaration in favor of the Susan B. Anthony Amendment, the N.W.P. saw in it a clear justification of the
organization's many years of emphasis on the President's
opposition to the Amendment as the great stumbling block
to the national enfranchisement of women. His long delayed espousal of the Amendment, which came January
9, 1918, won the Democratic votes needed to secure its
passage in the House the following day. The vote stood
274 to 136—just one vote more than the two-thirds majority required.

It was an interesting coincidence that this vote was cast
on the 10th day of January, 1918, the anniversary of two
significant dates in suffrage history. It celebrated the first
introduction into Congress of the Susan B. Anthony Amendment forty years earlier, and the appearance of the first
picket banner at the White House gates just one year before.

Since the President had made possible the passage of

the Amendment in the House, it now seemed reasonable to hope that he would press for action in the Senate. For the time being, the N.W.P. discontinued its dramatic protests and devoted its energies to bringing public pressure upon the President hoping thus to stimulate him to get favorable action on suffrage in the Senate as in the House. We worked also in other ways to win support from those Republican Senators opposing us.

Practically every national leader in the two majority parties was interviewed by the N.W.P. and his help was sought.

Colonel Theodore Roosevelt did most effective work in a determined attack upon the few unconvinced Republican Senators. He was said never to be too busy to confer with the suffrage leaders, and never to be dogmatic or patronizing in his dealings with them.

And special mention must be made of Colonel William Boyce Thompson of New York, who was later to become Chairman of Ways and Means of the Republican National Committee. Colonel Thompson had just returned from Russia where, with Raymond Robins, he had served as member of the United States Red Cross Mission. When the deadlock in the Senate was called to his attention, his quick response was most effective. He made one of the largest single contributions received during the national agitation. At a large mass meeting of the N.W.P. at Palm Beach, Florida, Colonel Thompson said:

> The story of the brutal imprisonment in Washington of women advocating suffrage is shocking and almost incredible. I became accustomed in Russia to the stories of men and women who served terms of imprisonment under the Czar, because of their love of liberty, but did not know that women in my own country had been

subjected to brutal treatment long since abandoned in Russia.

I wish now to contribute ten thousand dollars * to the campaign for the passage of the suffrage amendment through the Senate, one hundred dollars for each of the pickets who went to prison because she stood at the gates of the White House asking for the passage of the suffrage measure.

And Colonel Thompson, who had been a Suffragist all his life, not only became thus actively identified with the work for the passage of the Suffrage Amendment, but he continued to make generous contributions to the N.W.P. and, whenever it was needed, lent his political prestige to the campaign.

---

* Mrs. Lawrence Lewis was largely instrumental in obtaining this contribution.

10

POLITICAL LEADERS IN PENNSYLVANIA PLEDGE SUPPORT TO FEDERAL SUFFRAGE AMENDMENT . . . PICKETING RESUMED IN PROTEST AGAINST INACTION OF ADMINISTRATION 1918

Stirred by the exceedingly close vote in the House, January 10th, 1918, and by the difficulty faced in securing favorable action in the United States Senate, Pennsylvania sent special appeals for help to political leaders in the State, and received very gratifying responses.

Governor Martin G. Brumbaugh replied January 31, 1918:

> The people of Pennsylvania as a rule are conservative in matters affecting great social reforms but I am strongly convinced that they now sense the justice of granting suffrage to women, and I favor the Republican Party placing in its platform in the coming primaries and election a clearly worded statement that will commit the party to this important reform.
>
> It is my judgment that Pennsylvania should not be lax or slow in doing what the general judgment of mankind in these war times conceded to be the right thing to do, namely, to give women

the opportunity to express their views upon the type of democracy which this country should have and which it should be willing to offer in good conscience to the other peoples of the world.

I telephoned Governor Brumbaugh to ask if his letter might be used as a special message to a Conference of State Chairmen from the Eastern District of the United States which would meet in Philadelphia February 6th, and received his permission to do this. It was, of course, excellent publicity.

Mr. Joseph P. Gaffney, Chairman of Committee on Finance, City Councils, Philadelphia, wrote February 2nd, 1918:

> . . . I shall be pleased to be the mover of a joint resolution of Select and Common Councils urging the United States Senate to concur in the action already taken by the House of Representatives upon the Susan B. Anthony Amendment.

The Honorable A. Mitchell Palmer, Member for Pennsylvania on the Democratic National Committee, wrote February 13th, 1918:

> . . . I think at least two Pennsylvania Democrats, Mr. Vance M. McCormick and myself, have anticipated your desire that something should be done by Pennsylvania Democrats in securing a favorable vote on the Federal Suffrage amendment in the Senate.
> At the meeting of the Democratic National Executive Committee held last Saturday in this City [Washington, D. C.], I offered a resolution endorsing Women's Suffrage and urging favorable action by the Senate, and providing for a referendum of the question to the members of

the Democratic National Committee. A vote was taken by wire and the meeting of the National Executive Committee adjourned until Monday afternoon at 5:30, when the telegraphic answers were received. It appeared that twenty-eight members of the National Committee had voted for the resolution to fourteen against. We then passed a resolution in the Executive Committee, as you have doubtless seen in the papers, both Mr. McCormick and I voting for it.

This is an expression of the Democratic party of the nation through the only organization which can speak for it between national conventions. It was action taken upon the initiative and with the support of the two Pennsylvanians on the Committee. I think that kind of help is very much more effective than writing personal letters to Senators. In a resolution we spoke officially for the Party. Our personal views might not influence Senators much, but the Party's voice will.

In my letter of thanks to Mr. Palmer, I was glad to let him know that a press bulletin based on his letter had been sent over the country by Anne Martin, National Legislative Chairman of the National Woman's Party.

The Honorable Vance C. McCormick, in his letter of February 13th, 1918, wrote:

> . . . I suppose you have already noticed in the newspapers the action taken the other day by the Executive Committee of the Democratic National Committee, of which I am Chairman. I was very glad to record my vote in favor of the amendment, and am urging all the Senators with whom I get in touch to vote for the amendment.

April 4, 1918, the following letter was sent to Pennsylvania's thirty-six Congressmen and two United States Senators:

As Chairman of the Pennsylvania Branch of the National Woman's Party, I submit to you the following statement signed by seven members of our organization, and hope that you will give the request it contains your prompt and favorable consideration. An early reply will be appreciated.

"As citizens of Pennsylvania, who have endured a great wrong at the hands of the government of the District of Columbia, we ask you to take active part in advocating the passage of the bill to investigate the treatment of the suffrage pickets in Washington from June to November, 1917. The decision of the Court of Appeals in declaring the actions of the pickets to be lawful, orderly and according to the Constitutional rights of American citizens renders necessary a public investigation of the unlawful arrests by the Washington Police, the unlawful sentences of the Police Court and the unlawful imprisonments in the District Jail and Workhouse.

"These official acts have created a widespread misunderstanding and have reflected on our honor and patriotism. We cannot, therefore, rest satisfied with a legal decision, no matter how strong, but must also demand complete and public vindication which can only be given by the Congress of the United States.

"Lavinia L. Dock, Fayetteville,
"Kate C. Heffelfinger, Shamokin,
"Mary H. Ingham, Philadelphia,
"Dora Lewis, Philadelphia,
"Kathryn Lincoln, Philadelphia,
"Elizabeth McShane, Uniontown,
"Mary Winsor, Haverford."

Very truly yours,

Mary H. Ingham,
Chairman.

A Resolution to authorize an Investigation of the District of Columbia Workhouse at Occoquan, Virginia, had been introduced in the House by Jeannette Rankin, Representative from Montana. And a Resolution to authorize an Investigation of Mob Attacks on Suffragists had been introduced in the House by John Baer, Representative from North Dakota. Also, the Court of Appeals had handed down a decision holding that the arrests, convictions, and imprisonments of the Pickets were unlawful. Suffragists naturally felt that there should be a thorough, public investigation into all the facts.

July 5, 1918, the following resolution was unanimously adopted at a meeting held under the auspices of the National Woman's Party in the Hotel Walton, Philadelphia:

WHEREAS, The war is demanding of American women every kind of public and personal service, especially in relation to the fundamental civic problems of food, health and public morals,

BE IT RESOLVED, That this meeting of Pennsylvania men and women earnestly request President Wilson to do his utmost to hasten the passage of the Federal Woman Suffrage Amendment by the Senate of the United States as a war measure demanded for the public welfare. Also

RESOLVED, That we strongly urge upon our Pennsylvania Senators, the Honorable Boies Penrose and the Honorable Philander C. Knox, that they abandon a position which, in the face of present conditions, cannot but be considered as inconsistent with true Americanism, and by a straightforward change of determination make sure the prompt passage of the Federal Suffrage Amendment as a war measure for the efficiency of the nation.

RESOLVED, That these resolutions be forwarded to President Wilson and to Senators Penrose and Knox and that Senator Penrose be asked to read them into the Congressional Record.

To be within sight of our goal and yet not able to reach it; to pass the House and be blocked in the Senate; to be forced to continue suffrage demonstrations, which were costly in time, strength, and money, seemed an unnecessary burden for women to have to carry. But since the spectacular had paid handsomely in the past, we could not surrender the tool that seemed the most valuable one in our political chest.

Because the demonstrations of the N.W.P. were planned with such care and were carried out with such effectiveness the public did not realize how much work lay back of them. The following letter that Alice Paul sent me July 31, 1918, will throw light on what went on behind the scenes at National Headquarters:

. . . The success of our meeting will depend, of course, upon having a number of speakers, and of the people who have so far felt able to take part in the demonstration, almost none can speak. We have at present, forty-two in all, who are pledged to carry banners but only two of these, Miss Hill [Elsie Hill] and Miss Dock [Lavinia L. Dock) can speak and only one of these can speak out of doors very long. Miss Dock, I think, can speak for a few minutes but says she cannot undertake to hold a street crowd. We are planning to advertise her as a speaker and have her say a few words in order to have the publicity of her name. You can see, therefore, how much other speakers are needed.

Now that we have forty-two people taking part in the demonstration it makes it much less likely that anyone will be arrested and almost certain that if arrested, the terms of imprisonment will be very short. In view of this, we hope it will be much easier to secure participants.

Our answer to that urgent need for speakers was Elizabeth McShane of Philadelphia. Our records show that both Elsie Hill and Elizabeth McShane were sentenced to fifteen days in jail for that August, 1918, meeting.

It is pleasant here to interrupt the story of our battle with the United States Senate by presenting a letter from the Director of the Evening School of Accounts and Finance of the University of Pennsylvania, dated September 24, 1918:

Dear Miss Katzenstein:
This year for the first time the University of Pennsylvania has opened the courses of the Evening School of Accounts and Finance to women. This marks an educational epoch in the history of the University, and it would seem to me that some of your members might be interested in the opportunity thus afforded. I am therefore sending you, under separate cover, a number of copies of the Evening School Bulletin, and I shall be gratefully indebted to you if you will place the matter before those of your members who will be interested in the subject. I shall be further obliged to you if you will communicate with this office on receipt of this letter and let us know what, if anything, we may be able to do in this regard. We are ready and willing at all times to explain the Evening School to all those who desire further information in regard to it.

With many thanks for the courtesies with which I am sure you will treat this communication, I am

Sincerely yours,
Theodore J. Grayson
Director.

In my letter of thanks to Mr. Grayson I expressed the hope that the action taken by the University of Pennsylvania might mark the beginning of the end of woman's bitter fight for educational opportunities, and that Pennsylvania might lead other States in removing every obstacle to woman's full and free development along all lines.

Seven months after the House had passed the Susan B. Anthony Amendment, we found ourselves still lacking two votes in the Senate, and we were given no assurance by the President that he would exert himself sufficiently to secure these votes. Also, the Senate was about to recess and we had no promise from the majority party that suffrage would be considered either before or after the recess.

Patience seemed no longer a virtue. Was the Administration determined once more to test the mettle of the pickets to see whether they could stand the strain of still harsher prison treatment than they had already received? We had hoped that that phase of the campaign was a thing of the past and that it would never again be necessary to resort to it. Alice Paul had, the previous year, given expression to this hope, while at the same time making it plain that it was up to the Administration not to force us to go on with our demonstrations, when, November 27th and 28th, 1917, thirty determined Suffragists were unconditionally released from prison after going on a hunger strike. On leaving the prison, Alice Paul then said:

> The commutation of sentences acknowledges them to be unjust and arbitrary. The attempt to suppress legitimate propaganda has failed.
>
> We hope that no more demonstrations will be necessary, that the amendment will move steadily on to passage and ratification without further suffering or sacrifice. But what we do depends en-

tirely upon what the Administration does. We
have one aim: the immediate passage of the Federal Amendment.

A measure passed by one branch of Congress has to
be passed by the other branch during the same Congress
or the victory in the one house counts for naught. This
meant we had only a short time in which to act in order
to take advantage of our hard-won victory in the House
January 10, 1918.

The N.W.P. decided upon another national protest in
Washington, August 6, 1918. Led by a standard-bearer
carrying an American flag, women from many States, all
dressed in white, and carrying lettered banners and banners of purple, white, and gold, gathered at the base of
Lafayette monument in the park just opposite the White
House to hold their meeting. Fearless Mrs. Lawrence
Lewis of Philadelphia, the first speaker, began: "We are
here because when our country is at war for liberty and
democracy . . ." Not permitted to finish her first sentence,
she was roughly seized by a policeman and placed under
arrest.

One woman after another came forward and attempted
to take the place Mrs. Lewis had been forced to surrender, but not one was allowed to speak. In all, forty-eight
Suffragists were arrested and rushed to the police station.
The women were told that their arrest by the police was
under the orders of Col. C. S. Ridley, the President's military aide, and assistant to the Chief Engineer attached to
the War Department.

All of the forty-eight women were released on bail
and ordered to appear in court the next day. When they
appeared, the Government's attorney again postponed the

case. He did not know "what offense, if any, the women would be charged with."

"I cannot go on with the case," he said, "I have had no orders. There are no precedents for cases like these. . . ."

Among the forty-eight Suffragists arrested were the following ten Pennsylvanians: Cora Crawford, Lavinia L. Dock, Christine M. Doyle, Mrs. Edmund C. Evans, Kate C. Heffelfinger, Mrs. Lawrence Lewis, Dr. Sarah H. Lockrey, Martha W. Moore, Ellen Winsor, and Mary Winsor.

In reply to the women's demand that their cases be dismissed, or that a charge be made against them, they were told to return the following Tuesday. So much indignation was aroused against the Administration for taking this action that Senator Curtis of Kansas, Republican whip, could say publicly:

> The truth of this statement is made evident by the admission of the court that the forty-eight suffragists are arrested upon absolutely no charges, and that these women, among them munitions workers and Red Cross workers, are held in Washington until next Tuesday, under arrest, while the United States attorney for the District of Columbia decides for what offense, "if any," they were arrested.
>
> The meeting was called to make a justified protest against continued blocking of the suffrage amendment by the Democratic majority in the Senate. It is well known that three-fourths of the Republican membership in the Senate are ready to vote for the amendment, but under the control of the Democratic majority the senate has recessed for six weeks without making any provision for action on this important amendment.

Some of the Suffragists were tried August 13th, 1918, and some August 15th. The charge was "holding a meeting in public grounds," and for eighteen of the forty-eight, an additional charge of "climbing on a statue" was brought. After answering the roll call, the women remained silent, and the usual farcical procedure followed. For lack of identification, some of the women were released. Of the remainder, those who had only assembled to hold a meeting were sentenced to ten days in the District Jail; the others, whose additional *crime* was that they had "climbed on a statue," were sentenced to fifteen days in jail.

Situated in the swamp of the District prison grounds was a building formerly used as a man's workhouse—a place declared unfit for human habitation by a committee appointed under President Theodore Roosevelt in 1909 and unoccupied thereafter. Nine years after this condemnation of the building, it was re-opened for the incarceration of twenty-six women that had tried to hold a meeting in one of the public parks of the nation's Capital! When the united demand of the women that they be treated as political prisoners was again refused, all of them, except two elderly women too frail to stand the strain, protested by going at once on a hunger strike.

The long room in which the women were placed was below the ground level and the small section of grating in the cell doors admitted only a little light. There were small, unsightly wash-basins, iron cots without springs and with only a straw pallet. The toilet had no covering. Despite the summer heat of Washington, this unsanitary place was always cold; and nauseating odors permeated it. These conditions, plus the unfit drinking water, which came through pipes long unused, made a number of the prisoners ill.

Seeking some relief from the revolting odors, the women moved their straw pallets from the cells to the stone floor outside and refused in a body to go back to their cells when ordered to do so.

And all of this took place more than a year after Dudley Field Malone, in his famous interview with President Wilson in July, 1917, had stated unequivocally that it was the District Commissioners of the city of Washington—men appointed to office by the President—that had laid plans resulting in the outrageous manhandling of the Suffragists by the police and a court trial that was a perversion of justice. Surely the President could no longer have pleaded ignorance of what was being done to silence women in their legitimate protest against the Government's continued refusal to grant them justice, nor could he fail to know where the responsibility for this action lay.

The threat that Superintendent Zinkhan made to the pickets before they were released from prison at the end of 1917 was not only carried out, but things were even worse for the Suffragists than he had said they would be. He had said: "Now don't come back, for, if you do, I will have a far worse place than the jail fixed up for you. I will have the old workhouse fixed up for you, and you will have cells without sunlight, with windows high up from the ground. You won't be as comfortable as you are here." Apparently the authorities had looked ahead and made plans they felt sure would crush the spirit of the women.

The hunger strike brought results. At the end of the fifth day, the Administration released the women, some of whom were ill with chills, and some with high fever. Only with difficulty could they reach the ambulance or the motor car that awaited them.

Two days after the women were released, the Republican Party, for the first time in the history of woman suffrage, caucused in the Senate in favor of forcing the Suffrage Amendment to a vote. The resolution, which was passed unanimously by the caucus, was not a direct attempt to win more Republican Senators, but it gave a decided tactical advantage to the Suffragists. It emphasized the fact that the Republicans were proud of their suffrage strength, and that they knew the Democrats had no right to be proud of theirs. The approaching Congressional elections spurred the Republicans to assist in holding up to the country the Administration's policy of vacillation and delay. This not only helped the Republicans politically, but it also served the Suffragists by goading the Majority Party into action.

Now, let us return for a few moments to the twenty-six imprisoned women. Before the Administration yielded to the hunger strike and released the Suffragists, the N.W.P. had announced that despite the previous arrests a second protest meeting would be held on the same spot in Lafayette Square. And the Administration actually granted a permit for this second meeting! Col. Ridley, already referred to, sent the following communication to Alice Paul:

> I have been advised that you desire to hold a demonstration in Lafayette Square on Thursday, August 22d. By direction of the chief of engineers, U. S. Army, you are hereby granted permission to hold this demonstration. You are advised good order must prevail.

And Alice Paul replied:

> We received yesterday your permit for a suffrage demonstration in Lafayette Park this afternoon, and are very glad that our meetings are no longer to be interfered with. Because of the illness of so many of our members, due to their treatment in prison this last week, and with the necessity of caring for them at headquarters, we

are planning to hold our next meeting a little later. We have not determined on the exact date but we will inform you of the time as soon as it is decided upon.

September 1, 1918, Alice Paul sent me the following letter:

We are planning another demonstration of protest over the delay in passing the Suffrage Amendment, on Monday, September 16th. It will be held at the Lafayette Statue in Lafayette Square, as on the occasion of all of our recent demonstrations.

I am writing to ask that you do everything possible to secure participants for this demonstration. Everyone who comes must be prepared for imprisonment. The Government authorities, as you know, gave us a permit for a meeting in August, but we think that, in spite of this, we shall be arrested at this next meeting.

I am sure that I need not emphasize to you the importance of having numbers take part in the meeting. We need most urgently the help of everyone you may be able to send. . . .

October 1, 1918, the Suffrage Amendment was voted on in the Senate and failed by two of having the necessary two-thirds vote. There were 54 yeas and 30 nays. The long-sought help from President Wilson came too late. His remarkable speech to the Upper House September 30th did not win us any support. The two votes that we knew we needed were not forthcoming.

From the beginning to the end of the President's address to the Senate, approximating 1500 words, his main accent was on Woman Suffrage as a war measure, as

"vitally essential" to the successful prosecution of the war.
He closed his appeal to the Senate in these words:

> The executive tasks of the war rest upon me.
> I ask that you lighten them and place in my hands
> instruments, spiritual instruments, which I do not
> now possess, which I sorely need, and which I
> have daily to apologize for not being able to
> employ.

Although he had, for five years, opposed the passage
of the Federal Woman Suffrage Amendment, he now told
the Senate that it seemed to him neither Party could justify
hesitation as to the method of obtaining suffrage for
women, whether by Federal initiative or State initiative,
and that there could be no Party issue involved in it.

In beautiful words he paid tribute to women's contribution to the war effort, and said the "war could not
have been fought either by the other nations engaged or
by America, if it had not been for the services of the
women—". . .

But each time I read his address, I wish the President
had seen fit to pay some slight tribute to the splendid fight
women had waged for nearly three-fourths of a century
for permission to share with men the privilege of serving
their country in times of peace as well as in war, and
that his plea for the granting of the suffrage to women
had been based partly on simple justice rather than on
expediency.

Our failure to pass the Senate October 1st did not
mean a break in the campaign, but an intensification of it.

The spirit of the renewed fight was exemplified in the
following letter to me from Alice Paul, dated October 25,
1918, which will help to lift the curtain on some of the

work that went on behind the scenes at our national Headquarters:

. . . . .

We have had someone see Pollock in South Carolina, who takes his seat in the Senate in November to fill the unexpired term caused by the death of Senator Tillman. Pollock has promised to vote for the national suffrage amendment. . . . Please do not publish in the papers that Pollock has come out in support of the amendment, as he thinks it would make it more difficult for him because of condemnation that might be brought upon his head from the people of South Carolina.

Senator Borah came to our headquarters on Sunday, and gave us a pledge to vote for the amendment after the elections. . . . He explains his change of front by stating that the platform upon which he was elected six years ago did not mention the national suffrage amendment, and, therefore, he was free to vote his own convictions; but the platform on which he is now running declares for the amendment, . . . In his own hand, he wrote a statement setting forth his position which he authorized us to telegraph to Idaho. We have asked Miss Whittemore who is campaigning in Idaho, to give the widest possible publicity to his statement and have his friends . . . congratulate him, so that he will be committed so thoroughly that he cannot retreat after the election is over.

Please do not give publicity in the Philadelphia papers to Senator Borah's position either, as we are not counting upon him as an absolute vote yet. Unless, however, he breaks his pledge, he is, of course an additional vote. If we have Borah's vote, it will give us the two votes we are lacking.

. . . . .
Please continue to have as many telegrams and
letters of protest as possible sent to the President
and your two senators protesting against the continued delay in the passage of the amendment,
and particularly against the arrests of women
at the Capitol who have been protesting by banners against this delay.

Practically every day that the Senate has
been in session since the defeat of the amendment,
women have been arrested. None has been imprisoned; all have been released after a few hours
detention. These demonstrations have undoubt-
edly served to keep the matter before the Senate
as a subject calling for settlement, but their power
will be greatly increased if they are backed up by
the country.

Fortunately for the suffrage campaign, there were at
this time two Senatorial contests for vacancies in the short
term—in New Jersey and in New Hampshire—and in
both these States it happened that the Democratic candidates were pledged to vote for the Amendment if elected,
while the Republican candidates were both opposed.

The N.W.P. campaigned for the election of the Democratic candidates. The President was urged to appeal personally to the voters of New Jersey and New Hampshire
in behalf of his two candidates, and the candidates themselves appealed to their leader to aid them. They asked
President Wilson's help on the basis of their advocacy
of woman suffrage. But the President at first refused to
lend any assistance in these two contests, although his determined help at that time might have won for us the
two Senate votes we needed.

Shortly before the election, President Wilson did send

carry them at our hearts and thank God that we can say that we are the kinsmen of such.

But the President had made no plan to have his words converted into action and so this second appeal to the Senate failed as his first one had. A determined assertion of his power as leader of his party was needed.

11

OTHER WORK FOR EQUALITY FOR WOMEN CARRIED ON IN PENNSYLVANIA IN CONNECTION WITH SUFFRAGE CAMPAIGN 1918-1919

Although the Pennsylvania Branch of the National Woman's Party concentrated its efforts on the passage of the Susan B. Anthony Amendment, it welcomed opportunities to assist when possible in local movements for the advancement of woman's position in various fields of activity.

Before the end of 1918, two very stirring appeals for such assistance came to us. One was from the Woman's Medical College of Pennsylvania, and one from the Women Teachers Organization of Philadelphia.

But even when the N.W.P. was nearing its goal of enfranchising the women of the whole country, the conservative Suffragists of Philadelphia were still bitter toward the more aggressive group of the movement for using a different route to reach the goal for which all Suffragists were working—a goal toward which they had worked for nearly three-quarters of a century. This antagonism was shown when the Woman's Medical College of Pennsylvania was trying to raise a $75,000 Endowment Fund.

Dr. Gertrude A. Walker, Chairman of the Campaign Committee, early in December, 1918, asked me to handle the campaign's publicity and to serve on its Executive Committee. But the influenza epidemic of that year somewhat upset Dr. Walker's plans and it was not until early in 1919 that things got well under way. By that time, news that I had been asked to take charge of the campaign's publicity caused some excitement among conservative Suffragists. Dr. Walker received the following letter, dated February 11, 1919, from a member of a Suffrage Team organized to aid in the campaign, and forwarded it to me:

I am sorry indeed to have to send you at this time anything of a discouraging nature, but under the circumstances I fear there is no alternative but to ask for the release of the Suffrage Team. After careful consideration on the part of the team and the alternates, the following conclusion was reached.

Inasmuch as the National American Woman Suffrage Association has officially repudiated the National Woman's Party, a group of fanatics whom we refuse to recognize as loyal suffragists; and particularly since their late disloyal attempt to burn the President of the United States in effigy—Officers of the Woman Suffrage Party of Philadelphia feel it necessary, though with sincere regret, to withdraw from the College Campaign—the publicity of which is to be handled by one, who in the eyes of the press and the public, is identical with the National Woman's Party.

We are all exceedingly sorry for this but we are thoroughly disgusted with the policy of the Woman's Party, and we find continually in our work evidence of the harm they are doing the Cause; also we are forced constantly to explain the difference in the two organizations and we wish to avoid any association or possibility of further confusion in the eyes of the public. The situation in this case would be particularly dangerous as the Suffrage Team included the two most prominent Suffrage Leaders of Philadelphia.

No doubt we shall all be able to do something individually to help the campaign—but a team is now out of the question. . . .

That I should be considered "in the eyes of the press and the public . . . identical with the National Woman's Party" was surely an undeserved but very flattering compliment! I knew, however, the value of team work in a campaign to raise money and I thought, under the circumstances, it would be best for me to give up my official connection with it. February 15th, I wrote Dr. Walker a letter releasing her and her Committee from the contract they had made with me.

Our work with the Women Teachers Organization of Philadelphia had a very different ending, as the following account will show.

In 1918, the public schools in Philadelphia presented this remarkable picture:

HIGH SCHOOLS	ELEMENTARY SCHOOLS
Number of men teachers 337	Number of men teachers 206
Number of women teachers ...427	Number of women teachers ..4,515
SALARY SCHEDULE	SALARY SCHEDULE
Minimum to men $800	Minimum to men $800
Minimum to women 700	Minimum to women 600
Maximum to men 2,700	Maximum to men 1,400
Maximum to women 1,750	Maximum to women 1,100

Smarting under this unfair use of public funds, for the raising of which women were taxed on the same basis as men, the women teachers of Philadelphia decided to organize and wage a vigorous campaign of protest against the injustice they suffered. By November, 1918, 3,300 women teachers were enrolled as members in the Women Teachers Organization of Philadelphia, as the new organization was called.

On the suggestion of an editor of one of Philadelphia's leading newspapers, representatives of the Women Teachers Organization came to the Headquarters of the Pennsylvania Branch of the National Woman's Party for advice on needed publicity for their campaign. The teachers' plight served as a challenge to us. With official approval of the National Woman's Party, I offered to handle the teachers' publicity as a contribution from our Headquarters to their campaign.

At first the women teachers met obstacles at every turn. Although they were working for equalization of salaries *upward*, many men teachers bitterly opposed their efforts, and also the school authorities were anything but favorably inclined toward them.

December 9, 1918, the W.T.O. held a public meeting in the auditorium of the William Penn High School at which Miss M. Carey Thomas was the principal speaker. As a result of this very successful meeting, which crowded the auditorium and received publicity not only in the Philadelphia papers but in the Bryn Mawr and Ardmore press as well, the teachers were forbidden to hold any more meetings in the high school auditoriums. In order to continue their campaign, the women were forced to hold their meetings in various other halls.

The Woodruff Bill, for which the W.T.O. had worked faithfully, was signed by the Governor July 10, 1919, and gave salary increases of from ten to twenty-five per cent to teachers throughout the State. Also, there was included in the reckoning a bonus of $100 for the Philadelphia teachers. This successful work of the W.T.O. raised its standing with the Philadelphia Board of Education and made the organization's work for equalization of salaries easier. In December, 1919, Mr. Simon Gratz, President of the Board of Education, invited the W.T.O. to resume its meetings in the public high schools.

December 11, 1919, Edith A. Sprowles, Chairman of the Committee on Equalization of Salaries, reported that all the members of the Finance Committee of the Board of Public Education said they favored equalization of salaries, considered the W.T.O.'s plan excellent, and would take it up as soon as they could get the money required. (The plan the W.T.O. had proposed was a graduated scale to reach equalization.)

The compensation of public school teachers was not based on preparation for the work, on special ability to impart knowledge to the young, on experience in teaching, or on their financial obligation and responsibility to others. A young man just graduated from the School of Pedagogy, with no financial responsibility except for his own support, was paid more than a woman with college degrees, years of experience in teaching, the added culture of foreign travel, who was, perhaps, helping to support an old parent, assisting in the education of a younger member of her family, or who might be facing the responsibility of raising her own orphaned child. The unencumbered young man was paid a larger salary simply because he chanced to be born a male. It might even be possible that he was not taking up teaching as a permanent profession but only as a stepping stone to some better paid work. The small percentage of men teachers in the public schools of Philadelphia in 1918 was evidence that the profession was not attractive to men from the point of view of compensation. They represented only about 10% of the city's teaching force. However, when the unjust discrimination against women teachers on the salary question was raised, the stock reply was that men were the heads of families and were therefore in need of higher compensation. This argument did not affect the compensation of widowed heads of families, but was somehow construed to apply to unmarried men. In other words, sex alone was the basis for the unfair treatment of women teachers in 1918, when the women took up the cudgels to correct that inequality.

Even when the equalization of salaries was admitted by the Board of Public Education to be inevitable, opposition to it was so great in certain quarters that approach to the reform had to be gradual. At their meeting May 13, 1920, the W.T.O. saw the wisdom of compromise. They decided to endorse the proposition made by Mr. Dick to read 1922 into the June, 1920, schedule if that would mean the greatest possible relief to the women teachers in June. But the women were working for more than equalization of salaries. At a meeting October 14, 1920, the Chairman of the Nominating Committee reported that every nominee for office had pledged herself to stand for the following principles:

1. Equal pay for equal work.
2. Equal opportunity in the teaching field for men and women.
3. Superior ability in teachers must be judged according to the terms of an acknowledged and accepted standard, and not according to the mere opinion of any person or persons in authority.
4. Recognition by the school authorities of our right to organize and to use the school buildings for organization work in any manner that does not interfere with school duties.

At that same meeting, October 14, 1920, Jane Allen, Chairman of the W.T.O., gave a résumé of the meeting of the Board of Education, at which victory for *equalization* was won, and at which Judge Dimner Beeber, a member of the Board, and a staunch supporter of woman's rights, befriended the women "at a most critical moment." The maximum salary for women high school teachers was increased January 1, 1920, to $3140. To stimulate advanced professional study, a plan to pay a small additional salary to a limited number, known as *Class C* teachers, was put into effect September 1, 1922. However, this method of reward on a percentage basis opened the door for favoritism and caused some dissatisfaction. The plan was discontinued in 1945. As of September 1, 1921, the maximum salary of elementary school women teachers was increased to $2000.

The Finegan Bill, which was signed by the Governor, April 28, 1921, provided for high school teachers in Philadelphia and other first class districts a maximum salary of $3200 with the provision that, subject to regulations prescribed by the State Board of Education and the local Board of Education, the maximum salary for high school teachers should be advanced to $3600.

Early in its campaign, the Women Teachers Organization endorsed the single salary schedule. This schedule, which provided the same salary schedule for teachers whether they worked in elementary or senior high schools, was adopted throughout Pennsylvania in 1947.

Now let us return to the publicity upon which the teachers were largely depending for the success of their campaign. They knew that their demand for equalization of salaries was a just one, and they believed that an awakened public would support their campaign. Day after day, representatives of the W.T.O. came to the National Woman's Party Headquarters to report any news available. Their appeal to prominent representatives of the business and professional world for statements in support of their campaign met with remarkable success, and the newspapers were generous in allotting space to this propaganda. But one day when the teachers seemed troubled because they had no news to offer, one of them chanced to speak of some women teachers that were eking out their inadequate salaries by working after school hours in a department store. This I felt sure was news that would surprise the public and stimulate interest in the teachers' campaign, and I let the teachers know they had told me enough for that day. The next day's publicity was the best we had had, one paper devoting a whole column to our story.

Although the following letter written by Jane Allen, August 16, 1919, was addressed to me, it belonged largely to the National Woman's Party without whose generous contribution of the facilities of the State Headquarters my handling of the teachers' publicity would not have been possible. A part of Miss Allen's letter follows:

Dear Miss Katzenstein:
    Many times since I left home I've wanted to write you, and before that time too, to tell you, if I can, that I feel warm gratitude to you for the splendid assistance you gave us last winter. We could never have launched a successful campaign unless we had had one of your experience and judgment to open the gates for us. I feel that our publicity campaign awakened the entire state; and the legislators were quick to capitalize public sentiment. The experienced lobbyists at Harrisburg who feel, and rightly feel, that our victory was largely due to their influence with the leaders, have failed, I think, to realize what Philadelphia, by its publicity campaign, did for the entire cause. But we need not worry as to who takes credit for the work; a few of us have been at least close spectators. I for one believe and am sure that the successful launching of the entire work was yours.

I wanted you to know that I appreciated what you did for us.

The outcome, I feel, has been very successful. We met with nothing but opposition in the closing days of the legislature, but we fought every bit and won.

Very sincerely yours,

Jane Allen.

But women teaching in the public schools of Philadelphia had to fight not only for equal pay for equal work, they had to battle even for the simple right to teach in the public schools if they had done the normal thing of getting married. A determined, rather prolonged, but unsuccessful effort was made to oust the married woman teacher from the Philadelphia public school system. That the husband might not have earned sufficient to establish a comfortable home for his family and might have welcomed the financial assistance of his wife, that the wife might have liked her profession so much that she preferred it to housework and felt that by teaching she was making her best contribution to society—neither of these points of view seemed to be considered when the plan was first proposed. The wife naturally rebelled against this attempted infringement of her right to plan her own life-work and felt that city officials had no more right to restrict a woman's activities than they had to circumscribe the activities of a man. Her home was her castle and she and her husband were the ones to determine the best method of running it.

In the Philadelphia *Evening Bulletin* of September 2, 1930, it was reported that Philadelphia's Director of Public Safety, Lemuel B. Schofield, had, in the last month, discharged six married women from his department.

A specific case much advertised in the press during this

controversy was that of a woman whose husband held a public office, owned an automobile, and lived in an apartment cared for by a maid. Director Schofield seemed to think such a woman did not need to earn money and by working in an office was keeping some unemployed person out of a job. Apparently he overlooked the fact that the maid in the case was a person, and that her employment might have been made possible by the work of her mistress outside her home.

When the Philadelphia *Record* asked me to comment on the situation, I pointed out the injustice of employing a woman that had passed a Civil Service examination and then dismissing her just because she was married and was, in the opinion of the Director of Public Safety, not in need of an earned salary.

In a free country like ours, I asked, hadn't a woman the right to decide whether she preferred office work to house work? Perhaps she was better prepared for the one than the other and could, in the Department of Public Safety, earn more than a maid's wages. Perhaps she and her husband were looking forward to owning a home of their own and his earnings alone were not sufficient to make this possible. Surely they were the persons best qualified to plan their present and their future without the interference of a public official.

I argued that Director Schofield's action had established a paradoxical and dangerous precedent. If it was fair to dismiss a woman whose husband earned a salary, why not dismiss any woman that had saved or inherited funds sufficient to yield her a living—even a bare one? And, to go a step further, why allow men similarly situated as to incomes to hold any public position for which they received financial compensation? And if such a plan were followed, might it not be necessary to appoint a commission to determine the basis on which men and women would be eligible for public office? Just how large a saved or inherited income would be considered sufficient to disqualify them for paid public service?

The *Record* of Sunday, September 7, 1930, not only used my comments on the situation that had arisen in Philadelphia's Department of Public Safety, but gave them generous space, big headlines, and a conspicuous place in the paper.

Director Schofield had inadvertently emphasized the need to pass the EQUAL RIGHTS AMENDMENT to the federal Constitution, a measure sponsored by the National Woman's Party. While the Susan B. Anthony Amendment secured to the women of the United States the inestimable right to the ballot, the passage of the EQUAL RIGHTS AMENDMENT, now before Congress, is needed to supplement the legislation enacted in 1920, and to win for women full equality with men under the law. It reads: "Equality of rights under the law shall not be denied or abridged by the United States or by any State on account of sex." *

* See Appendix III.

12

*WATCHFIRES OF FREEDOM
LIGHTED ... PRESIDENT WILSON
SECURES LAST NEEDED SENATE VOTE
1919*

At the beginning of 1919, the National Woman's Party faced a very difficult situation. The 65th Congress would soon end its final session; President Wilson was in Paris attending the Peace Conference; and without the aid of the President the Federal Suffrage Amendment could not possibly get favorable action in the Senate.

The N.W.P. knew that President Wilson, if sufficiently aroused, could at times accomplish almost the impossible. The organization therefore planned once more to emphasize his responsibility as head of the Party in power, and the imperative need for Democratic support of a vital subject already endorsed publicly by the President.

Why did President Wilson continue to postpone securing for the women of America the support in the Senate needed to pass the Amendment? He had successfully overcome much more difficult problems in solving public questions that faced him—questions, I might suggest, that really interested him. Almost immediately after the United States had voted not to enter the war in Europe, the President led us into that conflict. Over determined opposition to conscription in the South, he had been able to conscript southern men. He had managed to win mothers to his point of view in regard to the war after they had fought enthusiastically for his peace program at election time. He had surely proved his great ability as a leader.

How could the President be moved to speed the passage of the Susan B. Anthony Amendment during the life of the 65th Congress? As effective as the picketing campaign had been in the past, it might be that the time had come to supplement it with something new in the way of the dramatic.

On New Year's Day, 1919, the N.W.P. lighted the first of its "Watchfires of Freedom." In an urn dedicated to that purpose, wood from a tree in Independence Square, Philadelphia, was lighted, and this blaze was placed on the pavement in front of the White House in a direct line with the President's front door. Perhaps woman's demand for justice might thus be burned so effectively into the President's consciousness that he would be impelled to act to make that justice a reality. Into the flame, Mrs. Lawrence Lewis, of Philadelphia, dropped the President's most recent words on *democracy*—words spoken at various meetings in Europe.

Women holding banners and carrying torches stood guard over the watchfires all day and all night, and a bell hung in the balcony at nearby Suffrage Headquarters tolled when the watch began, when the watch changed, and when the President's beautiful (but to us empty) words on democracy and kindred themes in speeches before various European audiences were consigned to the flames.

The unquenchable spirit of the women seemed actually to have entered the flames of the watchfires, which burned as if by magic. When, on that New Year's afternoon of 1919, soldiers and sailors overturned the urn at the gates of the White House and stamped out the blazing wood, the watchfire was later relighted and, despite the rain, burned throughout the night as relays of women watched and fed the flame.

Crowds watched the demonstrations, the press publicized the drama, and the world knew that the United States lagged behind a number of countries whose women had full or some form of electoral rights. I wish here to pay a special tribute to New Zealand, the first country to give full suffrage to all women (1893) ; and to Sweden, the first country in the world to extend to women any measure of suffrage whatever.

While American women at the gates of the White House were pleading in vain for justice, President Wilson at Buckingham Palace toasted England's King with these fine words: "We have used great words, all of us. We have used the words 'right' and 'justice' and now we are to prove whether or not we understand these words." The suffrage bell tolled and these words were burned to ashes.

January 13, 1919, the day the great world Peace Conference began its deliberations at Versailles on administering "right" and "justice," 23 American women were arrested in front of the White House for asking for these same blessings.

January 25th, 1919, the President in Paris received a delegation of French women, who urged that woman suffrage be one of the points settled at the Peace Conference. To them, President Wilson expressed admiration for the women of France and told the delegation of his deep personal interest in the enfranchisement of women. Our oldest suffrage prisoner, who had passed her three score years and ten, Mrs. Mary A Nolan, a gentle but very courageous woman from Florida, promptly burned these words of the President in the Suffrage Watchfire. During January, Mrs. Nolan was arrested many times at the Watchfire demonstrations, and received one sentence of twenty-four hours in jail. In 1917, it may be recalled, she was given a sentence of six days in prison for picketing.

Through January and the early part of February, the Watchfire demonstrations continued and the N.W.P. protested vigorously over the Senate's delayed action. These protests in Washington were well publicized in the Paris papers, and cables were sent direct to the President at the Peace Conference demanding assistance from him. The seriousness of the situation seemed finally to impress President Wilson who, in turn, began to contact Senate leaders by cable. And the Senate leaders began to take action. February 2nd, 1919, the Democratic Senators favorable to suffrage called a meeting at the Capitol to "consider ways and means." February 3rd, Senator Jones of New Mexico announced in the Senate that the Amendment would be brought up for discussion February 10th. February 4th, a caucus of all Democratic Senators was called at the Capitol by Senator Martin of Virginia, Democratic floor leader in the Senate. This was the first Democratic caucus in the Senate since war had been declared. The Democratic Party was showing what appeared to be real interest in getting the two Senate votes the Amendment needed.

After hours of heated debate, Senator Pollock of South Carolina announced for the first time that he would vote in favor of the Amendment.

Even with the pledged vote of Senator Pollock, the Democrats knew that we were still one vote short of the two-thirds majority we needed. Yet, with no plans made for winning that last vote, they set February 10th as the date on which a vote in the Senate would be taken.

On the day preceding that vote, the N.W.P. planned to register indignation over the President's failure to convert his words on democracy into effective action. Following the precedent set by the Revolutionary fathers, who burned a portrait of King George because he "refused to reign over a free people," a figure of President Wilson, sketched on paper in black and white, was burned in the Watchfire Urn on the sidewalk opposite the White House. Sue White of Tennessee and Mrs. Gabrielle Harris of South Carolina dropped the figure into the flames. Preceding them were Elizabeth McShane, of Philadelphia, and Nell Mercer bearing an earthen urn filled with fire. On one of the banners displayed at this ceremony were these words:

THE PRESIDENT IS RESPONSIBLE FOR THE BE-
TRAYAL OF AMERICAN WOMANHOOD

It was, I suppose, to be expected that here and there an earnest and devoted member might not absolutely approve some daring act of the N.W.P., and might worry over it. Shortly after Mrs. Lawrence Lewis' release from prison I sent her a letter from one of Pennsylvania's most prominent Suffragists, who had served several terms in prison for her suffrage work. This fearless member was upset over the burning of the President in effigy. March 8th, Mrs. Lewis wrote expressing regret that the effigy burning had upset this member. However she "felt sure that feeling would soon pass." Mrs. Lewis added that while the writer of the letter "needs no reminder of the fact of Party responsibility, I think that her letter shows that she does not follow it to its logical consequences. Of course if our struggle was to secure some trifle, these unpleasant actions, such as burning speeches and effigies, would not be necessary. I cannot see, however, how anyone who cares as much for freedom as this splendid person does, should hesitate over what is after all, a very mild deed (in my opinion)."

All of us, of course, regretted the need to do these things, but the President could, at any time, have made them unnecessary. It was in his hands to let us know when we had sufficiently "concerted public opinion" to make him feel the time had come for him to aid us as he alone could. Suffragists could not forget that in the Civil War there was only a very small group of women, Susan B. Anthony and a few co-workers, that remained faithful to the cause of woman suffrage. Now, more than half a century later, during another war, thousands of women were holding aloft the banner of freedom for women. These thousands could see that victory was actually in sight, and that the time had come to speed the arrival of that victory by every legitimate means within their power.

Fifteen Pennsylvania women took part in the January and February Watchfire demonstrations and each of them except Miss Mary H. Ingham was sentenced to five days in jail. Miss Ingham was freed because there were no witnesses against her, but she had been held in jail for two days before she was brought to trial. The other fourteen Pennsylvanians were Jennie Bronenberg, Cora Crawford, Mrs. Mary Carroll Dowell, Mrs. Edmund C. Evans, Rose Fishstein, Mrs. Rose Gratz Fishstein, Reba Gomborov, Kate C. Heffelfinger, Marie Ernst Kennedy, Mrs. Lawrence Lewis, Elizabeth Mc Shane, Martha W. Moore, Mrs. Martha Reed Shoemaker, and Ellen Winsor.

William Jennings Bryan, like many other Democratic leaders, became disturbed over the suffrage situation. This is the argument he used in consulting with the Democratic opponents of federal woman suffrage— an argument he later gave to the press:

Woman suffrage is coming to the country and to the world. It will be submitted to the states by the next Congress, if it is not submitted by the present Congress.

I hope the Democrats of the South will not handicap the Democrats of the North by compelling them to spend the next twenty-five years explaining to the women of the country why their party prevented the submission of the suffrage amendment to the states.

This is our last chance to play an important part in bringing about this important reform, and it is of vital political concern that the Democrats of the Northern Mississippi Valley should not be burdened by the charge that our party prevented the passage of the suffrage amendment, especially when it is known that it is coming in spite of, if not with the aid of, the Democratic Party.

As necessary as it was for President Wilson to see this handwriting on the wall, his past attitude toward federal woman suffrage was coming back to haunt him. His early bitter opposition, followed later on by a distressing lack of interest; his support of members of his Party that opposed the Amendment; his reversal of policy only when forced by political expediency to make that change—these things were now making it difficult for him to influence his Party on this subject. Democrats that had, by their votes, publicly committed themselves as opponents of the Amendment did not wish to sacrifice their dignity by switching their position just to follow their leader. They had by this time built up a formidable resistance, which the President found it difficult to overcome. When on February 24, 1919, the President returned to this country from Europe, he had only seven days in which to act on the Suffrage Amendment, before the session of Congress would end, March 3rd.

Boston, the President's landing place, had arranged a great reception for him. A beautiful, sunny day had apparently tempted the whole city to turn out to welcome him.

When the President, heading the procession, arrived at the reviewing stand, a file of twenty-two Suffragists, who had managed to slip through the "deadline," marched silently up to the base of the reviewing stand and took up their post facing the marines, who were supposed to protect President Wilson from these intruders. There the women unfurled their brightly colored banners thus adding beauty to the occasion as they stood calmly triumphant in having, contrary to official orders, carried out at least a part of their program of greeting to the leader of a great political party. So quiet and dignified were the women that they seemed to be just a part of the elaborate ceremony. But a large lettered banner they held aloft explained that their greeting to the President had a special significance, and they had the pleasure of hearing people slowly read the clearly written and concisely expressed message it carried.

The banner read:

> MR. PRESIDENT, YOU SAID IN THE SENATE ON SEPTEMBER 20 "WE SHALL NOT ONLY BE DISTRUSTED BUT WE SHALL DESERVE TO BE DISTRUSTED IF WE DO NOT ENFRANCHISE WOMEN."
> ... YOU ALONE CAN REMOVE THIS DISTRUST NOW BY SECURING THE ONE VOTE NEEDED TO PASS THE SUFFRAGE AMENDMENT BEFORE MARCH 4.

Katharine A. Morey, a young Brookline woman, whose colonial ancestors lived in Concord, carried an American flag at the head of the picket line. After standing about three-quarters of an hour, the Suffragists were told by Superintendent Crowley that they could not remain there while the President went by. When Miss Morey explained that it was in order to be there at the time the President passed that they had come and that they could not go back until the President had gone by, the twenty-two Suffragists were, with unusual courtesy, arrested and taken to the House of Detention, charged with "loitering more than seven minutes."

Mrs. Agnes H. Morey, Massachusetts Chairman of the N.W.P., commenting later on this charge, said, "It is a most extraordinary thing. Thousands loitered from curiosity on the day the President arrived. Twenty-two loitered for liberty, and only those who loitered for liberty were arrested."

In planning the Boston demonstrations, the N.W.P. had given the program full publicity in advance of February 24th. They wished not only Boston but the whole world to know why they were there. The press had been told that in the morning there would be a line of silent pickets holding up lettered banners calling to the President's attention the demand for his effective aid; that in the afternoon there would be a Mass Meeting on Boston Common at which those parts of the President's speech that related to democracy and liberty would be burned. It was amazing how these announcements alarmed official Boston. For two weeks, the Boston papers were filled with suffrage publicity. As on the day of President Wilson's Inauguration, the N.W.P. was again his rival for front-page space.

Although Boston's police protected the President from the silent pickets, throngs of Boston's citizens were permitted to listen from three o'clock in the afternoon until six to suffrage speakers on Boston Common, who explained why the protest was made, what the status of the Amendment was, and who was blocking its passage through the Senate. But at six o'clock, the order came to arrest the speakers! Thus Mrs. C. C. Jack, wife of Professor Jack of Harvard University, Mrs. Mortimer Warren of Boston, whose husband was head of a base hospital in France, and Elsie Hill, daughter of the late Congressman Hill of Connecticut, were arrested and taken to the House of Detention where they joined their comrades.

The women were kept all night in the House of Detention under the Court House. Because of the condition of the place, they slept in their clothes, four women to a cell, on iron shelves two feet wide. The place was soon filled with "drunks" and disorderly persons. The next morning, over the protests of the women, Chief Bolster's decision to try each prisoner separately and in closed court was carried out. The guards took the women by force to a private room. On entering the judge's private trial room, each woman said, "As an American citizen under arrest, I demand a public trial." The trial in closed court proceeded with no coöperation from the women. Some were tried under wrong names; some, under different names, were tried more than once; but most of them were tried under the name of Jane Doe.

Some among the crowds that came to the court house to attend the trial protested so vigorously to the city officials that the last three women were tried in open court. With the exception of Wilma Henderson, who was released because she was a minor, all of the women were sentenced to eight days in jail, in lieu of fines.

A Boston reporter made this interesting comment: "Superintendent Kelleher didn't know when he was in Congress with Elsie Hill's father he would some day have Congressman Hill's daughter in his jail."

Typical of the support the women received from the folks back home was a telegram received by Mrs. Lois Warren Shaw from her husband. Mr. Shaw, a Harvard graduate, and a successful manufacturer in Manchester, New Hampshire, wired his wife: "Don't yield. I have competent nurses to look after the children."

A few days after Boston's imprisonment of the Suffragists, the "Prison Special," * a special car of Suffragists, who had served prison sentences, and who had been touring the country from coast to coast, arrived in Boston. A meeting was held in one of the theatres of that conservative stronghold and a crowd eager to hear more about their own fearless suffrage leaders filled the house to overflowing and cheered while former suffrage prisoners were decorated with the *prison pin*, which had now become famous. Also Boston had an opportunity to hear from members of the "Prison Special" about their sensational tour and their success in directing public attention, during the closing days of the session of Congress, to the suffrage situation in the Senate.

The Pennsylvania members of the "Prison Special" were Mary H. Ingham, Ella Riegel, Elizabeth McShane, and Mary Winsor.

When President Wilson arrived in Washington after his Boston reception, one of his first official acts was a conference at the Capitol with Senator Jones of New Mexico, Chairman of the Senate Suffrage Committee. Not only was the President disturbed over the Senate's failure to pass the Amendment, but he talked of ways and means of getting it through the Upper House. As a result of this conference, Senator Jones, who had refused just a few weeks earlier to re-introduce the Susan B. Anthony Amendment after its defeat in the Senate February 10th, now agreed to introduce a new suffrage amendment with slightly different wording but having the same purpose as the original one. However, this new Resolution, because of possible controversial points in the enforcement article, was not so satisfactory to Suffragists as the clearly worded one originally proposed by Susan B. Anthony.

This new Amendment was a concession to Senator Gay

---

* This campaign tour should not be confused with the one made by the "Suffrage Special" in 1916.

of Louisiana, a Democrat, who had voted against the Susan B. Anthony Amendment February 10th, but who at once agreed to vote in favor of the new Resolution. The last vote needed to pass the Amendment was thus won, and the majority Party began immediately on a last-minute attempt to have the Resolution passed.

March 1st, Senator Jones tried to get unanimous consent to consider it, but Republican Senator Wadsworth of New York, an anti-Suffragist, objected. The next day, consent was again asked, but another Republican anti-Suffragist, Senator Weeks of Massachusetts, objected. The last day of the session, March 3rd, a Republican Suffragist from Illinois, Senator Sherman, also objected. Thus the Democratic Congress closed without passing the Amendment. The support of federal woman suffrage by the President and his Party had been too little and again had come too late.

An unfortunate political system that prevailed in 1919—one that has since been changed—placed the Suffragists at a disadvantage. The Republican Congress elected in November, 1918, would not convene in regular session until December, 1919. The N.W.P.'s job was to induce the President to call a special session of Congress. The organization had taken a poll of the new Congress by personal interviews and by mail, and had found a safe two-thirds majority in the House, but there was still lacking one necessary vote in the Senate.

President Wilson left again for Europe right after the 65th Congress came to an end, but before sailing March 4th, 1919, he decided to speak at the Metropolitan Opera House in New York in behalf of his proposed League of Nations. The N.W.P. immediately arranged a demonstration in New York to protest against the President's leaving the United States without making any plans for a settlement of the woman suffrage question. Also it was planned that every word on democracy spoken by the President in the Opera House should be burned at a public meeting nearby. Twenty-five women left the N.W.P. Headquarters at 13 E. 41st Street, New York City, carrying a flag of the United States, the purple, white, and gold banners of the organization, and two lettered banners that read:

MR. PRESIDENT, HOW LONG MUST WOMEN WAIT FOR LIBERTY?
and
MR. PRESIDENT, AMERICAN WOMEN PROTEST AGAINST THE DEFEAT OF SUFFRAGE FOR WHICH YOU AND YOUR PARTY ARE RESPONSIBLE. WE DEMAND THAT YOU CALL AN EXTRA SESSION OF CONGRESS IMMEDIATELY TO PASS THE SUFFRAGE AMENDMENT. AN AUTOCRAT AT HOME IS A POOR CHAMPION FOR DEMOCRACY ABROAD.

Soldiers and sailors, just returned from abroad, joined with the police in attacking the suffrage demonstrators. Some of the women were knocked down and some were trampled upon and their flags were torn and broken. But one of them, Elsie Hill, who had managed to hold on to her torch, began a protest meeting. Before the police could interfere, she had burned some of the words the President had just spoken—words hurried out to her by a messenger from the Opera House. As usual, the women were arrested, but they were quickly released. When the women returned to their Headquarters, they discovered that persons had broken in, stolen a large number of banners, and burned them in the street.

Naval and military officers, sailors and privates, called at Headquarters that night and the next day to apologize for the way other men in uniform had acted and to assure the Suffragists that those men had not represented the attitude of service men generally.

Soon after the Pennsylvania State Chairman, Mary H. Ingham, returned from her cross-country campaigning on the "Prison Special" she had to make plans for the 4th Annual Convention of the Pennsylvania Branch of the N.W.P., which was to be held in Philadelphia, April 26, 1919. As the Call to the Convention covered much recent woman suffrage history in both State and national campaigns, I shall give it in full with a list of the State's Executive Committee members that signed it:

The Fourth Annual Convention
of the
Pennsylvania Branch, National Woman's Party
will be held in
Philadelphia, Saturday, April 26, 1919

To the Pennsylvania Members of the National Woman's Party:

American women have, during the long months of war, made unceasing demand for enfranchisement. Although the Federal Suffrage Amendment has been before the United States Senate for more than a year, women still find themselves outside the nation's organic life.

During these same months of international struggle, the governments of fourteen European countries have recognized in the enfranchisement of women a measure vital to the strength of the people and to the welfare of nations.

Every English-speaking people in the world, every one of the new democracies, and almost every constitutional monarchy in Europe has set up the standard of equal rights and responsibilities for men and women. But the Government of the United States lags behind European governments in meeting this "acid test" of the reality of its democracy.

As only fifteen of our forty-eight states have granted full suffrage, we still have fourteen million unenfranchised women who are denied the right to take direct and authoritative part in the solution of the great problems of civilization—problems that now press heavily upon the minds and hearts of men and women in this and other lands.

Within the last two years, the people of this country have registered their will through the favorable vote on the Suffrage Amendment in the House of Representatives on January 10, 1918, by the granting of full suffrage in four states, of Presidential suffrage in nine states, and of primary suffrage in two states. Twelve and a half million women will be entitled to vote in the Presidential election in 1920.

At this, our Fourth Annual Convention, the extraordinary events of our intensive campaign for National Suffrage will be put before the members of the National Woman's Party in true perspective. The demonstrations in Washington and the unremitting political work in Congress and in the Congressional Districts will be shown as equally necessary parts of a well-considered plan of action. The fact that the Federal Suffrage Amendment had, at the end of the 65th Congress, all of the votes necessary for its passage and lacked only the time for the vote to be taken, is convincing evidence of the success of the methods used in setting forward the enfranchisement of the women of America. The sacrifices made have been amply justified.

It is expected that the President will call a special session of Congress shortly. You are urged to come to the Convention prepared to work for the passage of the amendment and thus to hasten the end of woman's long struggle for liberty.

STATE EXECUTIVE COMMITTEE

Mary H. Ingham, *Chairman*
Mary E. Bakewell,
　　　　　1st Vice-Chairman
Joan L. Brumm, *2nd Vice Chairman*
Mary Churchman Morgan,
　　　　　Recording Secretary
Martha Davis,
　　　　　Corresponding Secretary
　　Rebecca D. Ernst, *Treasurer*
Alice Brock
Fanny Travis Cochran
Harriet W. Dulles

Katharine G. Halligan
Lucretia M. B. Mitchell
Florence L. Sanville
Georgie W. Yeatman
Cecelia P. Bass
Caroline Katzenstein
Mary A. Burnham
Lavinia L. Dock
Mary V. Grice
Marie Ernst Kennedy
Sarah H. Lockrey
Anna Lowenburg
Ella Riegel

To us, who were weary of "the law's delay" and of the "insolence of office" and who saw many interesting activities beckoning us, for which time could not be spared from suffrage work, the fearless, aggressive campaign of the N.W.P. had been a great stride forward. It gave us renewed hope that we might soon reap the reward that generations of women had been denied in spite of the splendid educational campaigns they had waged and in spite of the courageous, rebellious spirit that some of them had shown. The leaders of the N.W.P. had, from the beginning of their campaign, inspired us with a confidence that made following them a privilege. I recall a reporter's once asking me to comment on a dramatic incident in which Alice Paul and Mrs. Lawrence Lewis had taken part. I had to tell him that the incident was news to me—that I had had no advance notice it would take place. But I added that my superlative confidence in those two leaders made me feel safe in saying whatever they did was right.

On the other hand, many Suffragists of the conservative wing of the movement, had only censure for the N.W.P. and, in spite of all the evidence to the contrary, sincerely thought that the young organization was putting the movement back ten or twenty years, the time seeming to depend on the strength of their disapprobation. They actually felt such antagonism toward the N.W.P. that they thought association with us was a form of disloyalty, if not worse. An unusually significant instance of this mental attitude was shown in a letter written by a sincere Suffragist less than two months before the N.W.P. actually succeeded in having both Houses of Congress pass the Susan B. Anthony Amendment. It was to an invitation to our Convention of April 26th, mentioned above, sent by a member of Pennsylvania's Executive Committee, Mrs. Mary V. Grice, that the Chief editorial writer of the *Public Ledger* wrote the following letter:

PUBLIC LEDGER
Independence Square
Philadelphia

April 17, 1919

My dear Mrs. Grice,

I am so sure that you would prefer absolute frankness from us that I am writing in that spirit in response to your kind invitation for the 26th. It would be much easier for Mrs. Stirling and for me to plead a previous engagement for that evening, and we have one in the last of the symphony concerts. I cannot imagine a greater pleasure than that we both should gain from being with you and the other interesting people in your group, and we are flattered that you should include us in it. But we both feel so strongly that Miss Paul and those of her party have done infinite injury to the suffrage cause, that we are not willing to take part in a public function which even seems to be in sympathy with her and their methods! I think I am right in saying that both of us have open minds; it is not because we are unwilling to hear all sides of a controverted question that we feel as we do. But there is a difference in being willing to hear

discussion and in taking part in what may be
termed a party gathering. I hope you will appreciate that we *do* take sincere pleasure in your kind
thought for us, and that we regret that we cannot
enjoy an evening's intimate contact with you in the
way you suggest.

Very sincerely yours, and with Mrs. Stirling's
cordial regards, I am,

Edmund Stirling

For a short time after the Pennsylvania Legislature
ratified the Amendment, June 24, 1919, the Pennsylvania
Branch of the N.W.P. continued to maintain headquarters
in the Penfield Building. Later, when Alice Brock, a member
of the State Executive Committee, offered to give us the
use of the large old Brock stable on Chancellor Street at
the rear of her home, we gladly moved our Headquarters
to 1613 Chancellor Street. This saving in rent enabled
us to contribute more to the Washington work.

By October, ratification had progressed with such speed
that I was tempted to take advantage of an interesting
business proposition, and wrote to the national secretary,
Mabel Vernon, asking if she thought I might soon withdraw
from the campaign. The following letter from Alice Paul,
in reply, emphasizes her great ability as a leader—her keen
political insight, and her long-range planning. Less than
five months after ratification began, June 4, 1919, she could
look forward to the possibility of completing this big task
"next February." And yet she was planning if necessary
to continue the campaign until 1921. Here, in part, is her
letter of October 31, 1919:

I am replying to your letter to Miss Vernon, in
which you ask about withdrawing from the campaign after Pennsylvania's quota of $10,000.00
has been raised, in order that you may take up
other work.

We cannot form any idea as to when the ratification campaign will be finished. It seems to me that the earliest it is likely to be finished is next February. It may, on the other hand, drag on until 1921 when it would seem that ratification must certainly come. I do not feel like giving any advice with regard to your taking up other work. Since this work may be so nearly at an end, we do not, of course, want you to forego an opportunity of getting a permanent position which would be satisfactory to you. On the other hand, I cannot bear to think of your leaving the campaign. I am sure you know perfectly well that I have always felt you were one of the corner-stones upon which the work has been built. I think that ratification would go faster if you would continue, because of all that you can do in the way of keeping the Pennsylvania group interested; and also because of all that you can do in raising money yourself, and, indeed, of all that you can do in so many ways. I think it would be a calamity to have you leave; but still, we would not want you to lose an opportunity of a good permanent position.

So nearly right was Alice Paul on the question of time, that by February 27, 1920, we were actually within three Legislatures of our goal! And in less than one more month we had 35 Legislatures on our side. But in emphasizing Alice Paul's ability as a leader, I have anticipated events and shall now go back to the time of the receipt of her letter.

The reader will recall the assistance the N.W.P. was able to give to the Women Teachers Organization in 1918, when that group, led by Jane Allen, was working to improve the status of Pennsylvania's women teachers. November 4, 1919, Jane Allen sent a circular letter to the members of her large organization reminding them of our help in their successful campaign and adding:

Miss Katzenstein . . . has asked me to assist her in distributing the inclosed communication. I am glad to respond for several reasons. First, for the cause of Suffrage. If the Federal Amendment is ratified, our cause—the welfare of women teachers, will be greatly strengthened; if the Amendment is defeated our work may be hampered for many years to come. Secondly, there is only one piece of work now for all suffrage parties—namely, the ratifying of the Federal Amendment. Any effort to accomplish this most important piece of work should be encouraged.

Let us do what we can for the good cause.

Now, back to the Washington scene. The Republicans would be in control of the newly elected Congress. The suffrage Cause had won here and lost there. New Jersey had elected Senator Edge who was in favor of the Amendment and had defeated Senator Baird who was opposed; while South Carolina had elected Senator Dial who opposed woman suffrage and had defeated Senator Pollock whose favorable vote had been pledged. That left things even. But when Mississippi defeated Senator Vardaman who favored the Amendment and elected in his place a man non-committal on the question, Senator Harrison, Suffragists were again placed in the position of being short one vote. Then there were two States, New Hampshire and Georgia, where opponents of suffrage were defeated and men that had not announced their stand on it were elected. New Hampshire had defeated Senator Drew and elected Senator Keyes; while Georgia had defeated Senator Hardwicke and elected Senator Harris.

Through the President's influence, two of the new Democratic Senators, Harrison of Mississippi and Harris of Georgia, had been elected, but neither of these men had been won to favor the Amendment, and neither of them was committed against it. From the time of their election until early spring, the N.W.P. had brought constant pressure upon President Wilson to win one of them to the suffrage side for that last vote in the Senate the Amendment needed. Seeing, however, no activity on the part of the President to secure the support of either of these two Senators, the N.W.P. made public its determination still to hold the President responsible for the passage of the Amendment, and threatened to resume dramatic protests against the Administration if it failed them. Friends of the Administration were worried and realized the danger to the Administration's many other endeavors if its suffrage record invited renewed attacks.

Alice Paul knew that Matthew Hale, former Chairman of the Progressive National Committee, although not a Democrat, was influential with the Administration, and she also knew that he was a sincere Suffragist. He might be a valuable ally. She suggested to Anita Pollitzer that she see Mr. Hale at once and talk over the suffrage situation with him. Mr. Hale was eager to help. He and Anita Pollitzer studied the Senate poll and selected Harris from among the non-committal Senators as the man upon whom Suffragists might pin their hope for that last needed Senate vote. He was known to be a firm supporter of President Wilson's. This was early in May, 1919, and the new Congress would convene May 19th.

But both President Wilson and Senator Harris were in Europe. Quick action was imperative. The N.W.P. concentrated on trying to get President Wilson to influence Senator Harris to declare himself in favor of the Suffrage Amendment. And Mr. Hale, who began to work on persons close to the President, made excellent progress. This pressure ultimately resulted in a conference participated in by Robert Woolley, Democratic Publicity Manager in the

1916 campaign; Homer S. Cummings, Chairman of the National Democratic Committee; William J. Cochran, Director of Publicity of the Democratic Committee; Joseph Tumulty, the President's Secretary; and Senator Thomas J. Walsh, of Montana. The outcome of this conference was a cable sent by Mr. Tumulty to President Wilson suggesting that he confer with Senator Harris. At the President's request, Senator Harris, who was at the time in Italy, went to France. Immediately a cable brought back the welcome news that Senator Harris would support the Suffrage Amendment. President Wilson had thus won for the Susan B. Anthony Amendment that last needed vote, and on the night of May 20th, he cabled to the new Congress an effective message in which he referred to that Amendment as follows:

> Will you permit me, turning from these matters, to speak once more and very earnestly of the proposed Amendment to the Constitution which would extend the Suffrage to women and which passed the House of Representatives at the last session of Congress? It seems to me that every consideration of justice and of public advantage calls for the immediate adoption of that Amendment and its submission forthwith to the legislatures of the several States.
>
> Throughout all the world this long delayed extension of the Suffrage is looked for; in the United States, longer, I believe, than anywhere else, the necessity for it, and the immense advantages of it to the national life, has been urged and debated by women and men who saw the need for it and urged the policy of it when it required steadfast courage to be so much beforehand with the common conviction; and I, for one, covet for our country the distinction of being among the first to act in a great reform.

Thus was the 64th vote for the Susan B. Anthony Amendment won in the United States Senate! A cable sent to the White House brought to Suffragists the good news that the difficult final Senate vote had at last been made sure. And that cable was followed immediately by another cable calling the new Congress into Special Session May 19, 1919.

It may clarify the suffrage situation to explain here that one week after Senator Jones of New Mexico and his Democratic colleagues refused to re-introduce the Susan B. Anthony Amendment after its defeat in the Senate, February 10, 1919, Senator Jones of Washington, ranking Republican on the Suffrage Committee, obtained unanimous consent and re-introduced it, thereby placing the original Amendment once more on its way to early reconsideration.

Although the Amendment had been passed by the House of Representatives in the 65th Congress, January 10, 1918, a new Congress made it necessary for the Amendment to be voted on again by that body. As soon, therefore, as the Republican Congress convened in special session, leaders of that party, in control of the 66th Congress, held a caucus and made plans to pass the Amendment promptly. Two days later, May 21, 1919, the Republican House voted in favor of the Amendment 304 to 89, exceeding the necessary two-thirds majority by 42 votes. This was a contrast to the vote in the House, January 10, 1918, when, under a Democratic-controlled Congress, there was just one vote to spare.

After the 64th vote in the Senate had been secured, two Republicans, Senator Keyes of New Hampshire, and Senator Hale of Maine, eagerly joined the winning side and announced their support of the Amendment. When, therefore, June 4, 1919, the measure was brought up in the Senate, victory was assured. The Amendment was carried by a vote of 66 to 30, including all voting and paired—two more than the required two-thirds majority. Of the 49 Republicans in the Senate, all but 9 favored the Amendment; of the 47 Democrats in that body, only 26 favored it. Counting only the votes cast, there were 56 yeas, 25 nays.

Years of arduous campaigning had at last secured sufficient support from both major political Parties to make victory assured. The Susan B. Anthony Amendment was adopted by both Houses of Congress.

13

VICTORY ... THE SUSAN B. ANTHONY AMENDMENT IS RATIFIED
1919-1920

Although the 65th Congress, controlled by Democrats, had failed to pass the Federal Suffrage Amendment and had allowed that honor to go to the Republican-controlled 66th Congress, quick action by the Democratic National Committee helped in the ratification campaign. That Committee immediately after the Amendment passed Congress, passed a resolution calling upon the legislatures of the several States to hold special sessions, where necessary, to ratify the Amendment, and thus to "enable women to vote in the national elections in 1920."

Fortunately, we did not need to ask for a special session of the Pennsylvania Legislature, but we did need help in getting favorable legislative action on the Amendment; and the following letter from the Attorney General gave the Pennsylvania campaign an auspicious beginning:

Office of the Attorney General
Washington, D. C.

June 11, 1919

Miss Caroline Katzenstein,
   Executive Secretary,
      National Woman's Party,
         213 Penfield Building,
            Philadelphia, Pa.
Dear Miss Katzenstein:

I have your letter of the 6th instant.

I am very pleased to write at once to the Democratic Senators and Representatives in the Pennsylvania Legislature, urging them to vote in favor of the ratification of the Woman Suffrage Amendment. As long ago as 1912, as Chairman of the Committee on Resolutions of the Democratic State Convention, I reported a resolution in favor of Woman Suffrage, which was adopted by the Convention. In the campaign of 1914, when I was a candidate for Senator, I also advocated Woman Suffrage, and while a member of the House of Representatives I supported it on all occasions. I shall take great pleasure in continuing to fight for the cause.

With best regards, I am

Yours truly,
A. Mitchell Palmer

Our national Headquarters were humming with ratification activity even before the final vote on the Amendment had been taken in Congress. So sure was the National Woman's Party that the Amendment would pass the Senate June 4, 1919, that Alice Paul left Washington several days before that vote and began the work of ratification. Although no time limit had been set by Congress on ratification, Suffragists were eager to have it completed as soon as possible. Those that believed it would take twenty years to get three-fourths of the State Legislatures to ratify the Amendment did not realize Alice Paul's ability to overcome what sometimes looked like insuperable obstacles.

The first guns were to be fired in the four States where the Legislatures were in regular session—Illinois, Massachusetts, Pennsylvania, and Wisconsin; and in the three States of Michigan, Ohio, and Texas, where the Legislatures were in special session although they had not been called to consider suffrage. Then it would be necessary to have special sessions called in other States.

After the Amendment was passed by Congress, woman suffrage grew rapidly in public esteem. The President and political leaders generally seemed ready to become our allies, if needed, in the work of ratification.

The honor of being the first State to ratify the Amendment developed into a race among the three States of Illinois, Michigan, and Wisconsin, their Legislatures all ratifying the Amendment on the same day, June 10. However, the honor of being first went to Wisconsin. A former Chairman of the Wisconsin Branch of the National Woman's Party, Ada James, was assisted by her father, D. G. James, in winning the race for her State. Mr. James who was in Madison the day the Wisconsin Legislature ratified the Amendment, hurriedly left for Washington with a certified copy of the Joint Resolution, which his State Legislature had just passed, and obtained from the Department of State the following statement:

Department of State
Washington

June 13, 1919

By direction of the Acting Secretary of State, I hereby acknowledge the receipt of a certified copy of the Joint Resolution of the Legislature of the State of Wisconsin, ratifying the proposed Amendment to the Constitution of the United States extending the right of Suffrage to women, which was delivered by Special Messenger, D. G. James, on June 13, 1919, and is the first ratification of the Amendment which has been received.

J. A. Towner,
Chief of Bureau

While this statement was being photographed at the Suffrage Headquarters in Washington, Mr. James proudly told his story to the press.

Due to an error in printing the Amendment when it was first ratified, June 10, by Illinois, that State had to re-ratify, June 17, and thus leave the honor of being second in ratification to Michigan. In such quick succession did Kansas, Ohio, and New York ratify, June 16, that Illinois actually slipped into sixth place in the list of ratifications. Kansas was not only the first State to call a special session of her Legislature for ratification, but she was the first State in which the legislators paid their own expenses in attending the special session.

Pennsylvania's ratification campaign was not an easy one. Mrs. Lawrence Lewis, Chairman of the Pennsylvania Ratification Committee, sought and received aid from Governor Sproul; and then Senator Boies Penrose, who had vigorously opposed the passage of the Amendment in the United States Senate, was persuaded to support ratification. Mrs. Lewis was fortunate in having the assistance of Miss Ella Riegel, a member of the State Executive Committee; and Miss Mary H. Ingham, Chairman of the Pennsylvania Branch of the N.W.P., who gave personal and organizational support to the ratification work. So successful were these leaders that, June 24, 1919, Pennsylvania, by a vote of 32 to 6 in the Senate, and 153 to 44 in the House, became the seventh State to ratify the Amendment. Pennsylvanians were proud of the large number in each branch of the Legislature that approved the federal emancipation of women. The Senate Chamber, when the vote was taken, was ablaze with the purple, white, and gold colors of the N.W.P. and made a scene to be remembered. It all helped the workers to forget, at least for the moment, the many years of drab and difficult work that led up to this joyful occasion. After the victory was concluded by the vote in the House, there followed a colorful parade through the streets of Harrisburg, which was organized by Mrs. Lawrence Lewis and other Pennsylvania leaders of the N.W.P.

The following day, June 25, Massachusetts ratified. And three days later, June 28, Texas, in special session, became the first "one-party" State to ratify. When, in special sessions, Iowa ratified, July 2, and Missouri, July 3, the N.W.P. had achieved the remarkable record of eleven ratifications in one month.

By September 30, Arkansas, Montana, Nebraska, Minnesota, New Hampshire, and Utah had ratified. And when, November 1, California gave us a favorable vote, we passed the half-way mark in our ratification campaign.

At the end of 1919, four more States were in the suffrage column, Maine, North Dakota, South Dakota, and Colorado, making our total twenty-two.

The first three months of 1920 gave us thirteen more States, Rhode Island, Kentucky, Oregon, Indiana, Wyoming, Nevada, New Jersey, Idaho, Arizona, New Mexico, Oklahoma, West Virginia, and Washington. When Washington ratified March 22, we were within one Legislature of victory.

But side by side with the many victories there were some defeats. As was anticipated, the South was not a favorable battleground for support of federal action on woman suffrage.

Despite the attempts of President Wilson to win the support of Governor Kilby of Alabama, and of Mr. Merritt, Speaker of the House of Representatives in that State, Alabama was the first State to refuse ratification.

And Georgia's Legislature voted "No" on ratification, July 24, although National Democratic leaders were assisting the N.W.P. in that State, and although President Wilson had written to Governor Dorsey of Georgia ten days earlier closing his letter with this significant sentence, "It is absolutely essential to the future of the Democratic Party that it take a leading part in this great reform."

Other southern States that defeated ratification were Mississippi, South Carolina, Maryland, Louisiana, North Carolina, and Virginia. Virginia said "No" on two occasions.

When the Republican Convention opened in Chicago, June 8, 1920, the Suffragists were still smarting under their bitter ratification defeat in Delaware, where both the Governor and the Legislature were Republican. Mrs. Florence Bayard Hilles, State Chairman of the National Woman's Party, had conducted a brilliant campaign in Delaware and made two attempts to have her State ratify—April 1, and May 5. So important was this campaign that some of the ablest national organizers were sent from Washington to assist Mrs. Hilles, and three national officers, Alice Paul, Mrs. Lawrence Lewis, and Mabel Vernon, took part in the campaign. Winning a favorable vote in the last Legislature needed to complete the ratification of the Suffrage Amendment was, it appeared, to prove as difficult as was the winning of that last vote in the United States Senate before ratification could begin. And the outlook was not bright.

As Vermont and Connecticut seemed at the time the only possible States from which that thirty-sixth vote on ratification could be obtained, and as both States were Republican, the responsibility of completing ratification fell directly into the lap of the Republican Party. But as the many appeals from Suffragists to the National Republican leaders that they bring pressure to bear on the Republican Governors of Vermont and Connecticut had not brought results, some stronger protest had to be made. The National Woman's Party decided to appeal to the National Republican Convention.

June 8, the first day of the Convention, Mabel Vernon

led a long line of Suffragists, dressed in white and carrying lettered banners and the tri-color, from their Headquarters across the street to the Coliseum, where the Convention was held. Miss Mary H. Ingham of Philadelphia carried a banner that read:

> THE REPUBLICAN PARTY HAS THE POWER TO ENFRANCHISE WOMEN. WHEN WILL IT DO SO?

Doris Stevens' banner said:

> WE HAVE HAD ENOUGH RESOLUTIONS. GIVE US THE 36TH STATE.

Mrs. H. O. Havemeyer's banner carried this message:

> THEODORE ROOSEVELT ADVOCATED WOMAN SUFFRAGE. HAS THE REPUBLICAN PARTY FORGOTTEN THE PRINCIPLES OF THEODORE ROOSEVELT?

Mrs. M. Toscan Bennett's banner told this story of Republican opposition:

> WE PROTEST AGAINST THE CONTINUED DISFRANCHISEMENT OF WOMEN FOR WHICH THE REPUBLICAN PARTY IS NOW RESPONSIBLE.
> THE REPUBLICAN PARTY DEFEATED RATIFICATION OF SUFFRAGE IN DELAWARE.
> THE REPUBLICAN PARTY IS BLOCKING SUFFRAGE IN VERMONT.
> THE REPUBLICAN PARTY IS BLOCKING SUFFRAGE IN CONNECTICUT.
> WHEN WILL THE REPUBLICAN PARTY STOP BLOCKING SUFFRAGE?

Catherine Flanagan and Lou Daniels also carried the above banner.

For the first two days of the Convention these banners were held up to public gaze. On the third day a new banner appeared, carried by thirty women:

VOTE AGAINST THE REPUBLICAN PARTY AS LONG AS IT BLOCKS SUFFRAGE.

Among the other banners was this one with a quotation from Susan B. Anthony:

NO SELF-RESPECTING WOMAN SHOULD WISH OR WORK FOR THE SUCCESS OF A PARTY THAT IGNORES HER SEX.

A popular banner posed this pointed question:
REPUBLICANS WE ARE HERE.
WHERE IS THE 36TH STATE?

Before the Convention closed, the Republicans had inserted this plank in their platform:

We welcome women into full participation in the affairs of government and the activities of the Republican Party. We earnestly hope that Republican legislatures in States which have not yet acted upon the Suffrage Amendment will ratify the Amendment to the end that all of the women of the nation of voting age may participate in the election of 1920, which is so important to the welfare of our country.

In reply to this plank, Suffragists, on the last day of the Convention, hung a banner from the balcony in the Convention Hall which said:

WHY DOES THE REPUBLICAN PARTY BLOCK SUFFRAGE?
WE DO NOT WANT PLANKS.
WE DEMAND THE 36TH STATE.

The persistent agitation of Suffragists was followed by immediate action on the part of Republican leaders who urged the Governors of Vermont and Connecticut to call special sessions.

Attention should be called to a legal tangle that had meanwhile arisen in Ohio. In that State, anti-Suffragists had brought suit attacking the validity of the Ohio ratification. They argued, "As Ohio has the initiative and referendum on all acts by the State Legislature, it must have it on ratification if it is demanded by petition." A referendum on the ratification of suffrage was, therefore, demanded by the anti-Suffragists. To contest this suit, the National Woman's Party engaged three Philadelphia lawyers, George Wharton Pepper, William Draper Lewis, and Shippen Lewis. The case went through the Courts of Ohio to the United States Supreme Court where the validity of the Ohio ratification was sustained.

The effect of the Ohio decision was far-reaching. The anti-Suffragists, by attacking the ratification in Ohio had unintentionally aided the suffrage cause. Prior to the Ohio decision, it had been considered impossible for either Tennessee or Florida to ratify the Amendment. There were clauses in the Constitutions of those two States providing that between the submission of an Amendment and its ratification an election must take place. But in the Ohio case the United States Supreme Court had decided that ratification was an act of a Legislature that was not subject to a referendum. Now, therefore, both Tennessee and Florida could ratify legally.

The National Woman's Party made a quick decision to begin a ratification campaign in Tennessee, and, after consulting many distinguished lawyers on the subject, the organization pointed out that the supposedly troublesome clause in the Tennessee Constitution could not prevent ratification by the existing Legislature. Also, the National Woman's Party emphasized that that clause was equivalent to requiring a referendum before submitting a constitutional amendment to the Legislature.

The State Chairman of Tennessee, Sue White, immediately went to work to win the support of Governor Roberts. She talked over with him the Ohio decision which indicated that ratification in Tennessee was now entirely legal. Also she urged him to call a special session of the Legislature. And the National Woman's Party appealed to the National Democratic leaders to bring pressure to bear on the Tennessee Governor.

The scene was truly set for action. In San Francisco, leading Democrats were preparing for their National Convention. Homer S. Cummings, Chairman of the National Democratic Committee, called Governor Roberts on long-distance telephone asking him to call a special session. Also the Democratic National Committee passed a resolution calling on the Governor to convene his session. June 23, 1920, President Wilson wired Governor Roberts:

> It would be a real service to the Party and to the Nation if it is possible for you, under the peculiar provisions of your State Constitution, having in mind the recent decision of the Supreme Court in the Ohio case, to call a special session of the Legislature of Tennessee to consider the Suffrage Amendment. Allow me to urge this very earnestly.

And the President wrote to acting United States Attorney General William L. Frierson for his opinion on the constitutionality of ratification by a special session of the Tennessee Legislature.

Mr. Frierson's reply closed with this re-assuring sentence:

I am therefore confident that if the Tennessee Legislature is called in session, it will have the clear power to ratify the Amendment notwithstanding any provision of the Tennessee Constitution.

On the opening day of the national Democratic Convention in San Francisco, June 28, 1920, Governor Roberts stated that he would, August 9, call a special session. The Democratic Party wrote into their 1920 platform a plank endorsing the National Suffrage Amendment and calling for its ratification.

For more than four months, ever since the State of Washington had ratified the Amendment, March 22, 1920, the National Woman's Party had been struggling for that last State needed to complete the national enfranchisement of women. And now the Suffragists realized that with victory almost within their grasp they faced in Tennessee perhaps the most difficult ratification campaign of all. As in the hard-fought Delaware campaign, there was sure to be strong anti-suffrage pressure on Tennessee. To offset this, Alice Paul knew it would be necessary to bring tremendous national political pressure on the Tennessee legislators. Governor James M. Cox, the Democratic nominee for the Presidency, loomed large on the political horizon, and the National Woman's Party set out to try to make him realize that in the ratification campaign, Tennessee, a Democratic State, was his responsibility. July 16, the National Woman's Party had a large delegation of its leaders from all over the country call upon Governor Cox at his office in Columbus. Governor Cox not only said he would coöperate with the Suffragists in their ratification campaign, but he asked that a committee be appointed to confer with him on the Tennessee situation. Four days later, when the Democratic National Committee met, July 20, the National Woman's

Party succeeded in getting the Committee to pass a resolution urging immediate ratification in Tennessee. July 23, Governor Cox had a conference with Sue White of Tennessee, Anita Pollitzer of South Carolina, and Mrs. James Rector of Columbus, Ohio, the committee that Alice Paul had appointed in response to Governor Cox's request for such a group.

Two days earlier, July 21, a committee from the National Woman's Party had seen the members of the Republican National Committee and had secured from that body a resolution urging the Republicans to do everything they could to win the last State in the ratification campaign.

Right after Senator Warren G. Harding's nomination by the Republican Party for the Presidency, members of the National Woman's Party, led by Alice Paul, had an interview with him in Washington. Pennsylvania's representative in the delegation was Mary H. Ingham. Senator Harding listened, but was evasive, and the interview proved most unsatisfactory. Again, July 22, the date Senator Harding was notified of his nomination, two hundred members of the National Woman's Party from all over the country marched through Marion, Ohio, to Senator Harding's lawn. The women, dressed in white and carrying the tri-color, displayed lettered banners that read:

> THE REPUBLICAN PLATFORM ENDORSES RATIFICATION OF SUFFRAGE.
>
> THE FIRST TEST OF THE PLATFORM WILL COME WHEN THE TENNESSEE LEGISLATURE MEETS IN AUGUST.
>
> WILL THE REPUBLICANS CARRY OUT THEIR PLATFORM BY GIVING A UNANIMOUS REPUBLICAN VOTE IN TENNESSEE FOR SUFFRAGE?

Mrs. John Gordon Battelle, Sue White, and Mrs. H. O.

Havemeyer, in addresses to Senator Harding, pointed out that he, as leader of the Republicans, had the power to direct the vote of the Republican members of the Tennessee Legislature and would be held responsible for what they did.

While these efforts were being made to stimulate the interest of national political leaders and to obtain their help, the campaign in Tennessee was getting more and more hectic. It was being waged from three angles. First, Sue White, the Tennessee Chairman, whose keen political insight made her a valuable leader of her organization, was assisted by highly gifted and experienced national organizers from Washington in conducting the campaign on home ground. Also Suffragists from other States lent a helping hand. Among this latter group was Mary Winsor of Haverford, Pennsylvania. As soon as Sue White arrived in Nashville, she opened National Woman's Party Headquarters from which she conducted her campaign on State legislators.

The second field of activity was in Ohio where Abby Scott Baker, working with Mrs. James Rector, kept a watchful eye on Governor Cox and Senator Harding in order to get national help from them when special needs arose for their assistance in Tennessee.

And Alice Paul in Washington was acting as a sort of one-woman clearing house for all field activity and was, at the same time, keeping in close touch with political leaders that might influence Cox and Harding.

Soon it was found that defections were arising among Tennessee legislators whose excuse for not voting in favor of ratification in this session, despite their previous stand on the suffrage question, was that they believed it would be unconstitutional. Alarmed by this loss of votes, which was especially noticeable among the Republican legislators, Anita Pollitzer set out to combat it. She obtained from the most outstanding legal minds in Tennessee favorable opinions as to the constitutionality of ratification by Tennessee at this special session and she sent these opinions to every member of the State Legislature. Then she wired Abby Scott Baker in Ohio that Harding's active support was imperative and should be immediately obtained.

After seeing Harding, Mrs. Baker wired Alice Paul that he had telegraphed two Republican Congressmen to give their support to ratification, and his friend, ex-Governor Ben Hooper of Tennessee, to send him a poll of the Republicans. By telegram, Alice Paul immediately gave this information to Anita Pollitzer who set out at once to see ex-Governor Hooper. She went over the situation most carefully with him and found that he had had no previous first-hand information on the subject. This interview brought excellent results. Ex-Governor Hooper spent the whole day telephoning the doubtful Republican legislators and he also telegraphed Senator Harding that the Tennessee situation was critical and urged him to give it all possible aid.

Anita Pollitzer's next step was to emphasize to Mr. Hooper the need of a Republican caucus. Although Senator Candler, Chairman of the Joint Caucus Committee, was an anti-Suffragist, it was known that Congressman J. Will Taylor, who had voted for suffrage in Congress, had great influence with Senator Candler and would be a good person to see. Anita Pollitzer set out late that afternoon for Knoxville, saw Congressman Taylor that night, laid her case before him and got his promise to do all he could to help. When, the next afternoon, she went to see Congressman Taylor to learn what he had been able to do, she found that he was leaving the city in an hour and that his efforts all day long to get Senator Candler on the 'phone had been in vain. Anita Pollitzer then took things in her own hands, called up the telephone operator in Athens and said, "This is a matter of life and death. Congressman Taylor must speak with Senator Candler. I have been in Athens myself and I know it is such a tiny place that you have only to look out of the door to know where Senator Candler is. You must find him for me." Senator Candler was at the telephone in a few minutes and Congressman Taylor got his promise to call a caucus of the Republicans. That night Anita Pollitzer went to all of the papers with notices of this important news, and every Republican member was sent a telegram urging him to come to the Legislature in time to attend this caucus. But their coming was not left to chance. Anita Pollitzer and Catherine Flanagan apparently left no stone unturned—not even a pebble—in their effort to get a good attendance. These two women even got train reservations for the men and saw them on the train. They were all there! And Republican leaders let these legislators know that for the sake of the Party they wanted a majority of Republican votes in favor of ratification.

By the time the Legislature had convened, Nashville was filled with visitors. The anti-suffrage forces were there. Lobbyists for railroads, manufacturing interests, and corporations of many kinds were also there. And the Suffragists, of course, simply flocked to the Capitol.

The situation on August 9, when the legislative session began, was tense. The National Woman's Party was bringing unceasing pressure on Democratic Governor Roberts to make him feel that he, as leader of the dominant party in this Democratic Legislature, was responsible for ratification and could achieve it. And, at the same time, the suffrage organization was pointing out to the Republican minority that they were responsible for favorable votes from their men.

August 10, the ratification resolution was introduced in

both the Senate and the House. August 11, the House and Senate Committees to which the resolution had been referred held a joint hearing. At this hearing in the great Assembly Hall of the Capitol, both floor and gallery were bright with the colors of the Suffragists and the anti-Suffragists.

On paper, the Suffragists had a majority when the Legislature met, but from long experience they knew a paper majority was not a sure thing. In fact, the National Woman's Party soon found, in both the Senate and the House, that among the men that always supported measures approved by Governor Roberts there were many not supporting ratification. A list of these names was taken to Governor Roberts and the situation was discussed with him.

Through Mrs. Baker, who was still in Ohio, this news was passed on to Governor Cox, who urged Governor Roberts to do everything that he could for ratification.

As the National Woman's Party knew that ratification support in the Senate was much stronger than in the House they wanted the vote in the Senate to be taken first. This proved to be a wise move because the successful Senate vote had a wholesome effect on those members in the House wavering in their stand on ratification. When, August 13, 1920, the Senate vote was taken it stood twenty-five in favor of ratification to four against it.

Realizing at last that they could not alter the opinions of legislators strong in their support of ratification, the anti-Suffragists began to introduce measures which, if passed, would be equivalent to defeating the measure. An instance of this was a resolution suddenly brought up providing that, on August 21, the question of ratification should be referred to mass meetings to be held in every district. This, if approved, would, of course, have caused a disastrous postponement of ratification. But, fortunately, the Suffragists were able to muster sufficient strength to have the resolution tabled.

As the campaign neared its end, the situation became more and more complicated by unpleasant rumors. It was said that men were being bribed; and these reports gained in strength as the days passed. They were so persistent that legislators on the verge of declaring in favor of ratification became fearful that to do this might place them under suspicion. Things became so uncertain that neither Suffragists nor anti-Suffragists knew what to expect. Before the Legislature convened, the National Woman's Party had been working in the legislative districts, and now, when a man began to waver, Suffragists at once got in touch with the political leaders in control of his district. The situation became so unstable that members of the National Woman's Party met at short intervals during the day to compare polls and were thus able to give political leaders the exact position of each man in the Legislature. All during this confusion, the National Woman's Party kept fully informed, and on the morning of the vote they made sure all their legislative friends were at the Capitol. Not only did the Suffragists round up these favorable legislators, but they talked with them to make sure the men realized they were fully committed to the Suffragists and to their political leaders.

The Speaker of the House, Seth Walker, just before the vote was taken, ruled that all the women be barred from the floor of the House.

With the vote a practical tie, the nervous strain was hard to bear. Two of the men, one a Democrat and one a Republican, were causing the Suffragists much anxiety.

Banks Turner, the Democratic member of the pair, although one of Governor Roberts' closest friends, had never made his position on ratification clear. Suffragists did not count on him. The Republican, whose stand on ratification seemed as unpredictable as Banks Turner's and who was helping to keep the Suffragists on the anxious bench, was Harry Burn. Although the county chairman of Harry Burn's district had called him on the telephone one day while Anita Pollitzer waited, and had assured her that the Suffragists could count on his support for ratification, when Suffragists and anti-Suffragists questioned Mr. Burn after his arrival at the Legislature, he finally announced that he was uncertain. Mr. Burn, the youngest man in the Legislature, popular and greatly beloved, no doubt found it difficult to decide what to do when his vote was courted by both sides of an issue as bitterly contested as was this ratification. When he arrived at the House the day the vote was taken, he was wearing the red rose of the anti-Suffragists. And yet when an organizer of the National Woman's Party said to him just before the vote was taken, "We really trusted you, Mr. Burn, when you said that you would never hurt us", he replied, "I mean that—my vote *will* never hurt you."

Through the unceasing pressure of Governor Cox on Governor Roberts, the National Woman's Party was, of course, all this time continuing the work of keeping the Democrats true to their pledges, and it now seemed that Governor Roberts had finally realized his Party would, in the coming elections, be held responsible by the women if Tennessee failed to ratify. To hold Governor Roberts to a realization of this responsibility, members of the National Woman's Party reminded him of it before the vote was actually taken in the House. And they saw Governor Cox, to make sure that his thought on Party Responsibility was clear and strong. Also, they asked Governor Cox once more to get in touch with the Tennessee Governor on that subject.

On that fateful August 18, 1920, when the Lower House of the Tennessee Legislature had gathered to cast its vote

on the ratification of the Federal Suffrage Amendment, only
three of its ninety-nine members were absent, and the poll
indicated a tie vote.

Some one made a motion to table the Resolution for
Ratification. Soon the name of Harry Burn was called. The
red rose won. Mr. Burn voted "Yes". As the roll-call continued, the men voted just as it was anticipated they would.
How would that other doubtful Representative, Banks
Turner, vote? If he sided with the Suffragists, the vote
would be forty-eight to forty-eight and the motion to table
the Resolution would have failed. But Banks Turner did not
answer when his name was called and the vote seemed to
stand forty-eight to forty-seven for the motion to table.
However, before the final announcement of this vote, Mr.
Turner stood up, hesitated a moment, and then said, "I wish
to be recorded as against the motion to table."

While this tie vote kept the Suffrage Resolution before
the House, it made ratification look extremely doubtful—
one vote short of a majority. Even if Banks Turner, when
the vote on ratification came up, would sustain the favorable position he had just taken in regard to the motion to
table the Resolution, the Amendment would be lost unless
one more vote could be won. Perhaps Harry Burn would
grant his mother's request to vote in favor of ratification.
Many persons knew that his mother had written a letter
asking him to do this. His name was called. Would he or
wouldn't he vote in favor of Woman Suffrage? In a clear,
loud voice, his answer was, "Yes." An almost unbearable
stillness pervaded the anxious audience in the galleries as
the rollcall neared the name of Banks Turner. Would he
be consistent and vote for ratification as a follow-up to his
vote against tabling the Resolution? Yes, he would. In a
low, solemn voice, his answer, when the clerk called his
name, was, "Yes." By a vote of forty-nine to forty-seven,

the Susan B. Anthony Amendment was at last ratified—
August 20, 1920.

But the anti-Suffragists would not surrender immediately. Before the Suffragists could begin to express their great
joy over the victory they had won, Speaker Walker was on
his feet. His face was pale when he announced, "I change
my vote from 'No' to 'Yes'." His object was, of course, to
move for a reconsideration of the Resolution—an attack
that the anti-Suffragists had prepared in advance if the
Tennessee Legislature ratified the measure. But, as Robert
Burns wrote many years ago, "The best-laid schemes o'
mice an' men gang aft agley." Speaker Walker's change of
vote had given the Resolution a *constitutional majority,* not
just a majority of the membership present when the vote
was taken. With the Speaker's unintentional help, the vote
in favor of ratification now stood fifty to forty-six, a bare
majority of the ninety-nine members making up the Tennessee House of Representatives—a close vote, but enough!

Now the pent-up enthusiasm of the suffrage workers and
their friends could be freely expressed. State leaders, who
had helped in the campaign, clapped and stamped. Women
were almost hysterical in their joy. They laughed and they
wept. They cheered and applauded. A legislator had managed to procure a bell and rang it lustily to his heart's content. The suffrage workers were jubilant, especially the
Tennessee members of the National Woman's Party whose
pride in helping to make Tennessee the thirty-sixth and last
State needed to complete the enfranchisement of the women
of the United States knew no bounds.

A suit instituted by the anti-Suffragists against the validity of the Tennessee ratification is still pending. But a thirty-
seventh State soon ratified the Amendment, a story that
deserves to be told, at least briefly. This thirty-seventh State
was Connecticut and its Governor was one of the outstand-

ing anti-Suffragists in the United States. In order that legal machinery might be provided to enable the women of Connecticut to vote in the approaching elections, Governor Marcus Holcomb issued a call for the Connecticut Legislature to meet in session, September 14, 1920. Again an anti-Suffragist had played into the hands of the Suffragists, who immediately took advantage of this special session to wage a ratification campaign in Connecticut.

In addressing the Connecticut legislators, Governor Holcomb in effect warned them not to ratify at that session, that such action would not be legal because he had not mentioned ratification in his call, and that he would call them again in a week for that purpose. However, Connecticut did ratify September 14, and Catherine Flanagan, of the National Woman's Party, personally delivered to the State Department in Washington the ratification from the Secretary of State of Connecticut.

As the legality of that first vote on ratification in Connecticut had been questioned because Governor Holcomb had not mentioned the subject in his call for the session of September 14, one week later the Susan B. Anthony Amendment was ratified a second time in Connecticut.

Thus, in the year 1920, there was brought to a close a political campaign as brilliantly planned, as persistently and courageously fought, as dramatically and gloriously achieved as any, I believe, in the world's history.

After the Amendment had been passed by Congress, it required less than fifteen months for 36 State Legislatures, 29 of them in special sessions, to ratify it and thus to confer upon all the women of the United States the right to vote. Those prophesies of direful decades of delayed enfranchisement of women that would result from the aggressive campaign of the N.W.P. were never given a chance to be fulfilled. In less than eight years after that organization, in

1913, began its campaign for the passage of the Amendment, the measure was incorporated in the National Constitution.

But it should be recalled that forty-two years had passed since a federal suffrage amendment was introduced into Congress, January 10, 1878, through the efforts of Susan B. Anthony, Elizabeth Cady Stanton, and other pioneers.

And it should also be recalled that prior to the intensive campaign of the N.W.P. for the passage of the Federal Suffrage Amendment, generations of heroic women had worked valiantly in State campaigns and had won suffrage for women in a number of States. They had thus simplified the winning of national woman suffrage and had given to the N.W.P. one of its most effective political weapons—the use of millions of enfranchised women as a balance of power in elections. This was language that hard-boiled politicians could understand, which moved them to act when logic and appeals for justice failed.

Women, disagreeing sometimes in methods of work, but aiming always at the same goal, had, at last, achieved victory. And many men had greatly assisted women in both the State and national campaigns. Their strong belief in justice and democracy had stirred them to strive to make the United States in fact as well as in name the greatest democracy in the world.

The use of the ballot has equipped woman to work more effectively than ever before for that equality in every field of endeavor that will enable her to develop to her fullest capacity, to serve freely wherever her conscience dictates, and to work side by side with man, his equal and his partner in life.

END

APPENDIX I

RESOLUTIONS AND DECLARATION OF SENTIMENTS ADOPTED AT SENECA FALLS CONVENTION, JULY 18-19, 1848.

More than a century ago, led by Lucretia Mott, Elizabeth Cady Stanton, Susan B. Anthony, women began the "Equal Rights" movement in the United States.

Among the demands of the first Equal Rights Convention held in this country—The Seneca Falls Convention of 1848—were: Equal rights in the franchise, in education, in the professions, in political office, in marriage, in personal freedom, in control of property, in guardianship of children, in making contracts, in the church, and in the leadership of moral and public movements.

Resolutions Adopted at Seneca Falls Convention, July 18-19, 1848

Resolved, That such laws as conflict, in any way, with the true and substantial happiness of woman, are contrary to the great precept of nature and of no validity, for this is "superior in obligation to any other."

Resolved, That all laws which prevent woman from occupying such a station in society as her conscience shall dictate, or which place her in a position inferior to that of man, are contrary to the great precept of nature, and therefore of no force or authority.

351

Resolved, That woman is man's equal—was intended to be so by the Creator, and the highest good of the race demands that she should be recognized as such.

Resolved, That the women of this country ought to be enlightened in regard to the laws under which they live, that they may no longer publish their degradation by declaring themselves satisfied with their present position, nor their ignorance, by asserting that they have all the rights they want.

Resolved, That inasmuch as man, while claiming for himself intellectual superiority, does accord to woman moral superiority, it is preëminently his duty to encourage her to speak and teach, as she has an opportunity, in all religious assemblies.

Resolved, That the same amount of virtue, delicacy, and refinement of behavior that is required of woman in the social state, should also be required of man, and the same transgressions should be visited with equal severity on both man and woman.

Resolved, That the objection of indelicacy and impropriety, which is so often brought against woman when she addresses a public audience, comes with a very ill-grace from those who encourage, by their attendance, her appearance on the stage, in the concert, or in feats of the circus.

Resolved, That woman has too long rested satisfied in the circumscribed limits which corrupt customs and a perverted application of the Scriptures have marked out for her, and that it is time she should move in the enlarged sphere which her great Creator has assigned her.

Resolved, That it is the duty of the women of this country to secure to themselves their sacred right to the elective franchise.

Resolved, That the equality of human rights results

necessarily from the fact of the identity of the race in capabilities and responsibilities.

Resolved, therefore, That, being invested by the Creator with the same capabilities, and the same consciousness of responsibility for their exercise, it is demonstrably the right and duty of woman, equally with man, to promote every righteous cause by every righteous means; and especially in regard to the great subjects of morals and religion, it is self-evidently her right to participate with her brother in teaching them, both in private and in public, by writing and by speaking, by any instrumentalities proper to be used, and in any assemblies proper to be held; and this being a self-evident truth growing out of the divinely implanted principles of human nature, any custom or authority adverse to it, whether modern or wearing the hoary sanction of antiquity, is to be regarded as a self-evident falsehood, and at war with mankind.

Resolved, That the speedy success of our cause depends upon the zealous and untiring efforts of both men and women, for the overthrow of the monopoly of the pulpit, and for the securing to woman an equal participation with men in the various trades, professions, and commerce.

Declaration of Sentiments Adopted at Seneca Falls Convention, July 18-19, 1848

The history of mankind is a history of repeated injuries and usurpations on the part of man toward woman, having in direct object the establishment of an absolute tyranny over her. To prove this, let facts be submitted to a candid world.

He has never permitted her to exercise her inalienable right to the elective franchise.

He has compelled her to submit to laws, in the formation of which she had no voice.

He has withheld from her rights which are given to the most ignorant and degraded men—both natives and foreigners.

Having deprived her of this first right of a citizen, the elective franchise, thereby leaving her without representation in the halls of legislation, he has oppressed her on all sides.

He has made her, if married, in the eye of the law, civilly dead.

He has taken from her all right in property, even to the wages she earns.

He has made her, morally, an irresponsible being, as she can commit many crimes with impunity, provided they be done in the presence of her husband. In the covenant of marriage, she is compelled to promise obedience to her husband, he becoming, to all intents and purposes, her master—the law giving him power to deprive her of her liberty, and to administer chastisement.

He has so framed the laws of divorce, as to what shall be the proper causes, and in case of separation, to whom the guardianship of the children shall be given, as to be wholly regardless of the happiness of women—the law, in all cases, going upon a false supposition of the supremacy of man, and giving all power into his hands.

After depriving her of all rights as a married woman, if single, and the owner of property, he has taxed her to support a government which recognizes her only when her property can be made profitable to it.

He has monopolized nearly all the profitable employments, and from those she is permitted to follow, she receives but a scanty remuneration. He closes against her all the avenues to wealth and distinction which he considers most honorable to himself. As a teacher of theology, medicine, or law, she is not known.

He has denied her the facilities for obtaining a thorough education, all colleges being closed against her.

He allows her in Church, as well as State, but a subordinate position, claiming Apostolic authority for her exclusion from the ministry, and, with some exceptions, from any public participation in the affairs of the Church.

He has created a false public sentiment by giving to the world a different code of morals for men and women, by which moral delinquencies which exclude women from society, are not only tolerated, but deemed of little account in man.

He has usurped the prerogative of Jehovah himself, claiming it as his right to assign for her a sphere of action, when that belongs to her conscience and to her God.

He has endeavored, in every way that he could, to destroy her confidence in her own powers, to lessen her self-respect, and to make her willing to lead a dependent and abject life.

Now, in view of this entire disfranchisement of one-half the people of this country, their social and religious degradation—in view of the unjust laws above mentioned, and because women do feel themselves aggrieved, oppressed, and fraudulently deprived of their most sacred rights, we insist that they have immediate admission to all the rights and privileges which belong to them as citizens of the United States.

In entering upon the great work before us, we anticipate no small amount of misconception, misrepresentation, and ridicule; but we shall use every instrumentality within our power to effect our object. We shall employ agents, circulate tracts, petition the State and National legislatures, and endeavor to enlist the pulpit and the press in our behalf. We hope this Convention will be followed by a series of Conventions embracing every part of the country.

APPENDIX II

THE 19th AMENDMENT TO THE UNITED STATES CONSTITUTION EXTENDING THE RIGHT OF SUFFRAGE TO WOMEN

"ARTICLE—Sec. I. The right of citizens of the United States to vote shall not be denied or abridged by the United States or by any State on account of sex.

Sec. 2. "Congress shall have power to enforce this article by appropriate legislation."

HISTORY OF THE AMENDMENT

Drafted
   By Susan B. Anthony in 1875.

First Introduced
   January 10, 1878, by Hon. Aaron A. Sargent, in the Senate.

Reported from Committee, in the Senate
   1878, Adverse majority.
   1879, Favorable minority.
   1882, Favorable majority, adverse minority.
   1884, Favorable majority, adverse minority.
   1886, Favorable majority.
   1890, Favorable majority.
   1892, Favorable majority, adverse minority.
   1896, Adverse majority.
   1913, Favorable majority.
   1914, Favorable majority.

1917, Favorable majority.
1919, Unanimously favorable.

Reported from Committee, in the House
1883, Favorable majority.
1884, Adverse majority, favorable minority.
1886, Favorable minority.
1890, Favorable majority.
1894, Adverse majority.
1914, Without recommendation.
1916, Without recommendation.
1917, Without recommendation.
1918, Favorable majority.
1919, Favorable majority.

Voted upon, in the Senate
January 25, 1887. Yeas 16, nays 34. Absent 25 (of whom 4 were announced as for and 2 against).
March 19, 1914. Yeas 35, nays 34, failing by 11 of necessary two-thirds vote.
October 1, 1918. Yeas 54, nays 30, failing by 2 of necessary two-thirds vote.
February 10, 1919. Yeas 55, nays 29, failing by 1 of necessary two-thirds vote.
June 4, 1919. Yeas 56, nays 25, passing by 2 votes over necessary two-thirds majority.

Voted upon, in the House
January 12, 1915. Yeas 174, nays 204, failing by 78 of necessary two-thirds vote.
January 10, 1918. Yeas 274, nays 136, passing by 1 vote over necessary two-thirds majority.
May 21, 1919. Yeas 304, nays 89, passing by 42 votes over necessary two-thirds majority.

RATIFICATION BY STATES[1] OF THE FEDERAL WOMAN SUFFRAGE AMENDMENT

	House Vote	Senate Vote
1. Wisconsin, June 10, 1919	House Vote 54 to 2	Senate Vote 23 to 1
2.* Michigan, June 10, 1919	House Vote Unanimous	Senate Vote Unanimous
3.* Kansas, June 16, 1919	House Vote Unanimous	Senate Vote Unanimous
4.* Ohio, June 16, 1919	House Vote 73 to 6	Senate Vote 27 to 3
5.* New York, June 16, 1919	House Vote Unanimous	Senate Vote Unanimous
6. Illinois, June 17, 1919	House Vote 134 to 4	Senate Vote Unanimous
7. Pennsylvania, June 24, 1919	House Vote 153 to 44	Senate Vote 31 to 6
8. Massachusetts, June 25, 1919	House Vote 185 to 47	Senate Vote 34 to 5
9.* Texas, June 29, 1919	House Vote 96 to 20	Senate Vote 12 to 2
10.* Iowa, July 2, 1919	House Vote 96 to 5	Senate Vote Unanimous
11.* Missouri, July 3, 1919	House Vote 125 to 4	Senate Vote 28 to 3
12.* Arkansas, July 20, 1919	House Vote 76 to 17	Senate Vote 20 to 2
13.* Montana, July 30, 1919	House Vote Unanimous	Senate Vote 38 to 1
14.* Nebraska, August 2, 1919	House Vote Unanimous	Senate Vote Unanimous
15.* Minnesota, September 8, 1919	House Vote 120 to 6	Senate Vote 60 to 5
16.* New Hampshire, September 10, 1919	House Vote 212 to 143	Senate Vote 14 to 10
17.* Utah, September 30, 1919	House Vote Unanimous	Senate Vote Unanimous
18.* California, November 1, 1919	House Vote 73 to 2	Senate Vote Unanimous
19.* Maine, November 5, 1919	House Vote 72 to 68	Senate Vote 24 to 5

RATIFICATION BY STATES—(Continued)

20.* North Dakota, December 1, 1919	House Vote 102 to 6	Senate Vote 40 to 4
21.* South Dakota, December 4, 1919	House Vote Unanimous	Senate Vote Unanimous
22.* Colorado, December 12, 1919	House Vote Unanimous	Senate Vote Unanimous
23. Kentucky, January 6, 1920	House Vote 72 to 25	Senate Vote 30 to 8
24. Rhode Island, January 6, 1920 [2]		No roll call
25.* Oregon, January 12, 1920	House Vote Unanimous	Senate Vote Unanimous
26.* Indiana, January 16, 1920	House Vote Unanimous	Senate Vote 43 to 3
27.* Wyoming, January 27, 1920	House Vote Unanimous	Senate Vote Unanimous
28.* Nevada, February 7, 1920	House Vote 25 to 1	Senate Vote Unanimous
29. New Jersey, February 10, 1920	House Vote 34 to 24	Senate Vote 18 to 2
30.* Idaho, February 11, 1920	House Vote Unanimous	Senate Vote 29 to 6
31.* Arizona, February 12, 1920	House Vote Unanimous	Senate Vote Unanimous
32.* New Mexico, February 19, 1920	House Vote 36 to 10	Senate Vote 17 to 5
33.* Oklahoma, February 27, 1920	House Vote 85 to 12	Senate Vote 25 to 14
34.* West Virginia, March 10, 1920	House Vote 47 to 40	Senate Vote 15 to 14
35.* Washington, March 22, 1920	House Vote Unanimous	Senate Vote Unanimous
36.* Tennessee, August 18, 1920	House Vote 50 to 46	Senate Vote 25 to 4

* The starred States ratified at Special Sessions.
[1] As given in the official organ of the National Woman's Party, the *Suffragist*, of September, 1920.
[2] Letter from office of Secretary of State of Rhode Island, April 6, 1954, says action in House was "by a roll call vote of 89 to 3, under suspension of all rules."

APPENDIX III

EQUALITY OF RIGHTS MUST BE COMPLETED

The women of the United States, in their struggle for complete equality with men, made a great step forward in 1920 when they won the right to vote, but that important advance left much to be accomplished. There still existed laws, both State and Federal, that discriminated against women.

Immediately following the enfranchisement of women, the National Woman's Party began to campaign for the removal of these discriminatory laws, and in 1921 was reorganized as a permanent association to raise the status of women throughout the United States. Here are a few of the developments of that campaign and of the international campaign that soon followed it.

Just as it proved to be too long and too unstable a process to obtain suffrage for women State by State, so it proved to be too long and unstable a process to remove discriminatory laws State by State and law by law. The National Woman's Party returned to the philosophy of the great pioneers and decided to attack the rest of the problem by a Federal amendment.

Such an *Equal Rights Amendment* was drawn up and proclaimed at a national convention on the seventy-fifth anniversary of the Seneca Falls Convention, July 19, 1923. This Amendment, often called the Lucretia Mott Amendment, reads:

EQUALITY OF RIGHTS UNDER THE LAW
SHALL NOT BE DENIED OR ABRIDGED
BY THE UNITED STATES OR BY ANY
STATE ON ACCOUNT OF SEX.

It was introduced into Congress in 1923. In 1944, it was for the first time included in the platforms of both major political parties.

Not content to work only for the complete equality of women in the United States, the National Woman's Party, at a Conference in November, 1923, made plans to do all in its power to bring together the women of the world "to deliberate upon problems of common interest to women and to aid the movement to end the present world-wide subjection of women."

In the beginning, this international campaign was carried on in the name of the National Woman's Party through its Committee on International Action; later through the World Woman's Party for Equal Rights, which was founded in 1939, and which, until the outbreak of the war, had headquarters in Geneva, Switzerland.

The equality cause has been carried by the National Woman's Party to the Conferences of the American Republics, to the Interparliamentary Union, to the Hague Conference on the Codification of International Law, to the Assembly and Council of the League of Nations, to the International Labor Organization. Its representatives have taken the equality message to gatherings of Governments and to gatherings of women in all parts of the world—Havana, The Hague, Geneva, Paris, Berlin, London, Edinburgh, Montevideo, Lima, Mexico City, San Francisco.

At the San Francisco Conference of the United Nations, representatives of the World Woman's Party for Equal Rights, and the National Woman's Party were again in the forefront in urging equality for women. The results at San Francisco marked a great advance in the march of the Woman Movement. The Charter, adopted in that city, June 26, 1945, opens with the words:

> We, the peoples of the United Nations determined . . . to reaffirm faith in fundamental human rights, in the dignity and worth of the human person, in the equal rights of men and women . . . have agreed to the present Charter . . .

But, here again, the United Nations Charter is only a milestone in woman's journey to freedom—not its end. The National Woman's Party and the World Woman's Party for Equal Rights must continue their work until every trace of the subjection of women is wiped from the face of the earth.

One of the finest tributes to the National Woman's Party came from that great leader in education and in equal rights for women, Miss M. Carey Thomas. Her confidence in the organization, and her recognition of the ability of its leader were evidenced by the following excerpt from "LEGACIES OUT OF SURPLUS," in Miss Thomas's will, which was filed for probate in Philadelphia in 1935:

Article Seventeenth

> In case my net estate shall prove to be sufficient to pay in full said legacy of $4,860 more or less and said legacy of $100,000 more or less and all other legacies hereinbefore bequeathed by me and still leave a balance, then after the payment in full of all said legacies I direct my Executors to apply such balance to the payment of a legacy of

Fifty Thousand Dollars, which I hereby give and bequeath to the Woman's Party (a corporation whose headquarters are now in the City of Washington, D. C.), and whose founder is Alice Paul, to be payable only out of said final balance, and to be held and invested by said corporation in safe English or American securities and the income therefrom to be used only to meet the administrative expenses of said Woman's Party.

Unfortunately, Miss Thomas's net estate when final settlement was made did not make possible the payment of any part of the Fifty Thousand Dollars she had wished to bequeath to the National Woman's Party.

Largely through the generosity of Mrs. O. H. P. Belmont, at one time President of the National Woman's Party, the organization has been able to establish permanent headquarters at 144 Constitution Avenue, N.E., Washington, D. C. This beautiful and historic building, known as the Alva Belmont House, serves as a meeting-place not only for the women of America working to raise the status of women, but for the women of all nations. And Washington, as the center of power for the forces of democracy throughout the world, is surely the logical capital from which to work for the extension of full democratic rights to women.

Those wishing to know more of today's activities of the National Woman's Party and the World Woman's Party for Equal Rights, than it has been possible to give here, will find a hearty welcome at the Alva Belmont House.

APPENDIX IV

WOMEN ARE PENALIZED FOR LIVING TOO LONG

In 1920, the year the 19th Amendment was ratified, I decided to enter the Life Insurance field and became associated with one of the largest New York companies. That company had offered me an unsolicited part-time contract while I was still at the Suffrage Headquarters and, although the day was then not long enough for additional work, it was, I suppose, natural to go to that company when I was in a position to accept a full-time contract.

The principle on which life insurance is based had always appealed strongly to me. Also, it seemed to offer an especially attractive means of earning a living because, as I naïvely thought, the question of sex discrimination would not be likely to enter into it. I thought that as the agent received no salary and earned commissions only as a result of his own labor he would be given a fair chance and would succeed if he had sufficient initative, determination, and information. I believed I had a fair amount of initiative and determination and I knew I would try to become informed.

Mrs. William B. Derr, an able and very attractive woman, and I were the only women in the agency, and we started out cheerfully to win our way.

Soon we heard rumors of an important luncheon-meeting the agency was planning, and that the agents selling a stipulated amount of insurance would be given the opportunity to attend it. As I recall, a representative from the Home Office was coming to Philadelphia to explain details of something new the company was placing on the market.

Mrs. Derr and I both qualified. Neither of us was invited. It was to be a stag luncheon!

Smarting under this discrimination, and disappointed at meeting so soon the old sex bugaboo, we went to see the agency manager to express our indignation. To go or not to go to a luncheon meant nothing to either of us, but to miss an opportunity to learn at first-hand about the business was extremely important. The manager did not seem to get our point at all.

Knowing that I could not work with enthusiasm under such conditions, I surrendered my contract and left to try for better luck elsewhere.

As more and more women were in those days entering the business and professional world and were succeeding, insurance companies naturally saw in them a new field of *prospects*. And they believed, I think, that women insurance agents might be successful in reaching these new potential buyers. I had no trouble in obtaining a contract with another large company and was just ready to sign it when I chanced to meet on the street a man from my home county who urged me to become a member of his agency with the Philadelphia Life Insurance Company. I liked the idea of being located at the Home Office of a Philadelphia company. Also I liked very much a folder the company had prepared for its agents that enabled them to present a few of the most popular policies with ease and clarity. With no training in the sale of insurance, I needed all the help I could get. I might add here that my undertaking the work without formal preparation was not unusual at that time. Many a raw recruit received a little help from the company, and learned the rest the hard way.* I recall that, when a pros-

---

* The American College of Life Underwriters, which later enabled insurance representatives to prepare themselves adequately before going out to meet their public, was not founded until 1927.

pect asked me a question I could not answer offhand, I did not hesitate to admit my ignorance and to ask permission to get the information from the office for him.

I am glad of this opportunity to pay a deserved compliment to the *Philadelphia Life*. I was shown beautiful courtesy by the officers and the employees, and was free to see any officer whose help I needed. Also I was cordially welcomed by the agents although I was the only woman in the group. I was even asked when I went to the first regular business meeting of the Home Office agency, a meeting attended by the President and Vice-President of the company, if I objected to the men's smoking. Of course my answer was "no" although I nearly always left those meetings with a "smoke" headache. I had made up my mind on entering the business world not to expect or accept special consideration just because I was a woman; but little courtesies were appreciated. Later on, I was elected president of the Plicos, as the agents' club was called.

Before long, I felt I had picked up sufficient information to solicit business with confidence, but soon I hit a snag. The Philadelphia Life Insurance Company did not permit the addition of the Disability Clause to policies sold to women although a number of larger companies were doing this. I wrote a long letter to the Manager of Agencies, Mr. A. M. Hopkins, and told him I had learned that several of the largest life insurance companies doing business in Philadelphia were then offering disability protection to women, and I added that I believed the time was not far distant when every first-class company would have to follow their example. I asked him whether he did not think the Philadelphia Life might see its way clear to "give to women, on the same terms that it gave to men, the benefits of the Disability Clause." I received the following reply from Mr. Hopkins:

It gives me pleasure to let you know that the Board of Directors of the Philadelphia Life Insurance Company have carefully considered your request to extend to women the full benefits of the "Disability Clause" that we now grant to men and have acceded to it.

It seems especially fitting that one who had devoted many years to the struggle of obtaining justice for women in the field of politics should be instrumental in helping to remove discriminations against them in the business world.

We are glad that you made the suggestion to us and congratulate you on gaining your object.

But there was a little fly in the ointment. As the Disability Clause covered *only total and permanent disability,* the cost to the insured was small—small enough, I thought, to make it attractive. But despite the remoteness of a claim, and despite the fact that women had to stand as rigid a medical examination for life insurance as men, women were charged a higher premium for this added protection. Insurance protection for women had a way of coming not only "too little and too late," but also too high.

When I had time to study my rate-book with more care, I discovered other things that troubled me. I knew that figures had managed to build up for themselves a very respectable reputation—*they did not lie.* But, lying as they did side by side in my rate-book, they told an ugly story. The little midgets glared at me as they boldly pointed out discriminations against women. And I found these discriminations against women were not peculiar to the rate-book I was using, but were to be found in the rate-books of the largest companies. It was plain that insurance companies were following the established practice of not opening wide the door to women, but of cracking it only a little at a time.

Would closed doors ever open wide to the mothers, wives, and daughters of men? In poetry, in prose, in art, woman over the ages has been apotheosized, but in the practical world she has been often defied, not deified. And in her effort to prove that she is "neither saint nor sinner," but just a human being with an earnest desire to develop and to assume her full share of life's responsibilities and opportunities, her every step forward has been blocked. Whether in the field of education or in the business, professional, and political world, whenever woman attempted to go beyond the narrow confines supposed to be her *only* sphere, it has been the same old story. But thanks to her own courage and to the help she has received from men of broad vision, woman is nearing the goal she has set for herself.

After that slight digression, let us return to the subject of Life Insurance. But before I present my "bill of complaints," may I, in as non-technical a way as possible, explain to the reader, who may not be familiar with the basic facts of Life Insurance, two of the fundamentals on which this splendid structure is built? I'd like first to emphasize that there is no hit-or-miss plan in arriving at the correct rates to charge for life insurance. These rates are built on a solid foundation that has required a tremendous amount of calculation. So thorough have these calculations been that Life Insurance has been defined as *the institution that eliminates risk or that substitutes certainty for uncertainty.*

The two fundamentals to which I refer are known as Life Expectancy, and the Law of Averages. Life Expectancy almost explains itself. Given a person's age, an insurance company can tell how long he is expected to live— not, of course, a specific person, but one out of the huge number considered in insurance companies' calculations.

To insure that person, let us say, under an Ordinary

Life Policy, the company must receive a large enough premium for a sufficient number of years to build up, through legal investments, a sum that will equal the face of the policy at the death of the insured. (Other elements entering into this complicated transaction need not be considered here.)

But just how, you ask, does the company know what the Life Expectancy of this person will be at any given age? The Law of Averages provides the answer. Insurance books describe this law as "A theorem that when the number of trials of an event of probability is increased indefinitely, the probability of any assigned deviation from the expected value approaches zero." In other words, it means, I think, that if a sufficiently large number of individual cases over a wide enough territory is carefully studied, it is safe to believe the information gathered from this study will be applicable to the whole group under consideration.

Now let us look at the two propositions, of Life Insurance and of Life Annuities. The latter are really Life Insurance in reverse.

When, for instance, you buy a Whole Life Policy, often called an Ordinary Life Policy, you pay the company annual installments, or premiums, on a lump sum of money to be paid at your death to some named beneficiary or to your estate. For this credit arrangement, you must pass a thorough physical examination. Also the company needs to know something about your character and your business standing in order to determine your fitness to become one of the millions of forward-looking persons who, through Life Insurance, have banded together for mutual protection. As every person applying for insurance has to undergo this test, regular inspection services have been formed for use by insurance companies. (They are akin to similar services in the financial world like that of Dun and Bradstreet, Inc.)

The *younger* you are, the *smaller* your annual premium will be. Your Life Expectancy indicates the amount of this sum.

When, on the other hand, you buy a Life Annuity,* you give the company a lump sum of money, and the company guarantees to pay you annually for the rest of your life a stipulated sum in return for the money you have deposited with it. For this, no examination is required because the company runs practically no risk. The *older* you are, the *larger* the return on your investment. Life Expectancy again comes into play and enables the company to know how much, on an investment basis, it can afford to pay you each year.

Life Annuities provide a definite and attractively large life income free from the care and danger of loss attaching to ordinary methods of investing money. For this reason, they fit well into certain situations, especially where the annuitant feels justified in looking out only for his own future, and wishes to make that future secure.

Now let us consider a case that might occur in the year 1955—a case covering both Life Insurance and Life Annuities. A brother and sister, twins, have reached the age of 65 and must retire from jobs they have filled for many years. They have worked hard, been fairly paid, and have, by strict economy, saved $20,000 each. They plan to arrange their affairs so as to get as generous a return on the money they invest as is consistent with safety. They own jointly their little home, do their own work, and believe they may be able to arrange their financial future with comparative confidence in a comfortable old age. Their wants are simple.

As neither of them has a dependent to consider, they both decide to place half of their savings in Life Annuities—

---

* No Payment After Death of Annuitant.

the kind of annuity that provides the largest income and returns nothing at the death of the assured. But when the insurance agent submits figures to the twins, they are surprised to see how much more the company will pay the brother than the sister. The agent tries to explain the situation, but is not convincing. The sister recalls that when they were young they took out small Life Insurance policies, each for the same amount, each one making the other the beneficiary. The premiums on these two policies were exactly the same. Why, she wished to know, should the company not pay her now as large a return on her money as it is willing to pay her brother on his.

Ever since 1920, when I began to sell Life Insurance, I had been asking this same question, but had never received a satisfactory answer. My thesis had run like this. Since Life Expectancy statistics prove that a woman lives approximately five years longer than a man, she will, in the course of time, have to pay approximately five more premiums on a Whole Life Policy than a man does. Both my arithmetic and my sense of justice indicated that her annual premiums should, therefore, be slightly smaller than his on the same basic contract. That is, I argued, her premiums should be smaller if the companies, in making up their Annuity rates, insisted on taking cognizance of woman's longer expectancy of life, and of giving her, in consequence, a smaller return than they give men on money invested in Annuities. If she *must be penalized on Annuities*, why not *give her an advantage on Life Insurance?*

The plain fact was that it seemed to me altogether unnecessary for Life Insurance companies to consider the sexes separately. Why not, rather, treat men and women as a group of human beings with common interests, each sex being naturally interested in the welfare of the other?

Wasn't the group composed largely of mothers and fathers; husbands and wives; sisters and brothers?

In our rate-books, the companies have, however, devised an easy way of handling this troublesome question. They simply list the Annuity rates for men and women in different columns, maintaining, all the way down, the five-year differential in their Life Expectancy. For instance, a woman of 70 receives on each $1,000 of invested capital only as much as a man of 65 receives. (It should be remembered that the older one is, the more one receives on a Life Annuity.)

The various companies have not, I believe, had time, or maybe they have not thought it worth the trouble, to catch up in their rate-books with the statistics on Life Expectancy made available in the year 1951. The figures for that year show that the life expectancy of both men and women has increased. The old figures (those in effect prior to 1951) were 67 years for women, and 62 years for men. The statistics of 1951 indicate that women's life expectancy had increased to 71 years, and men's to 65½ years.

Here are the amounts of income that $1,000 will provide annually if a male or a female at the ages of 65 or 70 purchased a Life Annuity from one of the largest three Pennsylvania companies, or from one of the largest companies in the United States:

	Penn-Mutual	Provident Mutal	Fidelity Mutual	Prudential
Male, age 65	$78.33	$78.33	$78.33	$78.31
Male, age 70	94.89	94.89	94.89	94.88
Female, age 65	$66.13	66.13	66.13	66.14
Female, age 70	78.33	78.33	78.33	78.31

I have given rates only on ages 65 and 70 because they will suffice to complete the fictitious story of the *twins*. For her $10,000, the 65 year-old woman would receive annually in any one of the three Pennsylvania companies $661.30;

in the Prudential, $661.40. For his $10,000, the 65 year-old man would receive annually in any one of the three Pennsylvania companies $783.30; in the Prudential, $783.10. At age 70, the woman's $10,000 would yield her $783.30 in any one of the three Pennsylvania companies; $783.10 in the Prudential. At age 70, the man's $10,000 would yield him 948.90 in any one of the three Pennsylvania companies; $948.80 in the Prudential.

Recently, when I talked with some one in the Actuarial Department of a large Life Insurance company, I asked if the attitude of life insurance companies generally had changed toward woman's position as a buyer of insurance. I shall refer to my informant as *Mr. X.*

Mr. X defended the plan of not charging women less for Life Insurance while charging them more for Annuities on the ground that a much smaller percentage of women than men buy Life Insurance, and that the average size of women's policies is much smaller than men's. Also, the per policy charges on the companies' books, Mr. X explained, are as much on a small policy as they are on a large one.

It seems to me Mr. X was making a question of book-keeping the defense of a principle that life insurance companies have adopted. If it costs as much to handle a small policy as a large one, why not charge both men and women a trifle more for small policies than for large ones? Why not, for instance, say that a policy of less than $5,000 should require a slightly higher rate to cover the proportionately higher cost to the company of carrying it on the books? I should prefer some other plan for adjusting this bookkeeping expense than the one I have suggested, which would increase slightly the cost of Life Insurance to the person of small means. But I am only trying to point out it does not seem right to seek relief from increased bookkeeping costs by putting the burden of it only on women.

Now, let us take up the second point emphasized by Mr. X—that fewer women than men insure their lives. As there are, I understand, about three times as many men as women carrying Life Insurance policies, and as a large proportion of these men carry only small policies, is it not reasonable to think that men are largely responsible for the extra costs that companies have to face in carrying small policies? Again, I ask, why should not men as well as women share this bookkeeping expense?

Now here is a cheering follow-up to this rather depressing presentation of the general practices of life insurance companies in regard to women. A large and progressive Canadian company now issues to women a *Preferred Risk— Life @ 85* policy, requiring a minimum contract of $10,000, at a rate actually less per $1,000 than the company's regular Ordinary Life policy. This better rate on the *Preferred Risk—Life @ 85* policy to women reflects what the company expects in "improved mortality."

As will be seen by the following letter sent me June 11, 1952, by a high official of this Canadian company,* the officer very honestly claims that the company's "pioneering in the women's insurance field" was prompted only by woman's becoming, through her successful entrance into the business world, a *prospect* worth "serving." However, the thing that especially interests me is that when woman's success in business stimulated a large insurance company to do some pioneering in regard to her, the company's first step in that direction was a recognition of the fact that woman's longer life expectancy was a factor to be considered. Here is the letter referred to above:

> I was interested in your inquiry about our pioneering in the women's insurance field. While

---

* The writer preferred anonymity.

it is perfectly true that women for many years have enjoyed a greater life expectancy—virtually always reflected in annuity rates—the development which prompted us to do something about it is of rather recent origin.

Traditionally the very large majority of our business in force on women was for small amounts, frequently one thousand or two thousand Endowments. On these plans the mortality element of the premium rate is at a minimum and the additional cost of handling small policies probably fully offsets any advantage in feminine mortality.

In recent years, however, the number of women in business who have been substantial purchasers of life insurance has been steadily increasing while the community property laws have focused new attention on the needs which many women have for adequate life insurance to meet their inheritance taxes. Our Company felt that this was a market which should be served and we were able to bring out our Women's Preferred Risk Policy with a minimum size of $10,000.00, on a basis which fully reflected improved mortality expected.

. . .

I trust this is interesting to you and appreciate your inquiry.

Although I know of no American life insurance company that has, at the time of this writing, followed the example set by our Canadian neighbor, I am glad to pay tribute to a large New York company that has for some time taken cognizance of woman's lower mortality rate by improving her position in life insurance *settlement options*.

The following letter came in reply to my inquiry as to what prompted the company thus to improve woman's insurance position:

THE MANHATTAN LIFE INSURANCE
COMPANY
120 West 57th Street, New York 19, N. Y.

August 6, 1952

Miss Caroline Katzenstein
3411 Powelton Avenue
Philadelphia 4, Pa.
Dear Miss Katzenstein:

We have found that women enjoy a lower mortality rate than men, whether they are insured under life policies or are annuitants.

It seems to be manifestly unfair to lump women together with men in the issue of life insurance policies, charge them the same premiums, pay them the same dividends, all without any recognition of the lower mortality among their sex, and then when they elect a life income settlement option insist that their income be reduced to the amount that the cash policy proceeds will purchase according to a female mortality table.

For many years, we have not followed this practice, of which we disapprove. I am,

Yours very truly,
Elder A. Porter
Vice President and Chief Actuary

In conclusion, I should like to say that during the eight years I remained with the Philadelphia Life such a friendly relationship was established that I still feel like a "member of the family" when I occasionally drop in for a little visit. At the end of that time, I decided I'd like to have a contract with one of the world's largest companies and chose the Prudential. I am glad to say, this association has been a very pleasant one. Although again I was the only woman member of the agency when I first joined it, I met no sex discrimination. Here, as at the Philadelphia Life, an atmosphere of helpfulness and friendliness prevails.

2167

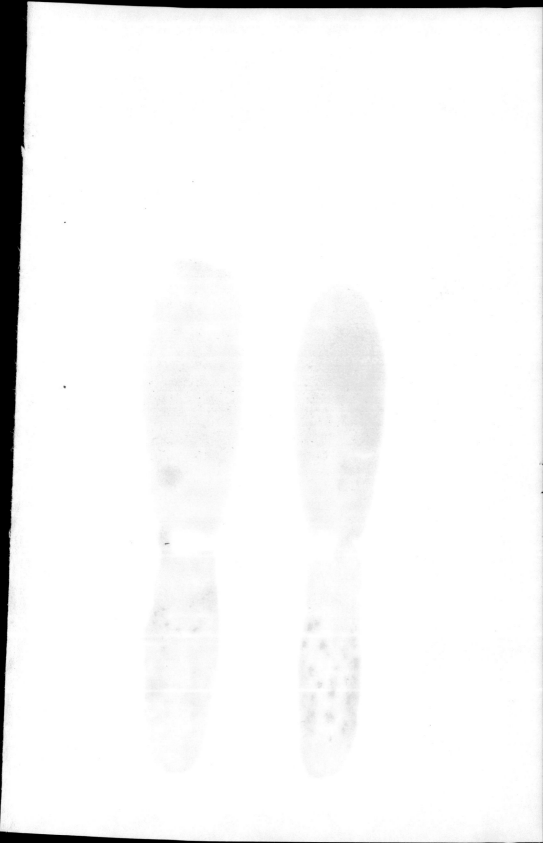

36740

KATZENSTEIN, CAROLINE
  LIFTING THE CURTAIN.